T0351461

SHEEPLANDS

SHEEPLANDS

HOW SHEEP SHAPED WALES AND THE WORLD

ALAN MARSHALL

2024

www.uwp.co.uk

British Library Cataloguing-in-Publication Data
A catalogue record for this book is available from the British Library.

ISBN: 978-1-915279-38-5

Cover artwork by Neil Gower
Typeset by Agnes Graves
Printed and bound by CPI Group (UK) Ltd, Croydon, CR0 4YY

The publisher acknowledges the financial support of the Books Council of Wales.

CONTENTS

PROLOGUE

The idea for this book came to me in a grassy field set on a tree-lined hill near the Welsh town of Carmarthen. Just behind were the earthly remnants of an ancient hillfort, well known in these parts as the original home of Merlin, the legendary magician of the Dark Ages, while just in front of me a relaxed flock of sublimely woolly sheep was grazing. In the summer sunshine, their curly threads dazzled in various shades of white. Despite living their days and nights exposed to the elements in a rustic rain-showered field, the sheep looked as fresh as the fluffy white clouds floating in mild array above them.

As well as the sheep, I had another companion: my six-year-old son Shelley. Like most children, Shelley is blessed with a sense of wonder about the natural world. As we gazed across the flock of friendly sheep and upwards to the hillfort and the clouds beyond, Shelley delivered a volley of left-field questions about the scene: 'Why does Wales have so many sheep?', 'Where did the sheep come from?', 'Where did Wales come from?', 'Did Merlin create clouds from sheep's wool?' Often, I would have to brusquely parry such random questions as I hurried through the day's tasks. Yet on this afternoon, resting with the idyllic Welsh landscape stretching out before us, I could hardly claim to be busy, so I slowly began to relate to Shelley what I knew about the origins of sheep, how they had come to Wales and how Wales grew to be a land of sheep. Shelley listened attentively with wide eyes – just the response a teacher might hope for. Because of this, I imagined the global history of the world's 'sheeplands' might be a commendable story to embrace and explore – then convey to the world. And so, after scouring libraries and museums and visiting many mountainous sheep places across Wales and the world, this collection of chapters came into being. Though Shelley should be thanked for providing the original inspiration, the good people at Calon and the University of Wales Press must be thanked for commissioning the book and bringing it to fruition.

Chapter 1
WILD SHEEPLANDS

THE MOUNTAINS OF WESTERN ASIA, 13000 BC

If you have had the good fortune to visit Wales, you'll know it to be a nation of mountains and hills. Indeed, over the ages, these mountains and hills have served to create then foster Wales as a nation. From prehistoric times to the Middle Ages, when invaders, conquerors and settlers arrived in Britain from Europe, they often found it relatively uncomplicated to move across the lowlands of central and eastern Britain. However, when they tried to take on the high peaks and hazardous weather of the Welsh uplands, the going was much tougher. The mountains afforded the Welsh people, the Cymry, a place of refuge. Protected by the mountains – and the rugged coasts and misty valleys that jutted into them – the Welsh evolved a distinctive and resilient culture.

The Welsh had an important partner in their national development: sheep. Like the Welsh themselves, sheep are creatures born of the mountains. These hardy, stalwart, intelligent, determined, beautiful creatures are made of sterner stuff than their fluffy appearance might suggest. Endowed with a grand coat of wool, sheep can handle the bitter sea-breezes of the Atlantic Ocean, the rain-soaked folds of the Welsh valleys and the snow-flecked peaks of the tallest Cambrian Mountains. As long as they can find grass to feed on, they manage to survive just about whatever conditions the hills might throw at them. Consequently, over time, Wales has become an archetypal 'sheepland'.

Wales is far from the only sheepland, of course. From Argentina to Australia and from Mesopotamia to Mongolia, just about any country with hills and meadows has adopted then developed sheep-farming as a key way of living. Today there are over 200 global breeds of sheep spread across six continents. Added to that, there are over 1,000 local breeds of sheep peculiar to a specific country or a single mountain range. This book outlines the journeys taken by some of these sheep as they voyaged across the world, both by themselves and with human shepherds.

We begin this series of journeys in the mountains of Western Asia. Here, around 15,000 years ago, every sheep was gigantic and wild, and humans had not yet become farmers. Striking into the Persian skyline of Western Asia is the 1,000-mile-long Zagros range of mountains. Within the range, there is a great array of settings: jagged snowy peaks, sloping woodlands and lush steppes, as well as deserted arid zones permeated by scrappy patches of pale grass.

At the northern end, the Zagros Mountains intersect with two other great alpine systems: the Toros Mountains, whose spine overshadows all southern Anatolia, and the Armenian Highlands, which dominate Armenia and northern Persia. This great confluence of mountains – interspersed with tens of thousands of valleys – provides the perfect habitat for a diverse variety of pastures and a superb array of hooved grazers and foragers: antelope, ibex, gazelle and wild sheep. The wild sheep may have evolved from goat-like ancestors in these mountains millions of years before, or they may have moved in from other parts of Asia. In any case, by the end of the Ice Age, wild sheep held these mountains as their home as they grew both gregarious and highly sociable.

During the Ice Age, although Wales was covered with a thick layer of glacial ice, the Zagros and Toros mountains and the Armenian Highlands were only patchily covered in ice and snow in their highest zones. Elsewhere, water flowed strong and grasses grew natural and abundant. The wild sheep that grazed these mountains were magnificent beasts called Mouflon. The Mouflon is a tall stout sheep covered in reddish-brown hair. When fully grown, the male Mouflon has enormous twisting horns jutting into full circles that curve out from the sides of its head. Its back is usually flecked with an uncanny whitish saddle as though enticing some brave Stone Age hunter to ride it. The females are also often horned – but without the gigantic twists of the males – and they lack the white saddle. The largest males like to think they are the bosses of the herds but for most of the year, the ewes and the lambs ignore them, going where they want and doing as they please.

Some old-style nature films present the male rutting process – when rams violently lock horns and butt heads – as determining the structure of wild sheep herds. Yet many zoologists believe that most wild sheep look to the understated leadership of the older ewes. It is often these ewes who choose where to find food and shelter and who guide their flock in migrating across the landscape. In the Zagros and Toros mountains, the Mouflon of the Ice Age migrated seasonally through the wetter grasslands in the valleys during winter and up on to higher slopes whose meadows were flush during summer. In both zones, they chowed down upon various wild grasses and the occasional leafy shrub.

Wild Mouflon were sometimes stalked by the big cats of these hills, including leopards, lions and lynxes, plus smaller wildcats. In addition, packs of wolves and wild dogs would often follow the wild sheep, usually targeting the lambs and the loners. Yet the alert nature of the Mouflon, their keen eyesight and their penchant for flocking enabled them to survive in this highly variable environment, prowled by predators and scavengers. The Mouflon's massive horns also allowed them to fight back when cornered, plunging their horns into the face of attacking cats to protect their lambs or butting wolves right off the side of rocky cliffs. However, their horns weren't nearly as important in dealing with predators as was their fleet-footedness. Mouflon could outrun most creatures on the slopes, bursting and bounding from a grassy knoll to a riverbank to the top of a boulder in moments: a strategy that would confuse and confound the best of hunters, including humans.

North Americans may be familiar with the Mouflon's cousin, the mighty Bighorn sheep, which inhabits much of the Rocky Mountains. The Bighorn sheep themselves are descended from Siberian snow sheep, which bounced across a land bridge to Alaska tens of thousands of years ago, perhaps tailed all the way by Stone Age hunters.

Nowadays, Mouflon have just about disappeared from the Toros Mountains and Armenian Highlands but they still roam freely in some southern parts of the Zagros range. They are just as wild as ever with hair for fleece – not wool – and always scrambling to keep out of sight.

If you are in Wales, you can visit the Stone Age Centre at Old Chapel Farm near Llanidloes in Powys to see a flock of semi-tame Mouflon. Further afield, there are also European Mouflon running feral in the highlands of the Mediterranean islands of Corsica and Sardinia. However, these Mouflon are not really pure wild Mouflon since they are the descendants of Mouflon that interbred with domesticated sheep brought to the islands by prehistoric farmers.

Right from their wild beginnings, sheep were always social creatures. Their sociability might be regarded as a survival mechanism since the many eyes of a co-living flock can spot trouble much more quickly than a lone grazer. Plus, during a snowstorm or rainstorm, a flock can huddle together to keep warmer and drier. At some point in their evolution, though, many creatures developed their social character beyond mere survival value – just because it is comforting and joyful to interact in a group.

Sociability also tends to make sheep quite smart. Any one sheep can learn an array of new skills from a multitude of trusted flockmates. Some people think sheep are stupid and that they just flock together in blind trust. Yet as social creatures ourselves, we share many 'sheeply' traits: intelligence, curiosity and a strong desire to be part of a group. Despite their essence as social creatures, each individual sheep – like each individual human – has its own character. This often makes sheep, whether alone or in flocks, behave in unpredictable ways, as many modern-day shepherds can attest.

As well as contending with big cats and wild dogs, the Ice Age Mouflon had to face human hunters. For this reason, wild Mouflon still regard humans as foe, not as friends, scattering into the hills upon first sight. Yet despite this, sometime long ago, a community of prehistoric peoples set out to tame Mouflon-like wild sheep. The next chapter offers a suggestion as to who these people may have been.

Chapter 2
VILLAGES OF SHEEP

THE LEVANT, 13000 BC TO 9000 BC

As congenial and woolly as they are now, there was once a time when every sheep in the world was wild and unfriendly like the Mouflon – and not at all fluffy. The exact geographical place where Mouflon were first tamed is not known for sure. Maybe it was within the valleys of the Zagros or Toros Mountains or within the upland steppes fed by the rivers of the Armenian Highlands.

One promising area where there is evidence of increasing closeness between sheep and humans is the zone where the Toros Mountains curve off from the lands of Anatolia into the Levant. The Levant comprises the easternmost parts of the Mediterranean: the lands of Israel, Lebanon and Palestine, as well as the distal south-eastern part of Anatolia. Here, at the end of the Ice Age, emerged a group of people we call the Natufians.

From around 13000 BC to around 9000 BC, the Natufians were transforming – ever so slowly – from living primarily as nomads to living primarily in settled sites. Near where the great ancient cities of Jerusalem and Jericho would be founded more than 10,000 years later, the Natufians were setting up vibrant settlements comprising many different families. These were the world's very first proper villages.

A typical Natufian village numbered around 150 people. From the grasslands and open woodlands surrounding their villages, the Natufians gathered wild plants of many kinds, including cereals, nuts and berries. From these, they baked the world's first bread and crafted the world's first beer.

Over countless generations, the Natufians became more and more anchored to the settled village lifestyle. Yet they still moved around to hunt and trap wild animals during different seasons. The southern Levant, where they first set up their villages, was then a patchwork of well-watered woodlands and grasslands interspersed with very dry or drought-prone terrain.

Within this mixed landscape, shrubs and bushes grew well enough that browsing animals like gazelle could survive and thrive. Because of this, gazelle became the wild game animal of choice for the Natufians, and the basis of their village economy. The Natufians became so dependent upon the gazelle that they even tried their hands at domesticating it. Probably, they kept live individual gazelle caught whilst hunting. If the gazelle of prehistoric times were much like the gazelle of today, they'd be disinclined to settle down within a human settlement, and prehistoric Natufians never tamed them. However, they did employ forms of wildlife management by sustaining the vegetation that gazelle browsed upon. The Natufians also likely frequented and sustained the watering holes where migrating gazelle would congregate. It's likely that this human control over the gazelle's environment pushed down the total number of wild gazelle but pushed up the average size of each specimen.

Suppose you were to visit an excavated Natufian village in the Levant today. You would likely find it nestled close to a cliff, possibly near a cave. It would be riddled with broken gazelle bones and exhibit a characteristic form of architecture. To get a feel for a Natufian home, you might have a go at making one yourself. First, dig a circular ditch into the earth some fifteen feet wide and two feet deep. Then pile large stones on each other on the inside edge of the ditch. As the piled stones reach the same height as the surface, keep piling them even higher, maybe another three feet. When the interior of the circular drystone wall is at about your standing height, lay out about half-a-dozen sturdy brushwood branches on top of the wall, from one side to the other, and arrange layers of brushwood twigs on top of these branches. This is your roof. Make the brushwood layers just thick enough to keep out the sunshine.

This fun project might puzzle onlookers but it serves as good training if you aspire to be an experimental archaeologist. If you are feeling really adventurous, go off and hunt a stag with flint arrows, then skin the beast and dry the pelt before stretching it out and interlacing it within the brushwood branches. Now your comfy little Natufian home will keep out the rain as well. I'm told by some archaeology students that they must do all of this – bar the butchery – to pass one of their exams.

As well as perfecting – then spreading – this architectural form, the Natufians shared a common fascination for sculpting bones and shells. The finished artwork then ornamented the insides and outsides of their half-sunken homes. Excavations also indicate that the Natufians were crafting early agricultural tools, especially sickles and grinding stones, to harvest and process cereals. These cereals were harvested from wild meadows but the Natufians sought to cultivate them near their villages as well. If we label them crop farmers, it was of semi-domesticated plants already growing in their chosen locality.

Despite never thoroughly domesticating their main economic animal, the gazelle, the Natufians nevertheless proliferated and their culture expanded. More and more Natufian villages were set up, growing further into the northern Levant. As the Natufians spread northward, they encountered more flocks of wild sheep venturing southward from the valleys and foothills of the Toros Mountains. Eventually, wild sheep eclipsed the gazelle as their main game animal. The Natufians in the north then re-applied the skills they had learnt in managing wild gazelle to managing wild sheep. Maybe there was some nascent domestication going on as well, whereby Natufian hunters captured and enclosed individual wild lambs before plumping them up for later consumption.

Of course, we should acknowledge sheep domestication was not some instantaneous moment whereby one particularly caring human befriended one particularly friendly sheep. Rather, it was a long and arduous process spread over thousands of years. The phrase 'Agricultural Revolution' is sometimes used to explain how humans transformed from nomadic hunters into settled farmers – but although it was revolutionary, it was a very slow revolution.

Given that nobody had ever domesticated a wild animal before, we might forgive the Natufians for taking so long to make progress – and then for never really fully succeeding. Doubtless they had to experiment with many techniques. Perhaps they kidnapped young lambs then let them bleat away in earshot of their mothers so that the ewes could be caught as well. Mouflon lambs are quite adorable – and probably scrumptious – yet the Natufians might have coveted the mothers' milk even more.

Another trick would be to let the milk flow the other way. Human mothers might have suckled orphaned lambs either to fatten them up or to make them more accustomed to human contact. As historian Philip Armstrong explains in his book *Sheep*, this tactic is still used by traditional village farmers in a few remote parts of the world today.

The more direct approach of imprisoning a wild flock in a cave or an enclosure was likely also attempted. Given the robustness and resourcefulness of wild sheep, this strategy would probably have failed far more times than it succeeded. However, the prize of having sheep graze quietly near the village instead of running free in distant hills was enough to encourage the Natufians to keep trying. By around 9000 BC, it seems late-stage Natufians had developed the art of 'sheep-whispering': enticing a flock of sheep to live permanently nearby, for example by burning away mature grasslands and shrublands so a verdant grassy regrowth would suddenly appear. These lovely fresh pastures would have been irresistible to wild sheep. The Natufians probably also dotted their villages with salted rocks – which sheep love to lick so they can dose up on essential minerals. If Natufian villagers just loitered about near a moving flock in a non-threatening manner over many seasons, they may also have habituated wild sheep to tolerate human presence, especially if the villagers acted to scare away predators.

The Natufians may not have laboured all alone to protect their wild and semi-wild sheep from predators. By this time, dogs had long been part of the village community as hangers-on. As scavengers, wild dogs likely domesticated themselves by following around human families, begging for scraps of food. Over time, friendly dogs came to see human villagers as their pack, appointing themselves to the role of camp guard and warding off competitors and predators.

To be classed as a proper sheep-farmer, it is not good enough just to collect animals from the wild and store them in an enclosure. You need to sustain multiple generations of self-reproducing flocks. It is not known for sure whether the Natufians ever managed to do this. Maybe they had to constantly hunt or gather new sheep from the wild every season. Regardless, the Natufians' skills in managing wild sheep would permeate other areas of the Near East and eventually give rise to sheep-farming proper.

Chapter 3
TOWNS OF SHEEP

ANATOLIA, 7000 BC

In central Anatolia, on the Konya Plain near the ancient Greek city of Iconium, there lies the remnants of a far more ancient settlement: Çatalhöyük. This settlement is about 9,000 years old and is located upon a pair of lonely flat-topped mounds that push out above flatlands. The flatlands today are barren and bare. However, in 7000 BC, the people there could look out upon a broad, lush river-soaked grassland extending to the Toros Mountains fifty miles to the south.

What is significant about Çatalhöyük is that it was the first town in human existence, becoming home to 10,000 people at its height. What is also notable – especially for us – is that Çatalhöyük's economy was based on sheep-farming. The inhabitants of Çatalhöyük lived in impeccable lime-washed clay-mud homes. These homes were nestled so tightly together that Çatalhöyük had no room for streets. Its occupants moved around upon the roofs of the homes.

Some archaeologists believe there is a connection between the people of Çatalhöyük and the earlier village culture of the Natufians; indeed, that the Natufians are the ancestors of the Çatalhöyük people. It seems that offshoots of the Natufian culture were drifting north to Anatolia sometime around 9000 BC. Maybe they were ethnically or culturally linked or maybe not. Certainly, there could have been intermittent trading between the late Natufians and the early Çatalhöyük folk as the 400 or so miles between the two cultures could have been traversed in weeks by intrepid traders or hunters. If so, then Natufians could have handed on their nascent sheep-farming knowledge, which was then developed in Anatolia to become fully-fledged sheep-farming. By 'fully-fledged' sheep-farming, I mean to indicate that Çatalhöyük eventually developed large self-reproducing flocks that lasted many generations. By 7000 BC, these flocks were so prevalent they formed the basis of the Çatalhöyük economy.

As sheep-farmers, the residents of Çatalhöyük would have selected the friendliest and tamest sheep, probably with a preference for diminutive specimens sporting minimised versions of those massive Mouflon horns. They also likely favoured ewes that were good milk producers. Whilst lamb and mutton would have been consumed occasionally, the milk products of sheep served as daily staples, including in the making of all kinds of yoghurts, cheeses and butters. When Çatalhöyük townspeople chewed on mutton or lamb, it was probably taken from wild sheep they'd hunted around the foothills of the Toros Mountains. The inhabitants of Çatalhöyük also knew how to capture and breed in wild sheep with their own domestic sheep – both to expand their flocks and to keep their sheep vibrant and healthy.

At this stage, all sheep – wild or domestic – were still hairy, not woolly. It would have taken quite some effort to pluck the hair off a sheep's back or cut it off with a flintstone blade. It's likely that the residents of Çatalhöyük used this hair to spin, twine and maybe weave various textile products – ropes and mats for example – for use in their homes and out in the field, although they probably didn't fashion clothing. Though textiles made from sheep's hair have yet to be unearthed from the Çatalhöyük site, woven plant fibres have been dug up recently and no doubt the people living there were utilising sheep's hair as well. Textile products made in Çatalhöyük also seem to have been traded to villages far and wide across Anatolia and into the Levant.

Although Çatalhöyük was humanity's opening foray into urban life, the homes were exceedingly well made and very comfortable. Inside each house was a special cooking area, a dedicated area for sleeping and a purpose-built spiritual zone. The latter involved a shrine-like emplacement embedded within the wall that also acted as a divider between sections of the home.

These homes were tended to with such devotion that they might have become spiritual spaces in themselves, serving as sacred zones of daily ritual for each family. Indeed, the residents of Çatalhöyük buried their dead relatives within the foundations below their homes so they might forever remain a physical part of the family. Often, the family would dig up their dead relatives decades later. They would then detach the skulls and place them as ornaments in the home, perhaps as a memorial of a dearly departed family member. In turn, the lime-washed walls were adorned with paintings depicting visions of their headless ancestors.

Up on the roofs of these well-made homes, the people of Çatalhöyük would dine and commune, as well as sleep during hot summer nights. The roofs were essential pathways into their homes, for each home's 'door' was a gap in the roof set around a ladder. From the top of their homes, they could also keep an eye on their flocks of sheep wandering about the pastures near the river.

Though the people of Çatalhöyük were very spiritual, they never built a central shrine or temple. Nor did they have a priestly class or religious elite. Çatalhöyük people shared the same religion yet their rituals were undertaken in a self-sufficient manner within each family home.

Another striking characteristic of Çatalhöyük was that each home was the same size and shape as the rest. In addition, all homes possessed about the same quantity of household goods along with a similar standard of cookware, matching washing facilities and comparable ornamental displays. No Çatalhöyük household appeared materially richer than another and all families seem to have held the same social status.

Scientific analysis of bones of Çatalhöyük's residents also shows they shared a common diet and enjoyed the same degree of health. Whether by design or by accident, Çatalhöyük was egalitarian. This situation is as fascinating as it is rare. As we explore the changing shape of human civilisation over the coming chapters, we will struggle through some 10,000 years of gross hierarchy and inequality before we chance once again upon other sheeplands embracing democracy and egalitarianism.

Like the Natufian culture in the Levant, the Çatalhöyük people did not just develop into sheep-farmers overnight. When they first settled this site, around 7500 BC, they were not farmers at all. They lived as urbanised hunter-gatherers before slowly transforming wholesale into dedicated farmers over the course of half a millennium. So why did it take so long? Perhaps the first cultures to explore agriculture did not see it as particularly valuable. Maybe the people of Çatalhöyük, and the Natufian culture as well, believed the 'settled hunter-gatherer' lifestyle worked for them just fine. As long as it kept raining in the Toros Mountains, the creeks and rivers would flow nicely for most of the year, and the grasslands and shrublands could flourish. Upon such verdant terrain, wild sheep were sure to move about in a fairly predictable manner. In such a garden of earthly delights, humans only had to visit a chosen meadow or river lea to shoot off an arrow or cast a net in order to secure enough food. Why would any villager or townsperson bother trying to solve the significant practical problems of farming sheep when nature was so providential?

It is also possible that farming was resisted for social reasons. As farming grew within settled communities, surplus food or materials might soon become managed and claimed by just one family. With this extra wealth, such a well-resourced family might start manipulating the group to their own advantage, asking for services or loyalty or payments in exchange for food or favours. Perhaps the pre-farming people of Çatalhöyük resisted this concentration of wealth and influence into the hands of a few by persistently laying their trust in nature's bounty rather than the vicissitudes of their fellow townspeople.

Eventually, though, Çatalhöyük sorted out a sustainable and equitable way to manage sheep stocks. Because of the economic equality within Çatalhöyük, some historians and archaeologists have suggested that its people had a robust ethic of sharing, in which one family were obliged to help another in times of need. Whether this sort of sharing behaviour was governed by social rules or by religious custom or just by a natural inclination for caring, we can only conjecture.

Perhaps, though, Çatalhöyük was only so egalitarian because no household or family could gain enough power and status to start effecting control over the food supplies. When wealthy people died, their flocks and grazing rights might have reverted to the community rather than pass on to their own children. Anybody who got too bossy or selfish and started demanding fees or privileges just because they owned a bigger house or managed a giant flock may have been communally censured or just ignored.

As profoundly ancient and quirky as it was, Çatalhöyük might still offer valuable insights on humanity. The longevity of Çatalhöyük's sheep-based economy, for instance, is impressive, lasting five centuries or more. When the Greeks and Romans and Spanish and British forged civilisations, many millennia later, they needed steel weapons, stone castles, plus armies and navies as well as book-loads of laws and huge unwieldy governments. The people of Çatalhöyük just needed sheep and an attitude of fairness.

Chapter 4

CITIES OF SHEEP

MESOPOTAMIA, 4000 BC

Let us now imagine we are travelling with a young shepherd living in the fourth millennium BC between the foothills of the Zagros Mountains and the mighty River Tigris. We shall call her Dumu, a name derived from Dumuzid, the Mesopotamian goddess of shepherds. Dumu spent most of her year roving slowly with her flock through dry pastures and wet meadows. Though just a teen, Dumu had learnt by now which basins and wadis would be sprouting verdant turf, which spring creeks would be swollen with water, and whence and where a flock of sheep would grow the fastest and the fattest.

The time would eventually come when Dumu had to trail her flock to the mighty gates of the city of Ur, located dozens of miles to the west. As Dumu approached, and with her dogs barking and her flock baaing, she paused by a watering hole to see for the first time an otherworldly glowing monolith deep in the distance. This radiant white tower was a gypsum-painted ziggurat: a gigantic temple that dazzled as a divine composition in the sunlight.

As Dumu drove her flock toward the thirty-foot-high walls of Ur, she met shepherds coming the other way. Most of them were leading sprightly fresh donkeys laden with beautiful woven cloth. These older shepherds assailed the young Dumu with advice, warning her of the stench and dirt crowded behind Ur's walls and the beggars and drifters crowded in front of them. Dumu was also warned off making deals with fake tax collectors outside the gates of Ur who occasionally attempted to wrestle away a sheep from passing shepherds as some kind of toll.

Armed with this advice, Dumu pushed past the ever-increasing array of hustlers, pedlars and roadside artisans until she had navigated her sheep into the city. Here, a shaven-headed priest-cum-taxman asked Dumu for her name then inscribed it into a soft clay tablet. The priest then handed the tablet to Dumu and told her to march the flock through the crowded, noisy streets of Ur, deep into its heart, until she came across the royal fields near the ziggurat.

As we saw in the last chapter, the Stone Age people of Anatolia had found a winning formula to prosper for untold generations – albeit in only one specific town. They founded their settlement on a well-watered plain not far from a rain-drenched mountain range. They grew cereal right next to their local waterways and shepherded large flocks in the drier pastures a small distance away. Over hundreds and thousands of years, this way of life was adopted by others so that full-scale sheep-farming slowly expanded across the landscape of the Near East, flourishing especially in open spaces where shepherds – and their canine companions – helped their flocks graze safe and content.

Mesopotamia was one area that successive generations of Anatolian sheep-farmers would expand into. As its Greek name denotes, Mesopotamia is a land zone between two rivers: the wide Euphrates and the fast-flowing Tigris. Both rivers begin as a network of tributaries in the mountains of Anatolia and Armenia then follow a near parallel 1,500-mile journey through the dry plains of what we now call Syria and Iraq before they converge to spill into the Persian Gulf. The nearby land either side of the rivers – and the hundred-mile stretch in between them – is blessed with rich soil perfect for farming. The soils have been lain down via the settling of a million years of silt and nutrients brought by the two rivers from the uplands where they began.

The forceful flow of the two rivers also made the region amenable to the construction of irrigation canals by arable farmers, which extended the range of developing farmlands. In this environment, sheep-farmers could slowly develop animal husbandry into a fine art. The rivers also acted as an excellent conduit for trade so that farmers could exchange livestock and crops up and down the Mesopotamian plain.

Around 4000 BC, something rather magical happened in Mesopotamia: the first woolly sheep came to be. Perhaps this was a surreptitious accident, via a spontaneous mutant variation, or maybe it was the culmination of gradual change brought about by farmers practising selective breeding. The Mesopotamians knew exactly what to do with this new curly wool springing out from the backs of their sheep, since they had been spinning and weaving flax into linen cloth for centuries.

If Californian technopreneurs had been around to witness the sheeply invention of wool, they would probably have labelled it the killer app of the sheep industry. Sheep could now supply not only milk and meat products – plus skins, bones, fats and guts – they could also provide a self-reproducing annual crop of highly useful and durable fibre. Harvested each summer, this wool could be homespun for domestic use or bundled up to be shifted and traded up and down the Euphrates and Tigris rivers over long distances. With the increased exchange potential that wool engendered, more and more small sheep-farming villages became larger and larger wool towns.

In ancient Mesopotamia, wool had obvious uses for all sorts of textile products – from cloth blankets to carpets, drapes and wall-hangings – and to make rope and fix sails. Sometime in the fourth millennium BC, the Mesopotamians also invented the first double-bladed scissors, which sped up wool harvesting markedly. These scissors consisted of two blades connected by a thin strip of flexible curved bronze, which allowed the blades to bounce open after every cut.

The durability and value of wool – and the fact it could be re-harvested from an already valuable animal – meant that the farming communities in Mesopotamia had an assured surplus of a highly regarded commodity every year. Because of this, wool towns in the southern stretches of Mesopotamia gradually grew into the world's first cities, like Ur. Nowadays, the remains of these cities are buried in the deserts of inland Iraq. However, 6,000 years ago, the climate was wetter, the soils richer and the sea levels higher – so these first cities were located right by the coast of the Persian Gulf.

We can afford to use the 'city' label for the likes of Ur since its population climbed to 100,000 residents. Ur also exhibited most of the hallmarks of modern-day cities, coming complete with grand markets, a busy port, specialised professional classes, distinct neighbourhoods, outlying suburbs, public monuments, international trade links and a sophisticated government that charged officials with collecting taxes, providing services and administering justice.

At about the same time that wool appeared as a major commodity, writing and mathematics were also invented. It would be nice to think that these came into being as creative pursuits of curious minds, but they were more likely practical innovations designed to keep track of the unprecedented civic and commercial activity that was then emerging. For instance, writing and maths were needed for essential tasks like counting sheep, apportioning grazing areas and recording wool revenues. They were also used in levelling taxes, distributing grain and applying the law. As our shepherd Dumu noticed when her flock arrived at the gates of Ur, the main writing medium for urban officials was the clay tablet. Cuneiform notes were inscribed onto tablets of wet clay. These tablets would soon dry – and could end up lasting centuries. Indeed, most of what we know about ancient Mesopotamia is because modern archaeologists can still read from these tablets today.

Ur was not the only city to spring up just when woolly sheep came into existence – the grand cities of Uruk and Eridu developed pretty much contemporaneously. We can therefore conjecture that wool stimulated urbanisation in ancient Mesopotamia. A corollary to this is that the wool trade funded the infrastructure of these cities, including their first temples. Some of the oldest human writing ever found, unearthed from the site of the city of Uruk, contains a telling three-word sentence. The first word is 'Inana', the city's goddess, followed by the local Uruk word for sheep, then the Uruk word for temple. If this does not show that sheep were regarded as divine beings, it certainly hints at their significance in ancient Mesopotamian society. Similarly, artwork excavated from Ur often depicts sheep at the heart of urban life.

Returning to the journey of young Dumu, you'll remember her goal was to shepherd her flock to the royal fields deep within Ur. This was no easy task. She needed to drive her noisy sheep through a labyrinth of narrow, crowded streets, and past busy markets. The flock would be stretched into a thin line, then knocked or blocked by aggravated townspeople, sending the sheep the wrong way. Dumu would have to use all her shepherding skills to keep the flock together and heading towards where they needed to be.

Although seriously attentive to her sheep, Dumu could hardly ignore how Ur was ablaze with industry. Butchers, millers, weavers, potters, bread-bakers and brickmakers – they all slogged away in crammed workshops or open-air manufactories. Some were private businesses, many were royal factories and all were heavily regulated by official accountants and tax collectors. The employees were generally paid with food, beer and cloth – and occasionally precious stones and metals. Over time, if they had worked hard enough over many years, they might save enough goods to trade them in for a one-roomed home within Ur's city walls. If not, they would probably have to commute from a suburban shanty village located somewhere outside the walls.

As Dumu weaved her flock through the streets of Ur, she could not help but notice the slaves as well. These poor souls were charged with some of Ur's worst jobs: shovelling manure, carrying grain sacks and moulding mudbricks. Their low status was evident to all because their owners branded them. When Dumu found the royal fields, she noticed that some shepherds were also branded. This sent a chill through her heart since she imagined this might be her fate should she slip up one day, for example, by losing her flock.

For now, all was well as her sheep rested in the royal fields. She joined other shepherds on rooftop pubs, sipping various honey-soaked beers from large communal pots. Some of the shepherds would quip about her gender but it was not very unusual for teen girls to be roving shepherds. Come morning, Dumu surrendered her flock to an agent from the Royal House. None of the sheep in her flock were legally hers: all sheep in the land were owned by the king. This was why it was so important she did not lose them. And all the wool on their backs was owned by the queen. Together the royal couple were nicknamed 'the Greatest Lambs'.

What this meant was that instead of selling her sheep at the market, Dumu just earned a wage to look after them for a year and bring them to the city. This wage she collected in the form of a significant bale of finished textiles and a precisely calculated number of flour sacks. Like the other shepherds, Dumu had to trade some of this booty for a donkey to carry the rest back to her village.

It is clear from this description of Dumu's journey that the economic and spiritual egalitarianism exhibited in Çatalhöyük – the world's first town – was long forgotten by the time Ur was founded. Mesopotamian cities were very hierarchical in formation and there was an enormous gulf between the elite and the workers, and between rich and poor. The royals also spent a lot of time and energy convincing everyone else that they were divine: or at least in league with the gods. The king and queen ordered their priests to get the population to go along with this idea as well as to oversee the sheep industry and the wool trade.

Royals in the greatest Mesopotamian cities adorned themselves with as much woollen cloth as possible to show off their riches and status, including an impressive array of cloaks, tassels, tufts and baubles. Meanwhile, the shepherds and weavers of Ur often toiled in the pastures and workshops in near nudity. At least during Ur's first centuries, woollen cloth was a luxury good. For all the wool that Dumu's sheep carried on their backs, not much – if any – would end up on hers.

As Mesopotamian towns and cities slowly increased their annual surpluses, woollen cloth did very gradually become more widely spread across all sections of society. After a thousand years, Ur became wealthy enough that the average person aspired to emulate the elite who wore woollen clothes from top to toe in all seasons. And after the people of Ur had covered themselves with woollen cloth, they took to decorating the inside of their homes with wool coverings.

The success and expansion of the Mesopotamian wool trade

during the fourth and third millennia BC meant that long-term credit agreements could be arranged across the full length of the two Mesopotamian rivers and then across mountains and seas to other cultures. With so many flocks producing so much wool – and with so many sheep reproducing every year – traders and merchants grew confident enough to take on the risk of granting credit to wool producers or clothmakers. The laws governing such creditor–debtor relations were carved into stone monoliths and scattered in public sites around various towns and cities. Some of these, dating back to around 2000 BC, are still legible today.

As our Dumu gained more experience as a long-distance mover of sheep, she may have found herself profitably employed to convey not only live sheep but also wool and cloth to the different city-states of Mesopotamia. Though land transport was the best option for live sheep, it was the amazing reed riverboats that did most of the work when it came to wool. In the early urban settings of Mesopotamia, wool was so durable and portable that wool bales or finished cloth often served as a form of currency, moving one way then back again, like a bullion of silver.

With all this wool trading going on between the city-states of Mesopotamia, and the taxes that could be drawn from it, cities like Ur and Uruk, then later Nineveh and Nimrud, invested in new forms of grand architecture. This included gigantic temples taller than medieval cathedrals, royal palaces with luxurious gardens, government warehouses staffed by thousands of people, and an array of piers, wharves, canals and dykes to serve bustling riverports.

Of course, as much as they were a hotbed for commerce and culture, the world's first cities also faced challenges related to their overcrowded conditions and dirty factories. Cities like Ur and Uruk had huge waste dumps, large amounts of pollution and high rates of disease and crime. Ur and Uruk were more complex than the towns and villages of earlier epochs but we must think carefully to classify cities as inherently superior compared to smaller townships. Indeed, they may have been a lot less liveable for most citizens.

Interestingly, woolly sheep contributed not only to the rise of the world's first city-states but sometimes also to their demise. Cities like

Ur and Uruk had accumulated so much wealth from sheep-farming and wool trading that they became a prime target for foreign raiders. A tribe of nomads called the Martu pounced on the southern Mesopotamian cities from the north, whilst other tribes, the Ghuti and the Elamites, did the same from the Zagros Mountains in the east. These tribes were also sheep-farmers, so they eyed the woolly riches of the cities with envy and repeatedly attempted to raid and then overrun Ur and Uruk. A few times, they managed to succeed, installing themselves as the city governors. It often took decades, centuries even, for the native Mesopotamians to get rid of these foreign governors and to reclaim their cities – and their sheep.

During the second millennium BC, many new sheep-powered cities had developed further north upon the shores of the Euphrates and Tigris. The most famous of these is Babylon, nicknamed the 'Land of Wool' in honour of its primary source of wealth. As historian Alan Butler explains, its renowned Hanging Gardens were lit up at night by tens of thousands of casks that burnt their way through tallow harvested from 50,000 slaughtered sheep.

By the time of Babylon's founding, the city folk of Mesopotamia were getting fussy with their wool, trying hard to breed white-wooled sheep. White wool was highly valued because it could show off vibrant dyes. When just about any citizen was able to cloak themselves in clothes made from brown or grey wool, the Mesopotamian elite set about distinguishing themselves by wearing woollen clothes coloured by expensive colourful dyes. This elitist desire for 'colour-coding' themselves above the masses would promote further international trade since most of the vital dyes had to be imported from faraway lands. It also prompted the creation of distinct sheep breeds: some producing dun-coloured wool – plus milk – for the working classes, while others were bred for white wool and meat for the elite.

Though shepherds like our Dumu would never have become part of the elite just by moving the king's sheep around, she might have ended up living an exciting life travelling the known world as one of Ur's wool dealers. She might also have had the opportunity to take up trading in commodities not claimed or regulated by the royal houses, such as exotic minerals or spices. As an international trader,

Dumu could have developed her own trade network, meeting with merchants and producers up and down Mesopotamia. If so, she could then gather valuable knowledge of various lands and peoples, including their customs and languages.

Travelling afar may also have removed her from duties owed to one royal house. Liberated in this fashion, Dumu could have roved – with sheep following her perhaps – to lands across the Near East. Maybe she even managed to find herself in ancient Egypt. I can plausibly suggest this because Mesopotamian architecture and pottery has been unearthed from the banks of the Nile, suggesting that some far-travelled traders from Ur or Uruk may have set up a trading colony there. Indeed, Mesopotamian ziggurats seem likely to have inspired Egypt's kings to build their first pyramids. At this time, too, someone like Dumu was impressing the first pharaohs with luxurious brightly dyed woollen cloth that they had never seen before.

Chapter 5

SHEEPLANDS OF STONE AGE WALES

BRYCHEINIOG, WALES, 3700 BC

If you wander up along the River Ennig from the Welsh market town of Talgarth into and beyond the fern-laden paths of the Pwll y Wrach nature reserve – with its waterfall, its singing warblers and its moss-laden banks – you'll eventually come to a sun-flecked stream called the Genffordd, which flows aside the crest of a ridge overlooking farmland. A prehistoric cairn sits upon this ridge. Cairns usually mark out an incredibly old ceremonial burial mound, and this seems to be the case here.

In 1972 an archaeological dig beside the cairn unearthed a Stone Age bone. The bone was carved into a musical instrument: a 5,700-year-old flute. The flute tells us that the people of Stone Age Wales were both musicians and craftspeople. The flute also indicates they were sheep-farmers, too, for this instrument is made from the bone of a sheep.

The flute is now on display at the St Fagans National Museum of History, near the Welsh capital, Cardiff. When I visited the museum as a student, many years ago, I was delighted to blow through some replicas to hear sounds from the fourth millennium BC come alive. That day also, accomplished modern-day musicians dressed up in prehistoric costumes and gathered around in the courtyard to play beautiful tunes upon all manner of Stone Age instruments, including those made of sheep bones.

So – we now ask – if one of the first sure signs of domesticated sheep in Wales is around 3700 BC, where did these sheep come from? Well, to make a very long and convoluted story somewhat shorter and simpler, we might present it as follows.

The ancestors of the first Welsh sheep would have left Anatolia about 7000 BC. This was around the time that the world's first town, Çatalhöyük, had peaked in population before its pasturelands started slowly drying out. After the sheep had migrated across the considerable expanse of the Anatolian plains, they would have come to the Aegean coast. Here, the sheep likely stared out at the clear blue Aegean Sea for a long while before being trundled by shepherds onto various tiny vessels around 6500 BC to island-hop to mainland Greece. They then island-hopped further westward till they landed on the Italian peninsula. After settling on the Italian coasts, new cohorts of shepherds then guided their flocks north, hugging the Mediterranean coast, until they ended up in southern France sometime around 6000 BC.

From the Mediterranean coast of France, the Stone Age sheep-farmers continued westward into Spain, colonising much of the grasslands of the Iberian Peninsula by 5000 BC. As you can see from the dates, this movement happened at a snail's pace across countless generations – of both sheep and shepherds.

Around 4500 BC, Stone Age farmers loaded their sheep on to rafts and paddled northward across the Bay of Biscay to the peninsula of Brittany. Eventually, sometime around 4000 BC, the first sheep sailed the Celtic Sea from Brittany to Ireland and then, not long after, they sailed to Wales.

The idea that a flock of sheep set out upon tiny boats for a 3,000-year-long odyssey from Anatolia to Wales is astonishing, I admit. And maybe a little wild and romantic. However, the voyage outlined above accords with the approximate dates of Stone Age sheep remnants found in the archaeological record. Landlubbers though might note that sheep flocks might have made the journey walking across dry land from Anatolia to Brittany, following the great river valleys of Europe such as the Danube and the Loire. Taking this land route, Stone Age sheep would again end up grazing upon the grasses of Brittany around 4500 BC before crossing the Celtic Sea half a millennium later.

The burial tombs of Brittany from this time resemble those of Wales, comprising great mounds of earth covering giant erect stones, and some pots dug up in Wales that date from this period resemble pots produced contemporaneously in Brittany. Given these common features, it is very possible that the first sheep-farmers of Wales are descended from the late Stone Age farmers of Brittany.

Interestingly, the prehistoric journey from Anatolia to Wales also seems to be recorded in the genes of people living in modern Wales today since many Welsh people share some pronounced genetic markers with those living in modern-day Turkey. Animal scientists are seeking to discover if this voyage is reflected in the genes of modern sheep as well. However, we may have to wait a few more years before they come up with anything conclusive.

Whether they arrived in Brittany via the Mediterranean or via an overland route, the exact manner that Stone Age farmers managed to get their flocks across the Celtic Sea is intriguing to ponder. What sort of water vessel could have conveyed the first sheep to Wales? Some have conjectured the original farmers in Wales arrived on a cwrwgl, or coracle. This is a small circular riverboat made from split wood and animal hide. These boats are still an icon of Welsh waterways nowadays. Recently, I boarded a fibreglass version with young Shelley on a small river in the south Wales valleys. Modern coracles are more stable than the traditional versions but still challenging to handle: Shelley and I ended up going in circles endlessly. Yet at least we managed not to capsize. Because they are so unusual and unsteady, needing experienced handling to go in a clear direction, outings aboard them are usually marketed as 'adventure boating' in Wales.

Yet coracles are known to have a long history. Julius Caesar, for example, noted their use in Britain in 56 BC. However, a traditional coracle is approximately three or four feet in diameter. If the first sheep-farmers migrated to Wales in these boats, it is hardly likely they could have brought flocks of sheep with them. Traversing open waters in a coracle would also be enormously risky. They are hard enough to keep afloat on a gentle Welsh river, let alone a raging Atlantic swell. A more likely watercraft for Stone Age farmers is a dugout canoe. These would have been crafted as one large log boat carved from one large tree – or maybe a couple of them bound together side by side. These log boats were big enough and sturdy enough to have transported adult sheep, and an entire Stone Age family, across a calm sea to a new land. Also, if a group of migrating farmers travelled in a flotilla, it would mitigate risk since capsized families and their sheep might stand a good chance of being assisted by their fellow sea-voyagers.

The first sheep to arrive in Wales are unlikely to have been woolly. As we saw in the previous chapter, woolly sheep only appeared in Mesopotamia around 4000 BC. The Welsh bone flute found near Talgarth dates at 3700 BC. The three centuries between the two dates is probably not long enough for a series of migrants or roving traders to have brought sheep from the cities of Ur or Uruk to the coasts of the British Isles. So, instead of looking all big, white and woolly, the first sheep in Wales would have looked small, hairy and brown.

We might get a good idea of such sheep by referring to a primitive hairy type of sheep called the Soay. These sheep are diminutive with rust-tinted wiry hair. They run semi-wild in the isolated Northern Isles of Scotland, munching on slow-growing Hebridean grass.

Though prehistoric hairy sheep did not provide lush wool, some types – like the Soay – had the handy habit of moulting off hair in clumps almost all at once. This hair would have been pressed into felt, spun into rope or woven into cloth. Possibly, the first Welsh sheep-farmers of the Stone Age sent their children out each morning during the moulting season to collect these clumps of sheep hair from the fields and woodlands.

With the coming of sheep into Britain around 4000 BC, the British way of life transitioned from hunter-gathering to settled farming. This transformation probably happened more quickly than its first iteration in the Levant and Anatolia. However, it still took many centuries.

During this transitional period, it is possible the incoming farmers might have slowly displaced the hunter-gatherers already living in Britain. With their newfangled techniques of food production, the farmers arriving from Europe might have secured larger supplies of food. If they ate better than the hunter-gatherers, then the farmer population likely grew faster, as did their expansion over the lands of prehistoric Britain.

However, the archaeological record is far from clear on what happened to the hunter-gatherers when the farmers from Europe arrived. Whilst there is evidence that farming was taking off in Britain at the time, this does not mean that the hunter-gatherers disappeared. Far from displacing the locals, it is quite possible that the immigrant farmers lived as neighbours with the native hunter-gatherers for a long time. If so, the two divergent groups would have developed relations through barter and through wedlock. Such entanglements would have seen the farmers teaching their skills to the hunter-gatherers. The hunter-gatherers would also have taught the farmers a thing or two about hunting for fish in the rivers and birds in the forest, plus important tricks about how to gather consumables from the woods and wetlands. This interchange of skills likely enhanced everyone's capacity to survive the ancient environment of the British Isles.

However, we should also admit that maybe the nomadic hunter-gatherers were pressured into adopting a settled lifestyle. As Britain became increasingly populated by farmers, some families and tribes would butt right up against each other. This may have curtailed the free-travelling nomadism of hunter-gatherers who once roamed far and wide to secure their essentials. In this case, stubborn farmers would have deterred and daunted wandering hunters so as to defend their valuable fields and livestock from intrusion or disturbance.

To avoid conflict, hunter-gatherers may have resorted to settling down in their own spot. So confined, they might not have found enough game and wild plants to survive unless they also took to farming. If this pattern emerged in Wales, then it was not that immigrant farmers fought against and purposely displaced the native hunter-gatherers but that they pressured them to convert to settled farming.

When the first farmers arrived in Wales – at the time the bone flute was making music in Brycheiniog – they would have encountered a very different environment from what we see today. At this time, forests and woodlands covered most of the land. What was not under wooded forest was usually precipitous mountainside, or coastal dunes, or boggy moors and wetland. Sheep are primarily creatures of the grasslands and meadows, not usually delighted to wander through woods or over bogs nor to browse among trees and shrubs. Thus, when sheep-farmers alighted from their log boats on the shores of Wales, they realised they would have to cut down the trees and burn away the woodlands to provide pasture for their sheep. With stone-bladed axes and firesticks, the first farmers initiated a protracted battle against the tree.

Clearing trees in wet places like Wales would have taken much more effort than tree clearance in the drier lands of the Mediterranean since wetter vegetation did not burn as readily. Also, unlike many Mediterranean woodland trees, northern European trees were not laced with flammable natural oils. This meant that farmers might have had to resort to chopping down the trees one by one, rather than clearing them with fires.

The forests were a significant resource for the hunter-gatherers, so this might also have led to conflict between them and the farmers. However, because the deforestation proceeded slowly, stretching out over untold years across the entire length and breadth of Britain, any violent competition between farmers and hunter-gatherers was probably very isolated in time and space. Indeed, there's not really any archaeological evidence of such fighting.

As we saw in Chapter 4, sheep-farming was such an all-important economic activity that it catalysed other human enterprises, ranging from accounting to architecture. In Stone Age Wales, it also served as a stimulus by encouraging flint mining. Stone Age farmers needed a sustainable supply of stone blades for their axes. They strongly preferred flintstone blades because these were the best at clearing trees and also in butchering animals. Because of this, farmers voyaged the length and breadth of the country to find flintstone. One flintstone quarry that attracted farmers from far and wide was Graig Lwyd in north Wales. This Stone Age quarry, located near the modern coastal town of Penmaenmawr, was a veritable axe factory. Stone Age axes made in Graig Lwyd have been dug up by archaeologists from sites all over the British Isles.

As well as flint mining, the Stone Age farmers of Britain took to building civic monuments. These monuments were mostly made of earthworks and megaliths: enormous sculpted rocks standing within or on top of mounds of earth. The purpose of such monuments in Stone Age social life was multiple. Some served as burial sites, some as meeting places, others as festival sites and trading posts, and perhaps as astronomical observatories. Some even seem to have been places of sacrifice. A trending theory these days is that these monuments were built by tribal 'founders' in order to stake a claim over land.

Wales is famously riddled with megalithic monuments. A perennial favourite is the Pentre Ifan dolmen in the Preseli Hills of Pembrokeshire. Here a giant sixteen-tonne capstone sits perched upon the tips of three standing stones. To casual modern-day observers, including the Welsh Mule sheep flocked in pastures nearby, it is not obvious how Stone Age farmers managed to get the capstone balanced up there more than 5,000 years ago. What is not visible these days is the earthen mound and rocky piles built to position the massive stones together and keep them in place, as these eroded away long ago. The giant rocks of Pentre Ifan seem to act as a portal to another world, the world of the afterlife, or so it is theorised. Incidentally, from these hills in Pembrokeshire, the remarkable blue stones of Stonehenge were quarried many centuries later before being rolled on logs and rafted across rivers – all the way to Wiltshire some 150 miles away.

Because these monuments started appearing in Wales at roughly the same time that farming was introduced, it is generally assumed they were built by Wales's first farmer communities. The message here might be that during the fourth millennium BC, farmers in Wales were producing enough surplus food that they could take a few months off from farming each year to devote themselves to constructing huge public monuments. Conversely, the hunter-gatherers at the time would probably have had to go hunting, fishing or collecting almost every single day to feed themselves – giving them no time for big side projects.

If you're curious about what a farming settlement in Stone Age

Wales would look like around about the time that Pentre Ifan was constructed, you might take a wander to Skara Brae in the Orkney Islands of Scotland. At this seaside site, dating from around 3200 BC, a small pastoral farming/fishing village was founded. The settlement comprised a cluster of ten stone buildings enfolded by earthen dams. The Stone Age villagers of Skara Brae depended upon flocks of hairy sheep and herds of hairy cattle plus the gathering of valuable marine resources that washed up on the nearby beach, primarily seaweed, which was used to fuel their hearths and warm their homes.

Despite being built on a wild and stormy coast, the Skara Brae homes were created for comfort. Each house had its own attached toilet whereby buckets of water washed waste through a perfectly crafted gap on a stone seat into covered sewage channels flushing into the sea. The homes also possessed comfy wood-covered furnishings from beds and dressers to chairs and storage boxes. Though Wi-Fi hadn't yet been installed, we know that such Stone Age pastoralists probably entertained themselves well enough with music and by spending many hours intricately decorating their homes, their pottery and themselves.

Although sheep-farming changed the landscape of the British Isles, the settlements that Stone Age sheep-farms gave rise to were only ever small scale, like Skara Brae. In Wales, too, the grandest settlements of the time were mere hamlets. Certainly, nothing remotely like a city, state or kingdom emerged in Wales in the fourth or third millennium BC. The story is very different in Africa and Asia, however, as we shall see over the following chapters.

Chapter 6
THE SHEEP OF THE PHARAOHS

___

EGYPT, 3000 BC

On the banks of the River Nile, within the Elephantine and Esna temples near the modern-day Egyptian city of Aswan, there stands a tall powerful sheep god, sculptured in granite. This god's name is Khnum. In ancient Egypt, Khnum was celebrated as the divine guardian of the Nile's headwaters. It was he who summoned torrents of silt-laden water to flood along the length of the Nile. And it was he who deposited the fertile clay soil upon the riverside plains upon which the ancients grew all their crops. It was also Khnum that moulded this silt into the first human form and breathed it into life – a craft he then practised within the womb of every subsequent pregnant woman.

Khnum is usually represented in ancient Egyptian art with a human body and the head of a ram adorned with a set of impressive corkscrew horns. For his role in building humanity – and each individual human being – Khnum was thought of as the primary creator god of ancient Egypt, often referred to as 'The Divine

33

Builder'. In honour of Khnum – and inspired by Khnum's power – the pharaoh that built the tallest of Egypt's great pyramids took on the name Khufu-Khnum as his royal designation.

As you might guess from this history of 'sheeply' power and divinity, the ancient Egyptians revered the ram for its virility and its creative power. Sheep-farmers in Egypt, as in other places, had adopted a model of managing flocks by allowing a single potent male to inseminate all the ewes with his 'creative essence'. Thus, the lone ram appears as a regal symbol of unique dominance and prolificacy. His impressive horns also showcased his usefulness in a fight.

Anyone who wanders around the many grand archaeological sites of the Nile valley will soon note how significant the ram was to the ancient Egyptians. As well as the statues, paintings and reliefs, the bodies of adored rams were often mummified and then covered with gilded masks and jewels. Around 1500 BC, another ram-headed god, Amun, became the god of the city of Thebes, which was then Egypt's capital. The entrance to Thebes's impressive Amun temple was flanked by equally impressive ram-headed sphynxes.

During this period, the Jewish citizens of Thebes noted the commitment of Amun's devotees and so refrained from the ritual of lamb sacrifice. If an Egyptian caught sight of such a ceremony, it might well provoke an angry mob reaction. Jewish scribes also noted the risk of showing off one's woollen wear in public. Because wool was the natural clothing of gods like Khnum and Amun, mere mortals – especially peasants, slaves and foreigners – were not supposed to flaunt it. In contrast, it was generally accepted that those Egyptians of very high station, who were on close terms with the gods, could cover themselves with flamboyant woollen cloaks. This convention was widely utilised by members of the royal house and the elite priesthood to graphically convey their sky-high sacred status.

Domesticated sheep had arrived in the lands of the Nile delta maybe around 5500 BC. Archaeologists and historians assume they trundled into the continent of Africa with Stone Age farmers migrating from the Levant via the Sinai Peninsula. However, modern-day sheep-farmers in Libya suggest that the first domesticated sheep in Egypt arrived from Libya. These Libyan sheep, it is said, were independently domesticated from some form of wild African sheep. Back then, the lands west of the Nile into Libya weren't Saharan sandy deserts as they tend to be now but an intermittent patchwork of dry grasslands and shrublands that could support sheep-farming.

Wherever they came from – the Levant or Libya – the domestic sheep of Egypt grazed upon the grasses of the fertile stretches of the wide Nile delta for millennia. These prehistoric Egyptian sheep were bred and rebred by a series of Stone Age and Bronze Age cultures, like the Badarians, the Gerzeans and the Maadi people. In a long slow series of interventions, these peoples transformed the Nile from a wild river filled with crocodiles and hippos into a managed waterway with levees, ports and irrigation systems. They also engaged in trade with the prehistoric cultures of Libya to the west and the Levant to the east, as well as up and down the Nile through North Africa. Textiles, mainly linen, comprised a considerable part of this trade. From the fourth millennium BC, woollen fabrics – and woolly sheep – were also traded from distant Mesopotamia, as we saw in Chapter 4.

Despite the divine status of the ram, sheep never came to dominate the agricultural economy in ancient Egypt as they had in ancient Mesopotamia. There were three main reasons for this. Firstly, the flax plant that produced linen grew just about everywhere up and down the Nile. Secondly, the climate of Egypt was mostly warm all year round, so linen clothing would have sufficed as an all-season covering. Thirdly, unlike the Mesopotamians living on the banks of the Euphrates and Tigris rivers, the Egyptian kingdoms on the Nile were thousands of miles away from wide grassy plains and mountain meadows. In Egypt, sheep had to share narrow riverside strips of farmland and orchards with cattle, goats and pigs – all of which might have been happier than sheep in the wet irrigated fields and groves. Also, given that it was somewhat taboo for the toiling masses to wear wool and slaughter sheep, the full economic potential of sheep-farming could never be realised.

Although sheep never became a mainstay of the economy of the Pharaonic Kingdoms, there is nevertheless nowadays a proper Egyptian sheep industry. Sheep's wool, for instance, is fundamental to manufacturing twenty-first-century Egyptian rugs and carpets.

The most popular of the present-day Egyptian sheep is the Rhamani, whose rugged and lush cream-brown wool looks like a shaggy carpet even whilst still on its back. The Rhamani cannot really trace their ancestry to ancient Egyptian epochs, though. They most probably came in from Turkey in early modern times when Egypt was ruled by the Ottoman Empire.

Another famous sheep breed in Egypt is the Barki, a tiny breed with all-over creamy wool except for a characteristic brown splotch on the neck. The Barki is the sheep of the modern Bedouin, Egypt's desert nomads. The Bedouin use Barki wool to weave their famous desert tents. Like the Bedouin, Barki sheep are hardy travellers – moving dozens of miles in a day across scorching sands and rocky arid lands. As we shall see in the next chapter, this ability to migrate over rugged terrain was also essential to sheep moving eastward from the Near East, and deep into Asia.

Chapter 7

SHEEPLANDS
OF THE INDUS VALLEY

PAKISTAN/INDIA, 2500 BC

The Urial is a tall, muscular species of wild sheep with a sand-coloured coat of dense wiry hair and deeply ridged horns spiralling from its head. A cousin of the Mouflon, the Urial split away on the Persian plateau untold thousands of years ago, then migrated eastward toward the foreboding Kirthar Mountains.

The Kirthar Mountains run along much of the western side of the Indus River, which twists and turns for a thousand miles from the Himalayas through modern-day Pakistan and India into the Indian Ocean. A keen-eyed Urial – and they do have keen eyesight – if perched on an outcrop in the foothills of the Kirthar Mountains sometime around 3000 BC, might well have spotted human settlements dotting the river. Some of these settlements comprised prosperous farms since the plains between the river and the mountains had highly fertile soils.

The same Urial, if it stood upon the same outcrop about 500 years later, would see not just villages, though, but also a massive brick-walled city, surrounded by enormous reservoirs of water and filled with a grand internal agglomeration of clay-brick houses. This city was Mohenjo-daro, part of the Indus Valley Civilisation. The civilisation ran just about the whole length of the Indus River and comprised five million people at its height. They lived in thousands of villages, and hundreds of towns, plus a small number of cities – the latter filled with up to 40,000 citizens each.

The ethnic origins of the people comprising the Indus Valley Civilisation are something of a mystery. They seem unrelated to modern-day peoples of Pakistan and India who now live near the river. Nor were they related to the Aryans who came from the north sometime around 1600 BC and whom some historians think overran and vanquished the city of Mohenjo-daro.

Some scholars suggest the Indus Valley Civilisation grew from the more ancient Mehrgarh culture, an early farming society localised to a few valleys squashed between the Kirthar Mountains of south Pakistan and the Hindu Kush mountains of north Pakistan. However, the origin of the Mehrgarh culture is itself not known. What's interesting, though, is that there is an indication the Mehrgarh culture was the first in the whole of South Asia to herd flocks of sheep.

As outlined in Chapter 1, the wild Mouflon is usually considered by scientists as the ancestor of all modern domesticated sheep worldwide. However, since the Urial long inhabited the mountain ranges just west of the Indus River, it is possible the Mehrgarh people independently domesticated the Urial. More likely, though, since the Mehrgarh culture also had some form of exchange with prehistoric peoples from the Persian plateau, they traded in domesticated sheep from Western Asia before passing on their sheep-farming skills to the succeeding Indus Valley Civilisation.

Wherever they and their sheep originated, the people of the Indus Valley Civilisation developed all sorts of technical innovations, including their own writing system. Indeed, they left behind tens of thousands of soapstone stamps carved with pictographic notes. However, unlike the cuneiform tablets of the Mesopotamians, the stamps of the Indus Valley Civilisation are pretty much indecipherable with archaeologists still guessing the meaning of the pictographs. Many of them display a grand assortment of animal symbols – including sheep. A few such clay seals have been found in the ruins of ancient Mesopotamian cities and in ancient ruins of seaports on both sides of the Arabian Peninsula. Though rare, these finds indicate that Indus Valley traders were probably travelling afar. A few Mesopotamian goods from the great cities of Ur and Uruk have also turned up in the remains of the ancient cities of the Indus Valley.

The Indus Valley people also left some fantastic stories written into their urban architecture. Firstly, they were a people who honoured water. They had huge pools within and without the city gates to collect fresh water from the Indus River. Their town sewage system was also formidable, with miles and miles of covered channels that managed to serve each household. They also had mighty public baths for all citizens to enjoy and to use communally. This devotion to water presages the Hindu water rituals that came thousands of years later.

Whilst their civic infrastructure was impressive, the Indus Valley culture as a whole was, in fact, stateless. There was no central authority as there was in the kingdoms of Mesopotamia and Egypt. Political power was devolved to councils or committees to oversee each independent village, town or city neighbourhood. As well as exhibiting egalitarian decision-making, each community had equal access to water supplies. There also appears to be no evidence of large-scale war or rebellion. The impressive walls surrounding their cities were built to defend against floods, not enemy armies or raiders. Whilst Mesopotamian city-states had endless confrontations with nomadic plunderers from the hills, the Indus Valley people seemed to live on good terms with their nomadic neighbours, trading with them and using nomads as a communication service between cities.

When the cities of the Indus Valley Civilisation first arose, sheep-farming seems to have been only a part of the overall economy, not a cornerstone. The residents relied more on the production and trade of cereals, dates and legumes, as well as water buffalo, than they did on sheep. They also devoted themselves to mining and trading in precious materials like silver and lapis lazuli plus the finished artefacts made from them. Cotton was the main material for textiles.

However, as Mohenjo-daro grew, its citizens at times relied upon both domestic and wild sheep as an important source of protein. This shows up when archaeologists look closely at Indus Valley pottery, which is often caked with thin layers of fat from sheep and their milk.

Unlike many shepherds and farmers in ancient Mesopotamia and Egypt, the shepherds and farmers of the Indus Valley likely had a more significant stake in their farming efforts, owning every sheep of their own flock or working as free agents when they transported them. The shepherds of the Indus Valley also seemed to trade in − and feast upon − wild sheep like the Urial.

Whilst sheep were occasionally very important, the Indus Valley Civilisation grew up more devoted to cattle herding. Cattle would have been domesticated prior to sheep in this part of the world since there were a number of species of easily tamed wild water buffalo hanging around near the river. Some historians believe the later Hindi respect for the cow was inherited from the customs of the Indus Valley Civilisation but this is by no means certain.

In some ways, the growing distance between the people of the Indus Valley and their sheep is a shame since their civilisation collapsed as the valley's environs slowly grew drier and drier. In such a situation, sheep would have been better able to cope with this climate than cattle, and sheep-farming would have exhausted the remaining grasslands much more slowly than cattle farming. Perhaps sheep might have prolonged the Indus Valley Civilisation for a few centuries.

Despite Mohenjo-daro crumbling into waterless dust, isolated meadows of the Indus Valley are today still grazed by sheep. Perhaps the most distinctive breed is the Lohi, which has very long floppy ears and a gormless look. The Lohi's dark tan head looks up from a slim frame draped in long white wool, usually shorn to make carpets. Like its ears, the Lohi's long wool droops off the sheep like soggy tassels rather than fluffing up into a rounded bulk. The Lohi is an important animal in some small lowland farms, providing enough milk for a family to produce their own cheese and yoghurt. One might surmise that the sheep of the Indus Valley Civilisation also had this function, and that it was perhaps only the wild Urial sheep that got turned into meat so readily.

Chapter 8

SHEEPLANDS OF THE BEAKER FOLK

GWENT, WALES, 2300 BC

One late spring afternoon, I found myself deep in the south Wales valleys on the edge of the quiet town of Blaina in Gwent. There, I perched myself at a table in a delightful limestone pub. Blaina is nestled within a melange of landscapes: abandoned industrial sites, regenerating woodland and a hillside of planted pine trees. Through the window flanking my table, a blooming juniper branch hung over yet another scene: steep green pastoral hills curving softly upwards for miles and miles, each hill speckled by vanilla-white sheep.

It is quite a typical environment for the valleys and the sheep are accustomed to human passers-by and act all approachable. Outside the pub, a few bleating lambs milled around over a stone wall encircling the pub's garden. Shelley, my co-traveller, was throwing crisps to these lambs as he tried to get them to come close enough to pat them on the head.

Inside the pub, prints of romantic eighteenth-century rural paintings were strewn dustily over the walls. Despite displaying an earlier age, some pictures were eerily similar to my view between the juniper branches. This set me wondering just how old such a scene of fluffy woolly sheep set on tranquil Welsh hills might be.

Luckily for me, a few years before, a team of archaeologists from Cardiff University had worked the hills surrounding Blaina and had thrown up an answer. On one of the nearby hills – the one that the locals call Cwmcelyn Mountain – a set of very distinctive ceramic beakers was found buried within an archaic village. These beakers served as ceremonial drinking vessels, and the people and cultures that made them are known as Beaker folk. Bronze Age Beaker folk once ranged across Europe. They began arriving in Britain around 2300 BC. This is also the approximate date of the prehistoric settlement near Blaina. If you gently climb Cwmcelyn Mountain, you can just about make out the remains of the settlement by noting several platforms upon which would have sat the Beaker folk's long-since decayed houses: their walls made from wattle and daub (sticks and mud) and the roof thatched in dried reeds.

The beakers of the Beaker folk could be used for processing or transporting food but they originated, it seems, as ceremonial vessels for the communal consumption of prehistoric beer. The ones that survive down through the ages have been kept intact because they were placed gently and carefully within burial sites. These beakers have a strange aesthetic allure. Sturdy yet graceful, their sides are inscribed with ancient patterns, often painted for ornamental impact. They are simple in form yet advanced in design.

Whilst this beaker design likely originated on the Iberian Peninsula, it was then taken up by separate ethnic communities in central Europe and the Low Countries. Some of these communities then crossed the English Channel in successive waves. When they arrived in Britain, they retained trading networks with the lands they had left. If there were fluffy white woolly sheep being farmed by Beaker folk in northern Spain or the Low Countries – as a few woollen fragments indicate – then woolly sheep were also probably landing not too much later in Wales. So, to answer the question I asked myself earlier, the Welsh landscape was probably first dotted with fluffy woollies around 4,300 years ago – give or take a few centuries.

Such a timeframe allows me to advance the idea that the farmlands of the archaic Welsh settlement on Cwmcelyn Mountain might have looked a little something like the scene viewed through the window of my Blaina pub.

At this time in the great cities of Mesopotamia, Egypt and the Indus Valley, artists painted woolly sheep on their walls and accountants inscribed sheep symbols into clay tablets. The Beaker folk, though, neither painted nor scribed any images or symbols of sheep on any of their many beakers and pottery. However, they did leave many spindles and loom weights within their archaeological sites across western Europe, so we might presume they had a wool-craft industry going – if only at a small village scale.

Given that wool rarely survives intact in the ground for thousands of years, it is nigh on impossible to determine if the ancient farmers of Cwmcelyn Mountain kept woolly sheep – as opposed to just hairy sheep. Over the course of millennia, wool is eaten by tiny creatures, broken down by soil acids and composted by microbes. Sometimes we only know of the presence of wool fibres in the deep past because of the impressions they leave on clay or mud, or maybe sometimes if they get frozen solid in everlasting ice or snow. However, such finds are rare, especially in wetter climes. When they are found, they are often microscopic in character, comprising little wool scratchings on tiny specks of dried clay.

In any case, wool would undoubtedly have been a significant benefit for the Beaker folk in Wales's cold wet weather. The lanolin oils within wool could easily repel a light shower of rain. And even when wool is soaked through by heavy rain, it still keeps those wrapped within very warm.

The Beaker folk of Cwmcelyn Mountain might have had to put up with more than just Welsh rain, though. They probably shared the landscape with wolves, lynxes and bears. Shepherds and sheepdogs would have had to work hard to keep their sheep from being carted away into the woods.

Over many centuries, though, the danger from predators would slowly decline as the Beaker folk attacked the woods and forests where the predators lived with bronze axes. These axes kept the trees at bay more effectively than the flint axes of earlier farmers. Whilst a flint axe might shatter into useless pieces if it struck at a stubborn piece of wood, a bronze axe would just deform. The Beaker farmer could then bash the bronze axe back into shape and attack the tree once more.

The Beaker folk's fondness for bronze tools may, in part, have attracted them to Wales in the first place as they searched for copper in the Welsh hills, copper being the main constituent of bronze. For instance, it seems pioneering Beaker folk developed an impressive copper mine in the Great Orme in Gwynedd.

As well as keeping the forests from returning to the lowlands – and very gradually clearing trees away in the uplands – the Beaker folk left their mark on the Welsh landscape with a fantastic array of monuments made of earth and stone. These included standing stones, cairns, cromlechs, henges, dolmens and barrows. Like the Stone Age monuments we noted in Chapter 5, these later Bronze Age monuments fulfilled diverse roles: staking out land claims, acting as calendars for the changing seasons and honouring various spiritual entities. Some were also burial chambers for chieftains and priests. A couple of great examples – backdropped by fluffy mountain sheep – include the giant diamond-shaped Maen Llia standing stone and the cairn on the top of the Corn Du peak, both in the mountains of Bannau Brycheiniog.

Earlier, I explored how the first Stone Age farmers might have brought the first sheep to Wales. Such a question emerges here again: how did the Beaker folk bring their woolly sheep across the seas from the continent? By 2300 BC, the boats of the day – and those likely used by the Beaker people – had grown stouter than the single-log dugout canoes used by Britain's first Stone Age farmers. The Beaker folk were attaching planks of carefully hewn wood to the sides of their boats. Unlike logs, these planks were pretty much uniform in dimension and crafted quite precisely and efficiently with bronze tools. Eventually, some Beaker folk abandoned logs altogether to fashion their entire boats with wooden planks. Such boats were also ribbed side to side with internal beams that made them stronger. Possibly the later versions also had sails since some prehistoric boats from the period have cleats, attachments to tie ropes to. Initially, these planked boats weren't much bigger than the dugout canoes. Still, they were much more stable in the water and offered more interior room to carry larger loads – maybe small flocks. Though starting off small, woodplank boats offered Bronze Age boatbuilders the chance to take their craft to larger scales as the centuries passed, since they no longer had to depend upon the size of one tree to fashion any one boat.

The arrival of the Beaker folk on British shores is sometimes looked upon as an invasion. According to some scientific studies, the Beaker folk – and their new woolly sheep – overran the British Isles, outcompeting Stone Age farmers and their small brown hairy sheep. Perhaps the Beaker folk stole the land of the Stone Age Britons, kicking earlier farmers off their land or enslaving them within bronze shackles and forcing them into servitude. Or maybe the newcomers assaulted the local population in an accidental manner by bringing in new diseases that wiped them out.

If we examine the genetic make-up of Britons from the period, there does seem to be a startling change. In 2500 BC, Beaker folk genes were present in zero per cent of the British population. By 2000 BC, they were present in 90 per cent of the population. Still, this seemingly massive penetration of Beaker folk genes could have been relatively slow, quite piecemeal and come about mainly via peaceful integration between the two cultures – primarily via intermarriage. And although Beaker folk DNA still runs rampant in modern Britons today, this does not necessarily mean it comes from the Beaker folk of Bronze Age Britain. It might well have come from later Anglo-Saxons – who themselves were maybe also descendants of European Beaker folk.

Whilst the bronze-working skills of the Beaker folk might have given them the edge in crafting superior weapons compared to those of Wales's Stone Age farmers, the archaeological record seems to indicate that the bronze tools of the Beaker folk were used only for agricultural and adornment purposes – not to wage war or fight battles. And if Bronze Age farmers were trying to kill off Stone Age farmers in some sort of mass genocide, it was a very slow and inefficient genocide, taking 500 years to accomplish.

Another likely explanation of why Bronze Age farmers seem to have gradually overrun Britain's Stone Age farmers is because the Stone Age farmer population was relatively low in the first place: only some

10,000 individuals at any one time. Quite possibly the somewhat clumsy Stone Age farming techniques – along with the absence of woolly sheep – kept the first farmers from growing to huge numbers. In contrast, the first waves of Beaker folk might have been relatively high, maybe 20,000 or more. And because successive waves of incoming Beaker folk organised themselves more and more into tribal groupings – rather than isolated farming communities – they could have exerted collective social power over the Stone Age farmers.

Of course, with improved woolly sheep at their side, Bronze Age farmers would also be more productive. Apart from anything else, wool would have offered the immigrant Beaker folk a competitive advantage over native Stone Age farmers as they fought through British winters. This is a potent explanation if we consider how woollen textiles can fend off bad weather and sickness for both mothers and infants.

Alternatively, the Beaker folk might not have competed much at all with Stone Age Britons. Perhaps they paddled their boats upriver into the unpopulated interior then chopped away at the inland woodlands with their Bronze Age tools. So cleared, the highly productive woolly sheep of Beaker folk could graze in hitherto unsettled lowlands. During occasional episodes of Bronze Age global warming, sheep-farmers may have sporadically settled their woolly flocks in the highlands as well.

All in all, the period we label as the Stone Age might also be aptly labelled the Hairy Age, and what we call the Bronze Age, we might as well label the Woolly Age. Of course, stone and metal are more durable than hair and wool over archaeological epochs, so we can forgive prehistorians for not wanting to give up their current designations.

We should also acknowledge the interdependence between wool and bronze as the Woolly Age/Bronze Age dawned across Eurasia. Bronze tools and blades would have made it easier to process wool, including cutting it off the backs of sheep. Conversely, with a surplus of wool and a massive sheep industry, there was a significant reinvestment in the bronze industry, including prospecting for copper and tin. This applies to mining operations set up in the mountains surrounding Mesopotamia in 4000 BC as well as in the hills of Wales when the Beaker folk migrated there some 2,000 years later. Alas, in Wales, this seems to have involved sending children down tiny cavities in the ground to dig out copper from the rocks, or so the archaeologists at the Great Orme mining site have suggested.

Back in twenty-first-century Gwent, this last thought makes me jerk my head away from my notes to spy Shelley's whereabouts. Slumped in the pub's courtyard, he had grown a little bored because the lambs were not interested in his crisps. So I decided to entice him on an adventurous walk up Cwmcelyn Mountain to lay our eyes upon the archaic village where the Beaker folk kept their Bronze Age sheep. If no one else believes my theory that woolly sheep may have ensured the Beaker folk's success in Wales, at least Shelley listened with wide-eyed attention as I talked him through it while wandering the mountain.

Chapter 9

LANDS OF THE GOLDEN FLEECE

ANCIENT GREECE, 2000 BC TO 323 BC

The idyllic islands rising from the clear Aegean Sea were probably the first parts of Europe to feel the hooves of domestic sheep as they migrated with their shepherds westward out of Anatolia. If not the Greek islands, then sheep would have trundled slowly around the rocky coastline of the Greek mainland. When shepherds first turned up in Greece, they would have encountered dry open woodlands, which were relatively easy to slash and burn away. This is one reason that sheep-farming was very common in this part of the world long before anyone in Wales had ever laid eyes on a sheep.

Around 3000 BC, a precursor civilisation to ancient Greece was forming off the Greek peninsula on the Mediterranean island we call Crete. This was the Minoan civilisation and on their island the first cities in Europe would emerge. By 2000 BC, the Minoan capital, Knossos, had a population of 20,000 – more than all Wales at the time.

The Minoans are better known for being 'bullish' than 'sheeply' – their name derives from the mythic bull-headed Minotaur. Yet they had always been great sheep-farmers. Just as woolly sheep had kickstarted urban civilisation in Mesopotamia, it did something similar in Crete when the first woolly sheep arrived there many centuries later. Using advanced sheep husbandry, sophisticated wool-crafting and a network of overseas wool trading, the Minoans of Crete developed an impressive civilisation. They built Europe's first great palaces, constructed its first large seaports and invented its first sophisticated writing system.

However, just as it scaled new heights in civic culture, the Minoan civilisation fell apart. Cities and towns were burnt to the ground, royal residences destroyed and ports abandoned. Similar devastation was wrought on other lands of sheep across the eastern Mediterranean, especially in the Aegean, the Levant and Anatolia. It seems many great wool-dependent, bronze-wielding kingdoms fell apart in the space of a few decades. This almighty crash of Mediterranean cultures has been dubbed the Bronze Age Collapse.

Some believe the Bronze Age Collapse was caused by a series of natural disasters: earthquakes, eruptions and tsunamis. Others believe it resulted from a series of exhaustive sackings by a massive band of pirates known as the Sea Peoples. Another increasingly popular idea lays the blame upon a mega-drought: a chronic drying of the eastern Mediterranean climate. Such a drought would have severely degraded the Minoans' ability to grow crops and to feed their urban population. Whatever the cause, the Minoans abandoned their cities.

What is interesting for us is that scientists have shown that modern-day Cretans are genetically related to the Minoans. Somehow, the Minoans persevered onward beyond the Bronze Age Collapse, not as city dwellers but as farmers. If there was a mega-drought affecting Crete, then there would have been no water to grow bumper crops. Thus, post-collapse Minoans would have relied upon pastoral sheep-farming to push through the long dry times.

As noted earlier, many varieties of sheep can survive admirably on degraded vegetation or dryland grasses. In post-collapse Crete, the sheep would probably have been sent on their own into the Cretan mountains to graze on whatever happened to be growing up there before eventually being rounded up and brought back to a farmstead to be milked or butchered.

Whilst the Minoans continued forward in time as sheep-farmers, the high culture of Minoan urban life was eventually rediscovered, adopted and developed by Mycenaean Greeks. Mycenaeans were ancient Greeks hailing from the mainland city of Mycenae. Not long after – or perhaps during – the collapse of the Minoan urban world, the Mycenaeans took it upon themselves to colonise the island and export the Minoan culture and lifestyle back to mainland Greece.

Like the Minoans, the Mycenaeans relied on sheep-farming and the wool sector to help grow their wealth. The Mycenaeans would take their sheep-based economy a few steps further though, building up a more substantial state, as well as a network of schools, plus large armies and navies, and an impressive capital defended by a gigantic wall. This defensive wall surrounded most of Mycenae, making it the first walled city in Europe.

The Mycenaeans also had a penchant for colonialism. They set up new colonies all around the Greek peninsula and across the islands of the Aegean Sea. Central to their success was their trade in olive oil, in pottery and in woollen cloth. Showcasing all these valuable trading goods together, the high-class olive-oil pots of the Mycenaeans were often adorned with beautiful paintings of nobles adorned in flowing woollen cloaks.

Though the Mycenaeans reigned as the premier civilisation in mainland Greece for hundreds of years, they eventually collapsed as well. The demise of the Mycenaeans is sometimes held to be part of the lingering economic impact of the Bronze Age Collapse, and it resulted in a fragmentation of central political power from their capital city to individual villages and towns of the Greek peninsula. Very slowly, over centuries, these separate villages and towns grew into solid independent city-states. These became the famous city-states we associate with classical Greece, such as Athens, Sparta, Corinth and Rhodes.

Once upon a time, in one such city-state called Iolcus, there lived a king named Aeson. King Aeson happily governed his sheep-loving subjects whilst always dressed in beautiful woollen cloaks. One day, though, he was suddenly set upon by an assassin. The assassin's paymaster was Aeson's own brother, Pelias. With Aeson gone, Pelias took the throne. Pelias then went on a killing spree, murdering Aeson's widow, her children, their servants and anybody thought loyal to the old king.

If this sounds ghastly, don't worry too much since we're moving from ancient Greek history into Greek mythology. This particular myth was scribed into text by Homer in the eighth century BC and I retell it here since it demonstrates the importance of sheep and wool to the classical world.

After settling into his kingship, Pelias decided he was not content to rule just his own city. He also wanted all the land of the Greek province of Thessaly. To bring Thessaly under his control, Pelias hired a mercenary army to unleash a reign of terror. This made him very unpopular, yet it also sent his enemies fleeing.

Unbeknownst to Pelias, though, Aeson had sired another son before he was assassinated. This secret child grew up on the slopes of Mount Pelion, where his guardians taught him that he was the rightful king of Iolcus and that he must one day reclaim the throne. The child's name was Jason. One day, when he had reached adulthood, Jason found himself in Iolcus on some random business regarding sheep. He decided then to head for the Royal Court. There, under public gaze, he openly confronted Pelias about his murderous treachery. A tense silence fell upon the court. All those armed reached for the handles of their daggers and swords. Half of them already distrusted and despised Pelias. But the other half were working for him.

To avoid a colossal fight in the court, King Pelias agreed to hand over his throne to Jason if Jason could bring to court the Golden Fleece of Colchis. This legendary symbol of regal power was purported to be in a faraway land across many seas. Thought by some just to be a myth, the Golden Fleece was believed by others to be a magnificent sheepskin sprouting gold wool. Even if it was real, the Fleece's exact location in the mysterious land of Colchis wasn't known. However, like Pelius, Jason didn't want a bloodbath at the Royal Court so he agreed to his uncle's proposal.

Jason then commissioned a boat called *Argo* and set sail with an array of eccentric sailors, the Argonauts, into the rising sun. The journey to Colchis would take them across three seas: first, the

Aegean, then through the Hellespont to the Sea of Marmara, then through the Bosporus Strait to cross the Black Sea.

As the epic unfolds, Jason battles all sorts of dragons and demons and monsters across many strange lands. Aided by the enigmatic Princess Medea, who claims to be the granddaughter of the sun god Helios, Jason eventually locates and retrieves the Golden Fleece from the land of Colchis. In time, he falls in love with Medea, marries her, then returns to Iolcus.

When Jason and his band of intrepid Argonauts bring the fleece to the Royal Court in Iolcus, Pelius at once backs away from his promise and refuses to give up the throne. All along Pelius had hoped Jason would get lost in some far-off place whilst on a fruitless search.

Like many in Iolcus, Medea is enraged by Pelius' betrayal of the agreement and she incites magic to have Pelius poisoned. She is not careful enough to hide her culpability, though. And because she is Jason's wife, he is also implicated in Pelius' death. The people of Iolcus could hardly welcome Jason as their rightful king when he too can be accused of regicide. Because of this, Jason gives up becoming king and drifts off on the *Argo* into exile.

If nowadays you seek out the location of Colchis, the ancient land of the Golden Fleece, you will find yourself in the pretty Georgian city of Batumi on the eastern coast of the Black Sea. In Batumi's central plaza, named European Square, you'll spot a slender statue of Medea on top of a splendid column, a glistening gold-painted fleece draped over her outstretched arm.

When Homer first recorded the story of the Golden Fleece, the economic value of sheep was plain for all Greeks to see. Sheep symbolised wealth − for both rich and poor − so it is no surprise that a fleece featured so heavily in this famous legend. In ancient Greece, the economy of most of the city-states was almost entirely based upon agriculture. Indeed, Athens was founded initially by shepherds and sheep-farmers who came together to develop communal livestock holdings and who shared the pastures around the Parthenon.

Over the centuries, the communal sharing of pastoral resources gave way to aristocratic control of the industry. Large farms and grazing lands were the most significant form of property owned by the Greek elite. Just as in ancient Mesopotamia, the wool industry of ancient Greece was dominated by aristocratic women. Under the patronage of a queen, Greek women of the upper classes would run their own weaving studios producing high-end dyed cloth for themselves and their high society friends. Homer notes this as the primary daily task of Helen of Troy, for example.

Another theme of Homer's epic telling of the Golden Fleece is that it foregrounds the nautical prowess of the ancient Greeks. With such nautical power at their disposal, ancient Greek city-states thought it logical to colonise the unsettled lands of the Mediterranean. The modern cities of Naples in Italy, Nice in France and Istanbul in Turkey started out as Greek colonies. The Greeks even managed to set up colonies in faraway Colchis as well, which is another reason why the city of Batumi celebrates the Golden Fleece.

In the fourth century BC, a Greek military leader emerged who was not content with just setting up colonies here and there on unsettled lands across the coasts of the Mediterranean. His title was Alexander the Great and his ambition was to conquer just about every land and kingdom in the known world. Interestingly, when Alexander moved to conquer Egypt in 332 BC, he became so enchanted by the ram-headed Egyptian god Amun that he made a pilgrimage to the Amun-Ra shrine in the oasis city of Siwa. In deference to Alexander's military power, the priests of Siwa took to calling Alexander the son of Amun-Ra.

Alexander was quite taken with this idea and he fostered a convergence between the Egyptian god Amun-Ra and the Greek god Zeus. As Alexander conquered more kingdoms across Mesopotamia and Persia and all the way to the Indus Valley, statues and paintings started appearing all over mainland Greece of this newly converged god who became known as Zeus-Ammon. In classical art, Zeus-Ammon looks exactly like the bearded god Zeus except he is adorned with amazing ram horns twisting out of his skull.

When Alexander the Great died in 323 BC, many of the lands that he conquered fell out of Greek control. Greece itself experienced something of a power vacuum as well. Barbarian tribes from northern Europe took advantage of this situation and swept down to sack Greek cities and temples. The most feared of these tribes were called the Keltoi by the Greeks – the Celts. As Celtic tribes were ransacking ancient Greek cities on the far eastern edge of Europe, on the far western edge of Europe, other Celtic tribes were building monumental sheep-farms. This is the story we shall cover in the next chapter.

Chapter 10

SHEEPLANDS OF THE CELTS

WALES, 500 BC TO AD 50

In the summer of 1846, deep in the Austrian Alps near the exquisite lakeside village of Hallstatt, a salt-mine manager was preparing to sink new shafts into a wooded hillside when he stumbled upon a long-decayed human body. Before returning to his drilling job, he decided to record his find by meticulously drawing it and noting the environment in which it was found. In so doing, he came across another skeleton. Then another. Then another. The manager and his workers soon uncovered layer upon layer of prehistoric humans – a thousand individuals in all, the older of them dating from around 1,000 BC.

Along with the bodies, many grave goods were also found: metal ornaments, decorative brooches and, in one case, an amazing sheepskin blanket. Some of the most elaborate burial plots also had swords and shields. There were also many tiny specks of spun wool. Whoever these people were, they kept plenty of sheep and wove wool into cloth. Because of the site's proximity to the village of Hallstatt, the inhabitants were designated the Hallstatt culture.

After decades of study – and a bunch of finds elsewhere in central Europe – Hallstatt was discovered to be the earliest known site for the pan-European people we call the Celts. As bronze was giving way to iron, the Celts spread westward from Hallstatt to form separate settlements in Switzerland, Germany, France, Spain and Portugal. Some Celtic tribes, though, went in the opposite direction, eastward along the Danube and into Anatolia (in a sort of reverse of the great Stone Age farmer migrations aeons before). In this way, the Celts became a dominant culture across northern Europe yet they never united politically into a single kingdom or empire.

From around 500 BC, successive waves of Celts also began crossing the sea to settle in Britain. During these waves, the Celts sometimes integrated with and sometimes displaced those already living in Britain, including the descendants of the Beaker folk. The most recent wave of Celts to set up home in Britain were the Belgae, from Belgium. The Belgae had only recently colonised parts of Hampshire by the time Julius Caesar invaded in 54 BC. As in previous human migrations to Britain, these Celtic settlers brought sheep, both for subsistence living and as an exchange commodity. The Celtic elite would also offer up sheep to each other as gifts as part of their diplomatic efforts. Often, Celtic tribes would count their wealth and power in terms of the number of sheep they owned.

As traders, the first Celts may have ended up in Wales far earlier than 500 BC, setting up coastal exchange posts from one of their many strongholds on the Atlantic Seaboard. Indeed, some experts believe that Celtic peoples originally emerged on the Atlantic coast of Europe and then spread to central Europe – rather than the other way round.

There is also a growing number of archaeologists and historians who posit that Celtic expansion around Europe resulted from cultural diffusion rather than actual migration. If this is the case, then the Celts comprised a loose multi-ethnic culture rather than a distinct racial group. The glue that held this culture together was trade – through which they shared their languages, their customs and their arts and crafts.

Whatever their origins, the Celts of prehistoric Britain were avid sheep-farmers and wool-crafters. In some modern-day museums, Iron Age Celts are represented by face-painted figures cloaked in woad-coloured woollen plaid. However, this may be just a projection of later clothing styles onto prehistoric Celts. Or it may reflect historical reality since smidgens of cloth from the late Hallstatt culture do sometimes exhibit a two-coloured plaid weave.

As mentioned earlier, complete woollen products do not usually survive well over the course of thousands of years. Sometimes a few scraps turn up underground here and there but these are usually very small. Much more commonly found are the tools of wool-craft: loom weights, spindle whorls, bone needles and sometimes sophisticated iron shears. These are quite regular finds in the Celtic archaeological record, including at Iron Age sites in Wales. Their abundance suggests that wool-working was ubiquitous at this time.

The most famous Celtic remains are their amazing hillforts. A hillfort is an enclosed settlement fortified with a stockade and located on a natural or artificial hill, usually surrounded by an array of earthworks, ditches and mounds. Because the earthworks are arranged within the hill's contours, the hillfort viewed aerially looks like it is perched upon a beautiful series of fluidic concentric rings. Wales is exceptionally well endowed with Celtic hillforts; at least a thousand dot the Welsh landscape. It is tempting to think that Wales has so many hillforts because it has so many hills, but it also attests to the strength and vibrancy of Celtic culture in Iron Age Wales.

If you want to view photogenic examples of the earthen remains of Welsh hillforts, you might like to seek out some built on top of promontories jutting out to sea, such as Dinas Gynfor in Anglesey, Llansteffan Castle in Carmarthenshire or Porth y Rhaw in Pembrokeshire. Some of these have medieval castles built upon them but they all give the air of a very ancient Britain.

Whether set on promontories or high in the mountains, Welsh hillforts come in all shapes and sizes. The smaller ones might have been fortified farming estates built for just one or two families. The larger hillforts are the size of small towns. It was upon the remains of one of these more formidable hillforts – later claimed to be the birthplace of Merlin the Magician – where I began writing this book.

Taking a slow exploratory stroll upon one of these larger hillforts rather floods the imagination. Looking at hillfort scenes shown in action movies, you might be inclined to imagine them purely as military enclosures from which painted warlords or warrior kings valiantly defend their territories against enemy attack. Indeed, a martial culture pervaded many Celtic tribes with warrior chiefs at the top. However, although there is evidence that tribal warfare grew more and more common as the Iron Age progressed, this does not mean that tribes were always at war with each other. For long periods of their history, most Celtic tribes lived in relative peace, the hillforts being sites of the inter-tribal exchange of wool-crafts and dairy products, rather than of clashing swords and pitchforks.

Celtic hillforts may have doubled as defensive structures when the need arose but many have a far more spacious feel as if they are primarily oriented to civic and agricultural roles. Such hillforts enclose entire villages and fields. In fact, the label 'hillfort' might seem out of place here. They are more like a 'hill village'. One of the significant roles for such civic hill villages would be livestock enclosure. Maybe, then, hillforts were built to keep sheep *in* rather than keep enemies *out*. As such, they also served to keep sheep secure at night when the Welsh hills were alive with predators.

Similarly, the gorgeous radial mounds and ditches that encircle many Welsh hillforts could be simple devices to pen and corral the livestock on their daily trips to and from surrounding pastures. Millennia after they were put together, visitors like Shelley and I can ascend easily along the circuiting paths of hillfort earthworks to the flat field on top. Celtic sheep likely did the same 2,500 years ago. For the Celts of Wales, corralling sheep would have been a critical economic activity to stop them from wandering off into the woods or from racing off to munch a field of cereal crops. Nowadays, the Welsh countryside is adorned with hundreds of miles of beautiful drystone walls laid out to keep sheep and cattle in the right place. In Celtic times, though, the earthworks of hillforts would have accomplished the same task.

As well as bustling with baaing sheep at night, the hill village would be scouted by barking guard dogs and rowdy shepherd dogs. Shepherds' dogs then may not have been as helpful, though, as sheepdogs are now. Iron Age sheepdogs could have driven sheep in one direction or another but humans and dogs probably hadn't worked out the sophisticated system of tricks needed to gather or disperse flocks into precise formations. This would take till well after the seventeenth century. It is also possible that the sheep of the Iron Age were just not as amenable to being pushed around and guided by dogs whom many sheep might not have viewed as worth their full attention. However, Iron Age dogs probably performed the role we generally attribute to cats, patrolling the hillforts and stables in search of rodents that could infest pantries and stores. Also, the dogs of the Iron Age often ended up on the dinner table – suggesting their usefulness in shepherding or hunting was not nearly as great as in later epochs.

Given the expansive character of some Celtic hillforts, where fields and villages co-inhabited the flat hilltop, we can surmise the whole gamut of sheep-related activity would have been present: folds and pens, shearing sheds, butcheries, meat-smoking huts, milking stalls, wool-craft workshops, marketplaces, as well as places to sacrifice the sheep for spiritual purposes. On this last point, Celtic Britons seem to have ritualistically offered livestock when new grain stores were dug, presumably hoping that some deity would respond by issuing bumper harvests in the future. The remains of sacrificed sheep have been excavated, for instance, from ground stores in the Danebury hillfort in Hampshire. In other Iron Age sites, similar ground stores had a mixture of animal remains: sheep bones, horse heads and the skeletons of dogs.

If the Celts loved and needed sheep, it is not so much because they enjoyed eating lamb and mutton but because they adored wool. As the Celtic prehistorian Miranda Green declares, the raising of sheep for wool was an essential aspect of their economy – for subsistence purposes and for surplus trading. Green asserts that wool was the primary product of Celtic sheep and they were only slaughtered for consumption as they approached the end of their wool-producing lives, long after the optimum time for meat had passed. The other vital Celtic sheep product was their milk. Sheep's milk is twice as rich in Vitamin D as cow's milk, so Green suggests it was probably crucial for Celtic health in cloud-covered Wales where the sun could hide away for most months of the year.

Other sheep products were also pretty useful. Sheep's dung could be dried and burnt in the hearth to heat the home or to cook meals. Wet dung, in contrast, could be mushed together with clay to produce daub, that organic mud the Celts slapped between wattle twigs to build the walls of their houses. Celtic sheep guts were used to make bowstrings and fishing lines. It is likely, also, that the Celts used sheep's tallow to make soap since, a few centuries later, Roman writers credited the Celts for teaching them this soapmaking process.

Given their success as farmers and the steady rise of the Celtic population, the Celtic tribes of Britain couldn't help but start brushing up against one another more and more often. This would prove beneficial by enabling increased trade and a more prosperous economy. However, it could also result in competition and conflict. Many a Celtic tribe took to sheep-rustling as an economic redress for land disputes, and perhaps as a business in itself. Far from being vilified as criminals and thieves, sheep-rustlers of the Iron Age tribes were sometimes celebrated as sheep warriors. Although the Welsh Celts did not have a written culture to record specific incidents, sheep-rustling is embedded in the oral storytelling traditions of nearby Celtic Ireland, ranging from the heroes of *Táin Bó Cúailnge* to the ballads of the Borderers.

Worse than all the sheep-rustling going on, though, was the practice of people smuggling. Some Celtic tribes would abduct women or children from other tribes before forcing them into marriage and slavery. In their new tribal setting, the children would be charged with shepherding and the women set to spinning and weaving wool.

Sometimes as well, there would have been all-out warfare between tribes. In these times, the pressure was on to shore up the hillfort defences with ramparts, spikes, hidden pits and mazes. It also meant either evicting all the livestock and sheep to lowland fields or more likely – since they were so valuable – corralling them together in a pen or fold at the top.

Given their prevalence in Celtic archaeology, sheep seem like they were not just part of the economy – they were the basis of it. Indeed, the archaeologist Umberto Albarella prefers to call the Iron Age in Britain the 'Age of Sheep'. Across the Channel, in the final century BC, the Romans pushing into Gaul soon noted Britain as a veritable land of sheep. For example, the Roman writer Strabo comments: 'They have such enormous flocks of sheep … so that they afford a plenteous supply of woollen coats.' Strabo would go on to write that there was no need for Rome to colonise Britain since a brusque trade between the island and the Roman Empire had been forced open by Julius Caesar. However, Strabo had yet to reckon with the ambitions of Emperor Claudius who was soon to fix his steely eyes on the sheepland he called Britannia.

Chapter 11

SHEEPLANDS OF THE ROMAN EMPIRE

WALES/EUROPE, AD 50 TO AD 383

If you walk east along a country lane through Yewtree Wood from the pleasant Welsh village of Hyssington, within about fifteen minutes you will cross the border into England. Although, if you do the same walk with a six-year-old boy playing dress-up as a Roman legionnaire, the walking time more than doubles.

In any case, as you stroll into the superb Stretton valley of Shropshire, you will soon come across a stunning green shield-shaped mountain in the distance. To reach the mountain's broad peak, you must trek a gentle incline that meanders upward through miles of meadows stippled with black-faced Shropshire sheep. This mountain is called Caer Caradoc and its folding slopes have been a summer sheep pasture for thousands of years.

Caer Caradoc is named for an ancient Celtic warrior: Caradog. The Romans, though, called him Caratacus. By this name, he was notorious across the Empire, a fearless barbarian who had attacked and wounded Roman legions more than once. In the AD 40s, the Roman army

62

swept into the lowlands of eastern Britain. One by one, various Celtic tribes fell under Roman conquest. However, by AD 50, Caratacus had managed to unite the Silures Celts of south Wales with the Ordovices Celts of north Wales. Together they set about making a final stand, here on Caer Caradoc, to stop the Romans from overrunning Britain.

From the crest of the mountain, Caratacus and his Celtic warriors could see 10,000 Roman infantrymen as they approached across fields and meadows – the sheep scattering to avoid them. When they reached the foot of the mountain, the soldiers halted.

The Roman commander in charge was a general named Ostorius. He gazed at the hastily built wooden fort on top of the mountain. Hordes of woad-faced Celts screamed and yelled abuse at him. Ostorius could see nervousness on the face of his troops. Most of the Roman soldiers had fought Celts before and knew them to be unreserved in their attack – and recklessly wild in hand-to-hand battle. None were keen to advance uphill, especially as they could see the Celts preparing to hurl various missiles at them: rocks, stones, flaming arrows.

However, General Ostorius had no intention of retreating. To do so would end his career. He ordered his legionnaires into a 'testudo', or tortoise formation. Pressing together and with their shields interlocked overhead, the Romans began walking up Caer Caradoc. Their progress was unhurried and gradual. Tortoise-step by tortoise-step, the Romans pushed slowly but relentlessly to the top of the mountain.

My own ascent up Caer Caradoc with six-year-old Shelley was equally slow. Shelley actually started the climb in a raging run but was soon waylaid, intent on slashing his plastic gladius into each and every small landmark: gateposts, bushes, boulders. The sheep were only spared because they could run faster than him. The day before, we had visited the National Roman Legion Museum at Caerleon in Gwent. The museum's enthusiastic guides were dressed up in period costume. Within minutes, they had psyched up Shelley into warrior mode by lending him a centurion uniform before setting him to re-enact a massive battle with a dozen other excited kids. It was mayhem.

Halfway up Caer Caradoc the next day, though, he was all battled out, slowing to a dawdle then plopping to rest in a flowery meadow. I did give young Shelley the choice of dressing up as either a Celtic or a Roman warrior. However, he had learnt at the museum that the Celts went into battle completely naked. Since it wasn't much fun to play dress-up without a costume, he opted to be a Roman.

Though Shelley and I never made it to the peak of Caer Caradoc, the Romans back in AD 50 were far more disciplined in their ascent. Their interlocked shields fended off the Celtic missiles and eventually they approached close enough to climb through and around the Celtic ramparts. Then, the hand-to-hand combat began. The Celtic spikes and longswords might have been lethal if there had been enough space to swing or hurl them. However, by the time the testudo broke, the fighting was cramped and crowded. Now the Roman gladius proved its worth, stabbing ingloriously but efficiently with short thrusts into the bellies of the Celts. Maybe the Silures and Ordovices warriors were naked or maybe they were clothed in sheepskin or plaid. Whatever the case, they could hardly match the Romans, who were clad in chain mail, shoulder-plates and iron helmets. Even when a Celtic warrior managed to get a good swing with their longsword, it might just clang against the metal armour and glance away.

As the Romans overtook the crest of Caer Caradoc, the Celts had to choose between being sliced down where they stood or escaping fast down the other side of Caer Caradoc. They decided to run – breaking their engagement and scattering into the Welsh countryside. Caratacus himself fled north to another Celtic tribe, one ruled by a Celtic queen called Cartimandua. Fearing the wrath of Ostorius, she promptly handed Caratacus over to the Romans. Before long, he was deported as a war trophy back to Rome.

This defeat neutralised the ability of the Welsh Celts to wage proper war against the Romans. However, it did not diminish their desire to fight for independence. For two decades, the Celts in Wales staged guerrilla attacks as the Romans tried to build forts and roads in Welsh territory. Eventually, sometime around AD 80, either through exhaustion or under a treaty, Welsh military resistance lost steam, and the Romans began setting up colonies in Wales.

The Roman governors, though, were not about to underestimate the Celtic desire to regroup and rebound from Wales, so they committed tens of thousands of auxiliaries into Welsh territory over the following decades. The Romans also demolished anything that looked like a Celtic hillfort so that any native resistance could not resurge using a hillfort as a stronghold. The Romans also built some twenty-five new fortresses of their own in Wales, often on top of demolished Celtic hillforts. They then linked the fortresses together with an impressive set of Roman roads.

The new Roman forts were constructed of wood to begin with but some were slowly reconstructed in stone. One of the biggest of these was Isca Silurum, built in the heart of Silures territory. It eventually became a township of 2,000 people but its remains now lie buried within the modern Welsh town of Caerleon. On site, there are outstanding remnants of a Roman amphitheatre. The amphitheatre's gorgeous circular shape has convinced many locals over the centuries that it was the site of King Arthur's famous Round Table. Nowadays you will often see the grassy innards of the Round Table being dutifully mowed in organic style by creamy Dorset sheep. Located right next to the site is the National Roman Legion Museum where Shelley learnt to wield a gladius.

The Celtic sheep farmed in and around Isca Silurum would have produced meat and cheese for the individual soldiers of the fort and wool for the Romans across Wales. The Roman navy may also have used wool to augment their linen sailcloth to propel their ships across their empire.

Judging from standard patterns in various provinces across the empire, Welsh sheep would probably have been 'requisitioned' by the Roman army: that is, stolen from local farmers during times of crisis. In peacetime, though, Celtic pastoralists around Isca Silurum could have traded their sheep at fixed prices set by administrators back in Rome. Ancient scribbled notecards found near Roman forts also suggest a flourishing black market existed in Britain at this time as well. Thus, Welsh farmers could probably rely on the desperation of well-to-do Roman soldiers to sell woollen cloth or sheepskins at inflated prices, especially as the wintry nights started to bite and shipments from other parts of the province were delayed.

Along with Isca Silurum, the Romans set up a fortified town called Venta Silurum. Like Isca, Venta Silurum has impressive remains, notably an excellent Roman wall. Again, the modern-day grasses surrounding the site are often organically mown by beautiful sheep, tan specimens of a breed called Glamorgan Welsh. Both these Roman towns became important centres of trade and administration. From them, Rome governed the Silures Celts into the second and third centuries AD.

However, whilst Roman strongholds like Isca Silurum and Venta Silurum dominated the nearby countryside of south Wales, many Welsh farms and settlements far away largely carried on with their traditional way of life without Roman interference. In areas not close to a Roman fort or a Roman road, Welsh farmers could raise their subsistence flocks without ever seeing a Roman soldier – let alone having their sheep forcibly taken. The twenty-five Roman forts in Wales may have looked impressive when plotted on a map but they were hardly substantial enough to oversee every single inhabited area. If a Celtic farmer desired to stay outside of Roman control, they could do so by casting away from the lowlands and heading into the hills with their livestock. The hills weren't great for growing crops but they were good places to let sheep roam to feed themselves. Secure with self-sustaining sheep, those living within – but isolated from – Roman Britain would feel little pressure to change their Celtic customs or language.

Even within the lowland zones of Roman Wales, some farmers may have carried on as usual without drastic lifestyle changes. One ancient sheep-farm in Wales that spans both pre-Roman and Roman times is the Thornwell Farm site in Gwent. The farm is better known in the world of archaeology for its Stone Age barrows yet during the late Iron Age it was occupied by a series of enclosed sheep-farms, that is, farms fortified by walls. By good management or good fortune, the farm survived unchanged well into the Roman occupation of Britain, carrying on as an independent Silures concern for hundreds of years. The site shows that Roman goods, Roman money, and Roman authority as well, may have only very slowly become part of Welsh Celtic life, intruding piecemeal over the course of centuries.

For sure, there is a chance that Thornwell Farm was located outside of a well-managed Roman administrative area or maybe it was just too insignificant for the Romans to care much about. Regardless, it is interesting for us to contemplate that Celtic-style farming was able to endure at the height of Rome's presence in Wales.

From the Roman side, it is likely that entrepreneurial soldiers with enough 'coins and contacts' probably engaged in many side ventures in an effort to make the most of their far-flung posting. This may have included trading Welsh-made textiles into other parts of the empire. One popular wool garment made in Britain at this time was the burra, a hooded cloak. It was much in demand across the Empire's northernmost provinces and if Wales had something special to offer at the time it may have been this. Over time, wealthy Roman-Britons with decent-sized villas also welcomed the chance to get their hands on locally made tapetia – woollen rugs – to adorn their couches and as saddle-wear for their horses. These woollen products would eventually earn high regard throughout Roman Europe, being listed in state-sponsored compendia as well as commercial handbooks that detailed which products each imperial province excelled at. By the third century AD, British wool became so well known that the great Roman administrator Dionysius Alexandrinus noted: 'the wool of Britain is often spun so fine that it is in a manner comparable to the spider's thread.' By this time, it seems, wool from Britain was not just being bought by the Roman army in Britain but by the Roman elite all over the empire. The former sought something functional for the weather and the latter sought the finest woollen garments money could buy.

Very possibly, these different wool products came from different kinds of sheep. When the Romans first 'tortoised' their way up Caer Caradoc, the Celtic sheep they scattered in their wake were probably brown or pied sheep, with some being woolly and some hairy. A few decades later, sheep-farmers in Wales were interbreeding their extant Celtic sheep with newly introduced varieties, including Rhufain sheep, Rhufain being Welsh for Roman. Rhufain sheep were hornless, white-faced, short-wool sheep whose wool came in many a colour. Many British breeds of sheep developed over the centuries can claim Rhufain sheep as their ancestors, including the Badger Face Welsh Mountain sheep and the Cotswold sheep just across the border into England

Though the Rhufain sheep came in all colours, careful Rhufain breeders could transform their flock into being mostly white-wooled so they could increase their sales value around the Empire. Like the Greek and Mesopotamian elite before them, well-off Romans wanted to be able to dye their clothes any colour they desired and white fleece made this much easier.

As well as new sheep, the Romans brought into Wales some new wool technologies, including the two-beam loom and a diverse assortment of iron scissors. With these new instruments, wealthy Romans could decorate their British villas with elaborate tapestries and artisanal furnishings. The Romans also brought their sophisticated know-how in water engineering to slowly drain some of the wetlands of south-eastern Wales, thus opening up more places to develop sheep-farming in their new dominion.

Sheep-farming and the wool trade were not only important in Roman Britain. They were also crucial industries throughout the Empire. The chief librarian of Rome, Marcus Terentius Varro, wrote in the first century BC that for all their showy architecture and grand cities, the Romans 'were first and foremost shepherds'.

In fact, just about all of Rome's famous statesmen, generals, engineers and philosophers were from families that owned vast tracts of land upon which they practised industrial-scale pastoral farming. The profits they accrued were spent on massive villas and palaces plus the buying of all sorts of civic favours. And if official coins fell into short supply, due to political unrest or natural disaster, the landowners could still buy everything they needed by paying in wool or sheep. This included sacrificial payments to the gods so that a prosperous future could be assured.

Well before their conquest of Britain was complete, the Romans had established a woollen mill near Colchester, their provincial capital. Evidently, they understood the importance of keeping their armies warm and clothed in Britain's rainy, chilly environs. Another woollen mill was set up in Winchester as the Romans moved westward. Some records suggest wool mills were operating on the Welsh side of the Severn, as well, most probably in or around Venta Silurum, where numerous Roman-era carding combs and loom parts have been dug up. All these Roman mills together increased British wool production and created a more robust international textile network across the empire.

As well as promoting the international wool trade when they colonised Britain, the Romans also seem to have disrupted it. In this regard, the long-established trade routes between Celtic tribes in Wales and Celtic tribes in Ireland, Scotland, Gaul and Galicia were either broken up or taken over by the Romans. So much for imperial progress.

Of course, the Roman economic interests in Britain were not confined to wool. Before their conquest of Wales, the Roman invaders would have been more interested in Welsh metal ores. The copper mines in Gwynedd would have been particularly enticing since they had been well known as productive sites for many centuries. The Romans also scouted for gold in the Welsh hills. In this regard, there was an initial rush at the Loventium goldfields in Carmarthenshire, but this soon petered out to render gold mining revenues secondary to the wool industry.

Another industry that flourished across the provinces of the Roman Empire, including Britain, was slavery. As well as enslaving vanquished Celtic warriors, the Romans imprisoned and trafficked young men and women as agricultural labourers across the Empire. Along with iron scissors, the Romans left plenty of iron shackles around their provincial farm sites for future generations to find. Welsh shepherds that had crossed Roman officials in some way probably ended up caring for sheep in Pannonia whilst Welsh weavers might have ended up in sweatshops in Hispania. Probably, neither would ever see the green hills of Wales again.

During the fourth century AD, the Empire's economy stagnated then gradually declined – as did its military power. Rome found it difficult to keep Britannia secure. At this time, Romano-Welsh towns had to be fortified as best they could to stave off various threats, especially marauders from Ireland. Eventually, around AD 383, the Roman army marched clear out of Wales altogether.

Sheep-farmers living alone in the wild west of Wales probably could not have cared less that the Roman army had departed. Indeed, many would have celebrated it since they were freed from tax burdens and could also lay claim to abandoned lands. However, since the Romans had been in Wales for three centuries, much of the population had grown to consider themselves Roman, either in whole or in part. These Romano-Welsh therefore dreaded what might come next – and who might assault their undefended shores.

Chapter 12
THE FLOCKS OF PATRICIUS

BANWEN, WALES, c. AD 383

One fine day around AD 383, a young Romano-Welsh teen was jauntily walking down the banks of the River Dulais in south Wales near his father's estate of Bannavem Taburniae. The teen's name was Patricius. For a long time, his father had been a wealthy Roman official until the garrisons were pulled out of Wales rather abruptly. After the imperial army had left, Patricius' father then assumed the role of deaconate in one of Wales's very first Christian churches.

Patricius took his family's wealth for granted, happily hunting for sport in the nearby woodlands every morning when he should have been attending to his duties on the family's estate, then joyfully fishing all afternoon even when his father commanded him to attend church events. You can't really blame Patricius; the River Dulais has so many great fishing pools. Even nowadays, the place is well known amongst Welsh anglers and back in the fourth century AD, these pools offered Patricius far more fun than his father's preaching. Some might call him spoiled. Others would call him carefree. Alas, his life-world would change in an instant.

As Patricius stepped out of a shallow river pool, a club-wielding assailant knocked the fish he was carrying from his hands. Patricius had but a moment to look up – spying a band of raiders – before he, too, was knocked into the water. Before he drowned in the river, the pirates lifted Patricius up and piled him half-conscious onto a boat. Then the boat cruised a little down the river until it met the ocean. When Patricius awoke, he was out to sea with no sign of land. Around him, through bleary eyes, he noticed other young Welsh captives cowering in the boat. After a few minutes, he surmised the worst had happened. He had been taken by slave traders and was on his way to the strange, wild, pagan island known to him as Hibernia – and to us as Ireland. Patricius knew that anybody taken in this manner never returned home.

In Ireland, Patricius was traded as a piece of property until he found his way to the rugged hills of County Mayo. He was sent there to tend to sheep on a lonely wet, cold, rainy mountain. Although at times he interacted with the Irish – and learnt their language – for many very long days and nights, only the sheep and the wild rain-soaked pastures kept him company. Shepherding then, as now, was a solitary, isolated existence, but one that allows time for the mind to meditate. Or to hallucinate. On one cool foggy night, Patricius heard the faint murmurings of God's voice in his head. Perhaps it was just half-remembered gospel utterings – delivered by his father – seeping back into his consciousness. Or maybe it was God taking pity on him and letting him know he was not alone. Or perhaps God was punishing him, telling him his new life as a slave shepherd was a response to how he'd wasted his youth.

Whatever the case, the fact that Patricius had been forced into shepherding might not have been an accident. Jesus Christ, even then, was often called the Good Shepherd and his followers his flock. To illustrate the traditional Christian message of shepherding, allow me to use the words of a modern-day Catholic priest, Father Michael Van Sloun of St Paul and Minneapolis:

> **Shepherding teaches self-sacrifice;** service is gladly given, and there is willingness to lay down one's life to protect the sheep from wild predatory animals and rustlers.

Shepherding teaches self-sufficiency. No one else is there to do the work. A shepherd accepts the task and completes it.

Shepherding teaches care and concern. Shepherds provide individualized attention, recognize differences in appearance and temperament, and work for the betterment of each sheep.

If these are the professed benefits of shepherding, then we might believe Patricius' abduction was more a blessing than a curse.

A full six years after being captured and enslaved, Patricius heard the Lord's voice once more. This time it conveyed a very precise instruction: to walk across Ireland to the furthest coast. There Patricius would find a boat and a crew prepared to take him home to Wales.

Taking heed, Patricius somehow managed to walk from County Mayo to the coast near St George's Channel. And, indeed, Patricius did come across a curragh boat being readied to set sail from a stony Irish shore, its tiny crew willing to ferry him across the Irish Sea: a great adventure itself. When he arrived home in Wales, his family greeted his return as a miracle.

However, by then, Patricius seemed a changed person. When abducted, he was a carefree teenager. Returned, Patricius was a fervent young Christian man. Not long after returning to Bannavem Taburniae, he set sail to France to take on many years of training to be a clergyman. Patricius proved an able student and then an expert Christian teacher.

However, the visions and voices in Patricius' head did not abate. In one vision, he saw a man approaching him upon a wave from Ireland, holding a pack of letters under one arm. He gave one of these letters to Patricius. The letter begged Patricius to return to Ireland to spread his Christian faith across the Emerald Isle. With little regard for his own safety, Patricius obeyed the message and returned to Hibernia to preach to the very people who had abducted and enslaved him.

With all the skills that shepherding had bestowed upon him – perseverance, patience, commitment and care – Patricius managed to spread the gospel throughout Ireland, converting all sections of Irish society from kings and warlords to peasants and slaves. Over the next few centuries, Christianity spread like wildfire and churches and monasteries popped up all over the island. Indeed, Ireland would be a beacon of Christian faith and learning for centuries to come.

Not long after he died, the Church pronounced Patricius a saint: St Patrick. The role of sheep in Patrick's personal transformation into a great holy man has been celebrated in both Ireland and Wales, where artistic renderings usually portray him caring for a lamb.

The remains of St Patrick's family estate at Bannavem Taburniae have since been built over to make the village of Banwen in Glamorgan. The modern-day residents commemorate St Patrick's life – and the role of shepherding within it – by parading through the village once a year with crooks in one hand and a fluffy toy sheep or a Bible in the other. Each year, more and more visitors from afar join in with them, often dressing up in ancient Welsh, Irish or Roman costumes to display the historical importance of his legacy.

Chapter 13

SHEEPLANDS OF THE DARK AGES

WALES/EUROPE, AD 400 TO AD 800

Like a cheerful woolly-white sheep, the previous chapter may have felt bright and warm. However, perhaps it was a tad too celebratory of the heroic stature of St Patrick and his role as a shepherd. As a contrast – and in the spirit of the darker times that we now enter – I will lay out an alternative interpretation of St Patrick's sheepish adventures.

The historian Roy Flechner has read through the writings of St Patrick with a fine-tooth comb and then compared them with the literary conventions of the rest of fourth- and fifth-century Europe. He then advanced the idea that St Patrick may have fabricated his abduction from Wales and his induction into Irish slavery. Flechner believes that St Patrick left Wales for Ireland because the Roman Empire laid too many responsibilities at his young feet. Since his family were the biggest landowners in the Banwen area – and his father the local Roman official – they were legally charged to collect all the taxes from the Roman citizens living nearby and to administer all judicial affairs as well. St Patrick would have inherited his father's estate and these burdensome duties. Given the crumbling Roman presence in Britain at the time, the economy was likely withering fast. Yet, despite this, Patricius would still have had to pester the locals to cough up tax payments. If he did a poor job of this, then – under Roman law – he would have to forfeit all his property to some higher bureaucracy back in Rome. Thus, according to this theory of events, Patrick fled the disintegrating Roman Empire.

Only after Patrick was sure the Roman legions had left Wales for good did he scuttle back there safe in the knowledge that he wouldn't be charged for absconding from his imperial duties. Patrick then took up the other profession handed to him by his father: a career as a Christian minister. And where else better to go to stake a claim in the Church hierarchy than a grand island of convertible pagans?

This might sound like a cynical interpretation of St Patrick's story. Still, Flechner's reasoning is based upon St Patrick's most famous piece of writing, *Confessio*. Though presented like a confession, the letter reads like a document submitted to his Church bosses on the continent to defend his reputation. The early Church was full of ambitious priests seeking to climb the corporate ladder. Evidently, one of St Patrick's peers was flinging mud his way suggesting he was in Ireland only because it served his financial interest and professional aspirations.

Although this narrative might be far less appealing spiritually than the traditional St Patrick story, it still presents him as a wily go-getter, someone dynamic enough to rain down the Christian message upon an entire island. And if we do suppose St Patrick fabricated his whole life-story, it still says a lot to us that he chose shepherding as a central part of his narrative. Evidently, sheep were embedded in the Christian culture of Britain and Ireland just as much as they were in their economies.

Another reason a shadow looms over the previous chapter is that we are entering a period of history dubbed the Dark Ages. Wales waved goodbye to the Roman army in 383 AD. The rest of Britain followed early in the 400s when Emperor Constantine pulled out the last legion stationed in Britain to fight against other Roman warlords in Gaul. With Roman authority in tatters, the imperial economy in Britain collapsed, and Roman high culture slowly languished too.

At this time, not many people in Britain and Wales had the need or desire to write things into script any more. Maybe the only people doing a lot of writing were the Christian elite, like St Patrick, who had to communicate with other Christian leaders in Europe. This dearth of written records to draw upon is why this era is called the Dark Ages since historians, who rely on written sources, have so little to work with.

For some people, the Dark Ages would have also seemed dark in other ways. Rome imposed a certain degree of orderly peace upon Europe so that when its empire collapsed, chaos and conflict often arose in its place. As the empire fell, international trade links were broken to bits, including the wool trade between Wales and the rest of Britain and between Britain and the rest of Europe. This impacted individual livelihoods as well as the whole economy. Many towns in Britain – and across Europe – were abandoned as townspeople moved into the countryside, reforming as agricultural communities so they could at least grow their own food. Others had to migrate to some faraway place to eke out an existence.

In fact, there was so much migration in the decades and centuries after the Roman Empire fell apart that the alternative name for the Dark Ages is the Migration Period. One part of the Migration Period was when large numbers of Angles and Saxons sailed from their Germanic homelands across the North Sea into Britain. By around AD 600, the pagan Anglo-Saxons came to dominate much of what is now called England – overwhelming the Christianised Britons living there. This takeover is often dubbed an invasion and represented as a barbaric conquest. However, if it were a conquest, it was not like the Roman invasion of the first century AD but more of a slow and gradual economic and cultural expansion proceeding over centuries. As such, it probably proceeded by peaceful means just as much as by violent.

The likeliest way the Anglo-Saxons asserted power when they arrived in Britain was by buying up good land using the prestige goods they brought with them from the continent. Amongst these goods were lovely long-wooled Saxon sheep. They probably bought themselves into advantageous marriages with nobles as well, propelling themselves up the social ladder quite quickly. The Britons, remember, were left relatively impoverished when the Romans abandoned the

British Isles. In this manner, the Anglo-Saxons pushed their way – in an economic sense – across England.

Since Anglo-Saxons seemed rich and influential to the locals, many Britons (except those in Wales) began to emulate them, slowly adopting Anglo-Saxon customs, Anglo-Saxon laws and the Anglo-Saxon language. In turn, Britons managed to convert Anglo-Saxons to Christianity.

Of course, given their abundant weaponry and their takeover of old Roman forts, it is hard to imagine the Anglo-Saxons never warred against the Britons. If a dispute between neighbouring Anglo-Saxons and Britons flared up, their military strength would probably have helped the Anglo-Saxons win the day. The Anglo-Saxons did not have it all their way, though. One legendary battle, the Battle of Badon, reputedly saw King Arthur inflict a grievous defeat upon the Anglo-Saxons as they attempted to overtake the western parts of Britain around AD 500. Though historians doubt the presence of King Arthur at the battle, most are convinced the battle was real. Archaeologists, though, are more circumspect since they've not yet found any such battle site.

Whether via economic takeover or via the sword, after a century or more, the Angles and the Saxons had subsumed the Britons to develop their own solid and assertive kingdoms across England. A number of these kingdoms pushed right up against the modern borders of Wales. For the Welsh, the contrast between their own way of life and those of the Anglo-Saxons was stark. As the Anglo-Saxon kingdoms grew stronger, the Britons of Wales fretted they would lose their lands, their laws and their culture. Legendary figures like King Arthur appeared at this time as a call to resist Anglo-Saxon expansion.

This resistance probably marks the birth of Wales as a nation. At this time, the Welsh word 'Cymry' emerged to describe the Welsh people, as did the English term for the Welsh whom the Anglo-Saxons called 'Waeles' – a Germanic word for 'alien' rudely applied to any person who did not speak in a Germanic tongue. The Anglo-Saxon advance across England also cut off the land connection between the Britons of Wales and the Britons of Cornwall and Scotland. The Welsh were now on their own as they forged a pathway out of the Dark Ages.

One of the few people writing down the details of life in Dark Age Wales was a Romano-Welsh monk called Gildas the Wise. Gildas studied at a legendary college in southern Wales called Côr Tewdws. Here, 'legendary' might be interpreted in either of its modern meanings. As a Christian Briton with Roman heritage, Gildas railed against the pagan Anglo-Saxons. To him, the Germanic pagans were brutal warring invaders. Gildas wrote that he and other Christians had to escape the Anglo-Saxon conquest by sailing across the Celtic Sea to Brittany. Indeed, this is how Brittany assumed its name, because so many migrants from Britain settled there during the Dark Ages.

In a hefty scripted sermon titled *De Excidio et Conquestu Britanniae*, Gildas also suggested the barbarian invasion was a punishment from God because the Britons were not taking their Christianity seriously enough. In the same work, Gildas diverts from his moral history lesson once in a while to relate something about ordinary life in Wales. He describes the Welsh mountains as 'particularly suitable for the alternating pasturage of animals'. Here, Gildas is pointing out the ongoing practice of transhumance when Welsh farmers would put their flocks into the mountains in the lush, warm months of the year and bring them back down to the valleys or lowlands during the months of snowfall and frost. This pattern continues today in the mountainous lands of sheep across the globe, including Wales.

In the century or so following Gildas' death, a geographical line between Wales and the Anglo-Saxon kingdoms did solidify. King Offa, ruler of the Anglic kingdom of Mercia, built a great embankment between his kingdom and the Welsh Britons lying to his west. Going by the name of Offa's Dyke, it ran more than eighty miles from the top of Wales to its bottom, just about from the Dee estuary to the Severn estuary. Nowadays, the dyke's striking linear remains still roughly mark out the borders between England and Wales.

Speaking of which, if you are ever seeking a sublime tree-lined Welsh trail to walk during a long weekend, Offa's Dyke offers a great route. This path combines an impressive Dark Age landform with astonishing vistas of rural idylls chock-full of amiable flocks of sheep. Eventually, you will find just the right spot where on one side of the dyke, charcoal-faced Llanwenog sheep bleat gently in Welsh and on the other side glaucous-faced Ryeland sheep bleat gently in English.

As peaceful and pastoral as it is now, Offa's Dyke in the Dark Ages was often full of action. Welsh warlords ran over the dyke to raid English farms and forts and to ransack English villages and towns. Sometimes, English warlords returned the favour in retribution. Some historians suggest the dyke was built primarily to stop Welsh sheep raids rather than to halt Welsh armies advancing into England. Yet, if this was the case, it may have only been partially successful.

Despite building a stupendous dyke, when King Offa began communications with Emperor Charlemagne, the ruler of the mighty Frankish Empire, it was not Offa's landscaping feats that Charlemagne wanted to discuss. Instead, what impressed the Emperor most about Britain were cloaks woven from local sheep's wool. Charlemagne wrote to Offa more than once about setting up a trade agreement to get more of these cloaks into his empire.

These woollen cloaks were commonly made by individual families for use by family members. Children of sheep-farmers would have learnt the whole process as they grew up: from shearing and spinning to weaving and later fulling. However, those capable of producing a surplus could do well in trading, especially if they had access to finer-wool sheep breeds whose woven cloth might fetch a premium price. Given this, Dark Age sheep-farmers bred for better wool in their flocks. We can surmise as much since the archaeological record indicates a gradually greater diversity of sheep types. We might therefore assume that some sheep varieties were favoured for their fine wool, others for their milk production and still others for their bulky meat. In the midst of a Dark Age, then, sheep-farmers in the British Isles were pushing forward with innovative ways of farming sheep.

Just as the Anglo-Saxons thought they had successfully claimed England as their own, they were besieged by gigantic bands of invaders from Scandinavia. These intruders were distant cousins of the Anglo-Saxons. We know them best as Vikings.

Chapter 14

SHEEPLANDS OF THE VIKINGS

ATLANTIC EUROPE, AD 793 TO AD 1066

Nowadays, Vikings are typically characterised as pillagers and plunderers. This characterisation is not entirely undeserved. In AD 793, a band of Vikings leapt from a dragon ship onto a Northumberland beach to pillage Lindisfarne Abbey. As well as making off with religious ornaments, the Vikings wrecked the abbey and killed many monks. This was the dawn of the Viking Age.

By the middle of the next century, Viking ambitions grew beyond raiding to include all-out invasion and colonisation. By AD 878, half of all Anglo-Saxon territory in England had succumbed to this ambition. It took half a century or more for the separate Anglo-Saxon kingdoms to unite and push the Vikings out again. If Wales was forged into being by the Welsh resisting the Anglo-Saxons, England was forged into being by the Anglo-Saxons resisting the Vikings.

England wasn't the only place the Vikings had had their eye on. Around the same time, Vikings were setting up colonies in France, Ireland, Scotland, Iceland and the riverine areas of European

Russia. Eventually, around AD 1000, a small fleet of Viking longships reached America. They had sailed there from Viking colonies in Greenland and tried their hand at setting up a settlement on the northernmost tip of an expansive island they called Vinland and we call Newfoundland. In due course, they created a village, Straumsfjord, with almost one hundred people. After ten years, the colony could not sustain itself and the Vinland Vikings went to sea once more to head back from where they came.

If you visit the archaeological site of the Viking town at L'Anse aux Meadows, Newfoundland, you will see an intriguing reconstruction of beautiful grass-covered rectangular longhouses on a foreshore overlooking a wide wild ocean. It looks like a stereotypical Viking village on the North Sea – except, there's something missing.

In a way, the failure of the Vinland colony is rather strange. The Vikings had successfully set up colonies across Europe's Atlantic Seaboard. How come they made such a bad showing in North America, whose climate and resources seemed amply suited to their traditional way of life? The medieval Viking Sagas that report their presence in America also sang the praises of Newfoundland, describing it as a fertile wooded paradise rich in resources, both on land and in the sea.

Well, maybe the Vikings failed in colonising America because they didn't take sheep. The L'Anse aux Meadows site is devoid of sheep bones and without any remains of farmyards. This is the 'something missing' from the reconstruction of the settlement, too, and why it seems odd to look upon. Typically, if you go to a historical village anywhere in the Viking world, a few sheep are included for a more realistic feel. But the North American Vikings didn't take sheep with them. Archaeologists found a single spindle whorl but that was probably used to produce rope from plants to effect emergency sail repairs whilst voyaging. In all other Viking colonies, sheep were an important tool of colonisation, providing food and skins to survive the frigid winters plus wool to weave the sails. Sheep products would also put Viking settlers into a good trading position as they interacted with the foreign locals.

As an interesting aside, we might note that 600 years after the Vinland Vikings had abandoned their L'Anse aux Meadows outpost, a Welsh settlement was set up in Newfoundland. This colony, founded in 1617, was organised and paid for by a Carmarthenshire landowner called Sir William Vaughan. Vaughan outlined his plan to foster a 'Little Wales in the New World' within a fantastic book called *The Golden Fleece*. The book used the story of Jason and the Argonauts to explain that a land of wealth and plenty beckoned in faraway America if only courageous Welsh worked together and braved the seas. The Newfoundland colony, dubbed New Cambriol, was planned by Vaughan to have fishing as its prime industry, not sheep-farming. Vaughan's *Golden Fleece* was a figure of speech whereby the *Fleece* stood for fish, not sheep. This passage from Vaughan's book indicates as much:

> This is our Colchis, where the Golden Fleece flourisheth on the backes of Neptunes sheepe, continually to be shorne.

Maybe because the sheep were but metaphorical, Vaughan's Welsh colony in Newfoundland could not sustain itself and collapsed within a few years.

Whilst Vaughan was very serious about his colony, perhaps the Newfoundland Vikings weren't that serious about colonising the New World at all. This is why they did not bring any sheep with them. Maybe the Viking stay in America was only ever planned to be temporary, just to collect scarce resources. In this regard, old-time Viking Sagas report that Newfoundland timber and wild berries seem to have been much coveted for boatbuilding and winemaking.

Though Viking voyagers might not have cared much for sheep on their boats, pre-Germanic Scandinavians had depended on sheep for a sustainable pattern of living since around 1700 BC: at least, that is when remnants of wool fibres and woollen textiles begin to appear in their archaeological remains. After a thousand years of adaptation to Nordic lands – and the odd seabound adventure as well – the Vikings were bequeathed very hardy and very woolly sheep, somewhat resistant to sleet and snow. There's evidence, though, that they had to be kept indoors during the winter but then who would not seek 'hygge' with a fluffy sheep on a frigid Scandinavian evening when even the fiords outside have iced over.

Like the Vikings themselves, their sheep were well travelled. Amongst the Viking sheep that have spread and bred across the North Atlantic are the stocky Icelandic sheep of Iceland, the scraggy Herdwicks of Cumbria, the four-horned Loaghtan sheep of the Isle of Man, the tiny but indomitable Ouessant sheep of Normandy and the beach-loving North Ronaldsay sheep of the Scottish Isles. All these breeds have modern-day fan clubs that promote them and their intriguing histories. For instance, the Orkney Sheep Foundation relates how the entire island of North Ronaldsay was transformed to manage the flocks of sheep freely roaming the island since Viking voyagers left them there. In the eighteenth century, the island's farmers built a twelve-mile-long drystone wall at the high-tide mark to keep the feral flocks out of the croplands and gardens of the interior. With only seaweed to feed upon, the North Ronaldsay sheep changed their diet from grass to kelp. In fact, they've become the first mammal in evolutionary history to subsist entirely by consuming kelp.

Another variety of sheep that was abandoned to its fate on a North Atlantic Island, and then re-domesticated centuries later, was the shrub-munching Faroese sheep of the Faroe Islands. Faroese sheep come in many colours and colour combinations – some 300 in all are recognised by expert wool-crafters, ranging from the whitest whites to the blackest black and all manner of creams, duns, tans, fawns and greys in between. Weavers all over Scandinavia use this natural colouring to design shaded, striped and patterned clothing whose intricate blends enchant and confound the eye.

As far as Welsh sheep are concerned, the Defaid Mynydd Duon, or Black Mountain sheep, is held by breeders to have descended from Viking sheep. If you are a visitor to Wales, you must seek out a flock of these beautiful sheep. With their tight black curls gleaming very slightly reddish in full sunshine, they are a treat to behold against the long stretches of Wales's green desert: that vast grassy interior highland in Wales populated by few people but millions of sheep. The wool of the Black Mountain sheep never attracted widespread commercial interest, since clothmakers generally prefer white wool. Yet today it is sought out by modern-day artisanal weavers who swear the red-flecked blackness is wholly unique in colour and also much firmer to the touch than other wools.

Some Welsh farmers believe that the Black Mountain sheep cannot possibly have Viking origins since Wales was never colonised by the Vikings. Nor was any Welsh kingdom overrun by the Vikings. However, in AD 850, a Viking horde out of Ireland raided Cardiff and a few other sites on the south coast. And in AD 854, a massive band of Viking marauders terrorised the island of Anglesey. Probably, they did not bring sheep with them since rams and ewes aren't known for wielding war-hammers. At times, though, the Vikings would camp out in foreign lands such as Wales for the whole season. Perhaps, then, they brought some sheep to bolster their food supply or to effect trade with the locals, thus introducing the ancestors of some Welsh mountain sheep to Wales.

Incidentally, the Welsh city of Swansea owes its first iteration to such a temporary settlement. It takes its name from a Viking pirate-king called Sweyn Forkbeard, who was shipwrecked in Swansea Bay and subsequently led a series of raids in the area before setting up a small Viking trading post.

Though the Vikings deftly navigated many British rivers, they seemed to have no interest in the riches of Wales's mountains. The seas and waterways were the preferred Viking domain, and if things got a bit hilly, they became nervous. So here again, the highlands of Wales might have acted as a natural defence for the territories of the Welsh.

On the water, though, the Vikings reigned supreme, perfecting an incredible array of longships big enough to carry small flocks of animal passengers. They had worked out that the most effective seaworthy boats were built in a clinker manner, whereby the flexible side slats would overlap each other rather than merely sitting flush together. This offered extra strength and flex as the Vikings ploughed through the waves – and as waves pummelled them back.

We should note, though, the pre-Viking Scandinavians never set sails upon their longships. They moved on inland waterways and at sea by rowing. Only when sails were finally added in the late 600s did the Scandinavians become actual Vikings – migrating and marauding around the North Atlantic and beyond. And here's the important point for us to restate: the sails were made of wool. And lots of it. One sail would need the clip of hundreds of sheep and required a year of spinning and weaving to fashion. The final product, though, was a formidable sail the likes of which the Atlantic Seaboard might never have seen – even in Roman times. So, alas, whether we abhor the Vikings for being marauders or admire them for being great explorers, they couldn't have done either without their sheep.

Despite their episodic raids and occasional settlement in Wales, the Vikings were far more aggressive in England. Worse was to come, though, when their longships arrived not laden with raiders but with colossal flocks of sheep. This would mean the Vikings had no intention of leaving. Eventually, via a series of wars and conglomerations, the entire northern half of England fell under the dominion of Viking kings. Sometimes Welsh kings would ally themselves with the Vikings to thwart the English, and other times the Welsh teamed up with the English to battle the Vikings. An example of the latter was the Battle of Buttington in Powys, in AD 893, when a coalition of Welsh and Anglo-Saxon warriors deployed under Aethelred, king of Mercia, defeated a giant Viking war band.

During the Viking Age, Wales was never a single kingdom. However, several kings managed to gain control over most of the Welsh territory for limited periods. Hywel Dda was one such king who, via propitious marriage, canny diplomacy and enormous luck, gained enough land west of Offa's Dyke to earn the label 'King of the Britons'. Hywel Dda took advantage of his great influence to codify the legal customs of Welsh lands into a proper series of common laws.

Like other Welsh kings before and after him, Hywel spent much of his time negotiating whether to work with the Anglo-Saxons against the Vikings or vice versa. Although Hywel felt the common Welsh disdain for Anglo-Saxon hegemony, he calculated that he and Wales would gain more if they supported the kings of England against the Vikings.

Despite working tirelessly to navigate this quandary, Hywel found time to consider the plight of Welsh sheep and sheep-farmers. According to the veterinary historian A. C. Kirkwood, the earliest attempt to pass laws against the common costly disease of sheep scab can be traced to Hywel, who, in AD 949, forbade scabby sheep from being traded at market. Hywel also ruled that flocks should not be settled upon land grazed by scabby sheep during the past seven years. As well, Hywel's laws pronounced that the pigs of a family farm – and the revenue they brought – were the domain of the husband whilst an estate's sheep was the domain of the wife. This was probably just a guide based upon customary division of labour but it took on great import when divvying up assets upon spousal separation.

Usually, when livestock roamed freely in the summer, the pigs were assigned to the woods while the wife took the sheep and the children to the high pastures. Once there, the wife began milking the sheep and processing the milk into cheese, curds and creams. It goes without saying that if sheep hygiene – and the inheritance of sheep – were being codified into law, they must have been a crucial part of the Welsh economy in the tenth century.

As Hywel was laying down innovative sheep law in Wales, across the Viking world there were innovations in what could be done with wool. As well as crafting their world-beating sails, Viking textile workers introduced a forerunner of knitting known as naalbinding (the Danish word for needle-knotting). Naalbinding involves the stitching of woollen fabric from short lengths of yarn using a single holed needle. Fragments of medieval cloth fashioned this way have been excavated from Viking sites across the North Atlantic, including naalbinded socks from the Viking-founded city of York.

With woollen socks keeping their feet warm and their woollen sails catching the wind, the Vikings worked their way all across Europe: southward into Frankish lands in the ninth century and eastward into Baltic lands and Russia in the tenth. For a long time, the armies of various Frankish and Baltic kingdoms kept them confined to coastal colonies. Still, when these kingdoms began weakening, the Vikings started rowing upriver to sack inland cities. The French cities of Paris, Caen and Nantes suffered this fate, for instance. This prompted the building of fortified bridges across French rivers to thwart Viking movements. Sometimes these bridges worked a treat, dissuading Vikings from heading any further inland. Sometimes they did not, since the Viking boats were so light they could be hauled up off the river by their crew then carried or rolled on logs around the bridge, and lowered back into the water.

Eventually, in AD 911, the Vikings signed a treaty with the French king, Charles the Simple, to give up their raids in exchange for land on the French coast. This land became known as Normandy – the land of the 'North Men'. Here, the Vikings built lively towns and sturdy castles. Eventually, they abandoned their piratical ways and adopted French culture and lifestyles.

They also embraced Christianity. Would this lead them to be peaceful, loving and tolerant? The answer lies in the next chapter.

Chapter 15

SHEEPLANDS OF THE NORMANS

THE WELSH MARCHES, 1067 TO 1154

A century and a half after the Vikings had successfully settled on the French coast, one of their descendants, a man nicknamed William the Bastard, rose to the noble post of Duke of Normandy. With the Viking blood of his forefathers egging him on, William set his sights on England, which lay visible just across a short stretch of the English Channel. In 1066, William and 10,000 fellow Normans put their boats into the water and – with woollen sailcloth catching the winds – crossed the Channel to land upon an English beach. Soon after, at the Battle of Hastings, the Norman invaders defeated the English army and killed the king of England. William the Bastard then became William the Conqueror.

To learn the lay of the land, William commissioned a survey of every farm and every farmyard animal in England. This would show him just how much money he might earn, either by direct dominion over the land or through taxing all the livestock. The resultant work of accounting is famously known as the Domesday Book. In it, it is recorded that 'Sheep dominated the countryside as there were more woollie beasts than all the cattle, pigs and goats of England combined'.

The Normans quickly saw the value of intensified sheep-farming in their new English territories. Before long, an organised programme of exports began with wools and felts being sent to Normandy and France. Norman wool technologies also arrived in England, including the introduction of a horizontal loom. This type of loom enabled faster weaving than traditional looms but also encouraged the slow transition of weaving from being primarily the domain of women to being primarily the domain of men since these looms required longer arm-lengths to shift the shuttle from side to side. This, in turn, prompted weaving to become more professionalised as groups of male weavers formed trade guilds to incorporate their power and to regulate the trade.

Beyond new looms, England and Wales faced a much more aggressive Norman technological project that went by the terrible name of 'encastellation' – the building of castles. From great towering stone strongholds, some the size of villages, the new Norman overlords planned to assert power over their new dominions in the British Isles.

When it came to Wales, William the Conqueror was too busy with matters in England and Normandy to lead a conquest in person. In his stead, he selected a group of his most savage soldier buddies, knighted them as English barons, and then granted them the right to go freebooting across Offa's Dyke to seize as much Welsh territory as they could take. William then allowed these Anglo-Norman adventurers to reign supreme over the land that they had managed to steal.

Here, I use the term Anglo-Norman not to denote a certain ethnic mix of English with Norman but to denote French-speaking warlords from elite Norman families who ran England and were attempting to overrun Wales. A whole class of bastards, if you like.

The first Anglo-Norman lord to complete a castle on Welsh lands was William FitzOsbern. A relative of King William, FitzOsbern fought for the Conqueror at the Battle of Hastings. In Chepstow, on the Welsh side of Afon Gwy, the River Wye, FitzOsbern constructed the first new stone castle that the country had seen since Roman times. Chepstow Castle is still fairly intact and casts a startling image over the cliff banks of the river. As the eleventh century waned and the twelfth century waxed, the Anglo-Normans would build many more castles in Welsh lands, helping Wales to become a world record-holder in terms of the number of castles per capita.

However, since castles took many years to build, a favourite resistance technique for Welsh rebels was to attack the Norman castles before they were finished. Depending on the situation, they could then either occupy or sabotage the castle. Another favourite tactic for Welsh resistors was to rustle away entire flocks of Norman sheep and cattle that were grazing unenclosed near the castles.

Those Anglo-Norman nobles that had been granted land on or across the Welsh frontier were known as Marcher lords. 'Marches' is an old French word meaning 'boundary' or 'border'. The Marcher lords were reviled by the Welsh for their greedy ambition, callous brutality and contempt for local laws and customs. They often forced out Welsh communities from the land they took over, pushing them from the lush productive lowlands into the interior rugged uplands of Wales. Because of this displacement, Welsh revolts – large and small – flared up repeatedly during Norman times.

One very significant revolt involved the Welsh king of Deheubarth, Rhys ap Tewdwr, the great-grandson of Hywel Dda, who faced off against an Anglo-Norman army in the Battle of Brycheiniog in 1093. His ally, Gruffudd ap Cynan, the king of Gwynedd, also successfully attacked Norman castles all over north Wales a few years later, sending Anglo-Norman troops back to England. Unfortunately, Welsh kingdoms were also doing battle with each other during the same period. This meant a unified Welsh resistance was mounted only episodically as the Anglo-Normans regrouped to press gradually further into Wales.

Though the Anglo-Normans were never loved in Wales, we might still credit them with helping to make the country we see today. Firstly, as they built their castles, small towns sprang up aside them. These new towns often stimulated the commercial development of the Welsh Marches by providing marketplaces and protected trading ports.

Secondly, the Anglo-Normans knew they could not conquer Wales without the help of God, so they built churches as well as castles. Often the churches were right by the castles and sometimes inside them. Though the Welsh were wary of Anglo-Norman theology at the time, the grandeur and beauty of some of their holy architecture still survives today. This includes major parts of Eglwys Gadeiriol Tyddewi, or St Davids Cathedral, often regarded as the premier cathedral of Wales.

Thirdly, the Marcher lords often set up new farms, especially sheep-farms, since there was a growing demand for wool in both England and Europe. Alas, on these new farms the Marcher lords usually pushed Welsh farmers into serfdom, forcing them to do all the actual farm work. Meanwhile the Marcher lords themselves paraded around in tournaments across England and Normandy on beautified horses in lavish armour.

Added to this, the Marcher lords often banned the Welsh from living in the newly set-up market towns, allowing only English traders and craftspeople to live and work there. In this way, over many decades, there was a relentless domineering intrusion of Anglo-Norman life into Wales, most especially in the south.

One part of Wales that was particularly inundated by English colonists was the southern coast of Pembrokeshire. Indeed, this area attained the nickname Little England beyond Wales as though it was a distant English exclave deep in Welsh lands. In this area, sheep-farming and clothmaking took off as important medieval industries. Numerous market towns developed and prospered because of this, all under tight English control. A slew of stone castles was also built nearby to protect the Anglo-Norman farming estates and English towns. These include Pembroke Castle, Manorbier Castle and Carew Castle, all standing today, plus dozens more whose remnants are in various stages of preservation and decay. If you visit any of these castles or their dramatic crumbling remnants, they are likely to be pleasingly foregrounded with various Welsh sheep, including Badger Face Mountain sheep and Brecon Cheviots, and it might have been somewhat similar when they were first built.

A relic of these times is a peculiar language border called the Landsker Line running between north and south Pembrokeshire. North of the Line, the Welsh language was predominant, whilst English dominated in the south. The Line is still noticeable today, when census maps show the preferred tongue of Pembrokeshire's northern residents is Welsh versus English for those in the south.

Surveys also find those south of the Landsker Line self-identify as British at a far higher rate than those north of the line, who primarily self-identify as Welsh. Along with cultural differences, some modern-day genetic studies suggest that Saxon genes are much rarer north of the Landsker Line, though ubiquitous south of it.

As well as helping transplant traders and craftspeople from England, the Anglo-Norman conquest of Marcher Wales meant boatloads of immigrants from Flanders also came as settlers. The story goes that William the Conqueror's son, King Henry I, invited a number of Flemish people to move to the towns of coastal Pembrokeshire since it produced lots of wool and the Flemish had renowned wool-crafting skills. It was a perfect match. The Pembrokeshire towns of Haverfordwest and Tenby are particularly proud of their Flemish ancestry and their association with textiles and wool-craft. Pembrokeshire historian Mary John notes that the dusty old medieval records from these towns are filled with European surnames redolent of clothmaking, such as le Taillour, Textor and le Webbe. A modern-day guided tour of either Haverfordwest or Tenby will also assail you with details of where the first artisans from Flanders set up their workshops and where distinctive Flemish-style homes were built.

However, it is possible that none of the Flemings who relocated to Haverfordwest and Tenby were wool workers at all. Instead, they could have been out-of-work mercenaries. As well as being famous for textiles, Flanders was also famous for its mercenaries. King Henry I was particularly fond of employing Flemish mercenaries in his military campaigns. Come peacetime, though, Henry wasn't sure what to do with them. They had been causing trouble in various English cities by ganging together to rough up and shake down the local citizenry. Because of this, Henry I issued a decree sending them off to faraway south-west Wales. At the time, Welsh attacks against the Anglo-Norman castles on the Landsker Line were becoming a problem. Perhaps King Henry thought if the Flemish mercenaries insisted on making trouble, they could make trouble for the Welsh – not the English.

And it seems they did. According to the medieval Welsh clergyman Gerallt Cymro, the Flemish settlers menaced local villagers, ordering them around and kicking out Welsh families from the best farms.

Gerallt's primary job was as Archdeacon of Brecon but his family estate was in Pembrokeshire. As an ardent advocate of the established church, Gerallt grew angry about how the Pembrokeshire Flemish weren't paying their annual tithes – that is, their church taxes. Usually, tithes were paid in kind to the local bishop in the form of a bag of wool or a bundle of cloth, or sometimes using live sheep. Local Welsh peasants, in turn, would usually pay tithes in cheese or butter, which the churches would often then trade for coin on market day. Whilst the Welsh dutifully journeyed to a faraway church or cathedral to deliver their tithe, the Flemish couldn't be bothered. When a tithe collector knocked at their gate, they would angrily convey they had no intention of paying the tithe and they'd quote some vague tax immunity agreed with King Henry.

It is hard to ascertain for sure if the Flemish settlers in Pembrokeshire were mercenaries that began sidelining as sheep-farmers and clothmakers or if they were full-time sheep-farmers and workshop owners who sometimes sidelined as mercenaries. According to Orderic Vitalis, writing in the 1130s, they made a habit of crossing over between the professions. For example, he noted the Pembrokeshire Flemish:

> are a brave and robust people but very hostile to the Welsh
> and in a perpetual state of conflict with them. They are
> highly skilled in the wool trade, ready to work hard and
> face danger by land or sea in the pursuit of gain. As time
> and opportunity offer, they are prompt to turn their hand
> to either the sword or the ploughshare.

As some British historians have noted, Anglo-Norman Wales was a bit like the Wild West. Robert Turvey, for instance, suggests places like Pembrokeshire were frontier societies, 'shaped by the ebb and flow of conquest and colonization'. So, if money was to be made in cloth, the Flemish made cloth. When money was to be made by oppressing the native Welsh, they did that as well.

Whatever the reason for their initial appearance in Pembrokeshire, the Flemish established themselves among the commercial elite, investing heavily in wool-shops and sheep. Yet the problem of tax avoidance only got worse, especially as they attempted to hand down their supposed tax exemption privileges to their children. Gerallt Cymro and others brandished warning letters from the Archbishop of Canterbury in the faces of wealthy Flemish townspeople but mostly it had no effect.

Eventually, the Flemish of southern Pembrokeshire would integrate with the English townspeople. However, this took centuries. The historian Lauren Toorians, for instance, uncovered how a wool trader from Ghent called Lucas D'Heere travelled in the 1500s all the way from Ghent to Norfolk, then London, then Bristol, to visit Pembrokeshire only to find he was able to chat in Flemish with some local merchants. This was more than three centuries after their ancestors had first settled there.

Interestingly, the Landsker Line that now serves as a language border between the Welsh and the English may have also been a language barrier that separated the Welsh from the Flemish. As well, we might regard the Landsker Line as a border separating how different communities value sheep. South of the Landsker Line, the Flemish and the English, plus their Anglo-Norman overlords, valued sheep as instruments to produce the vital international commodity that was woollen cloth. On the northern side of the Landsker Line, in north Pembrokeshire, sheep were valued mainly for producing the daily necessities of milk and cheese, plus some other sheep products like tallow and fat, which were used for soap and for making cheap candles. North of the Line, sheep products were used locally, but south of the Line, just about every sheep product would have ended up outside Wales in England, Flanders or France.

Nowadays, if you want to roam through just about any of the lovely towns of south Pembrokeshire, you are bound to chance upon one or more delightful wool-craft shops, often adjunct to a small cafe. Even if you do not plan to do any knitting or weaving, it is worth diverting into one of these shops to admire the bales of lush wool and beautifully arranged reels of spun fibre. If you prefer something north of the Landsker Line, then a visit to the farmers' market in places like St Dogmaels or Tyddewi will offer a chance to enjoy a variety of cheeses made from the milk of several local sheep breeds, each with its own distinctive taste.

Chapter 16
THE SHEEP OF CHRIST'S SERVANTS

TINTERN, WALES, 1131

By the sixth century AD, the city of Rome had degenerated from a bustling metropolis of a million people to a decaying old town holding just a fraction of that number. Even so, it was still too decadent and salubrious for one particular Roman: a wealthy, pious young Christian called Benedict of Nursia. Dismayed by the physical and moral degradation of Rome, he set off into the mountains of Italy to live a simple earthly life, all alone. In solitude, Benedict would escape the noise and distractions of the city to listen clearly to the voice of God.

However, Benedict made the mistake of performing a set of marvellous deeds as he travelled. These were much confabulated by the villagers along his route. By the time Benedict found himself a serene spot in the mountains, he had attracted a growing retinue of fans and followers. Resigned to his popularity – as a miracle-working ascetic – he invited his followers to build a fabulous monastery in Monte Cassino.

After his death in AD 547, Benedict's ideas about monastic life were written up by some of his followers. This book became sought after throughout Europe whilst Benedict himself was venerated as a saint. Since then, thousands of religious establishments bearing his name have been built around the world, including a few churches in Wales.

As the Middle Ages progressed, monasteries were set up by monks who strictly adhered to Benedict's guidelines on austere Christian living. Together, these monasteries formed the Order of St Benedict, its monks nicknamed the Benedictines. Because of their discipline and piety, the Benedictines gradually attracted patronage from wealthy landlords and sovereigns, including Emperor Charlemagne. Because of this – and despite their commitment to modest material well-being – the Benedictine monasteries slowly became very wealthy. Their earthly riches enabled them to buy up lots of land that they could rent out to make even more money. Meanwhile within the monasteries, the monks began feasting on rich meals taken from silver plates just about every day of the year. After hundreds of years of growing evermore wealthier and fatter, the monks of the Benedictine Order became infamous for their greed.

Intent on reform, some monks broke away from the Benedictines to strike up their own Order. The breakaways set up a monastery near the French village of Cîteaux, so they became known as the Cistercians. The best known feature of the Cistercian reformers was their commitment to manual labour, especially agricultural work. This was in contrast to many religious orders whose monks only used their hands when placing them together for prayer. The Cistercians would work all day in the fields before returning to chant in a chapel for many hours then retiring to eat a simple meal of bread and cheese in silence.

This daily regime became an acknowledged feature of Cistercian life across much of the Christian world. If Cistercians produced some sort of material surplus from their exertions, this was to be donated to the poor. And if Cistercian monks found themselves with spare time on their hands, it was supposed to be spent caring for the sick and the old or teaching the young.

Alas, Cistercian monks ended up following the path laid out by their Benedictine forebears. The Cistercians lived in such a well-organised fashion and managed their estates so efficiently that they began bringing in loads of money. Sheep-farming was a Cistercian specialty; because they had been granted so much pastoral land, they could regularly produce lots of surplus wool every year. Like the Benedictines, the Cistercian monasteries also received grand donations from dead and dying nobles seeking the good graces of the angels.

The Cistercians were supposed to reinvest their profits in their local communities. However, more often, they spent big on grand architecture, plus silver church ornaments and expensive gold-painted Bibles. They also reinvested heavily to expand their wool businesses. Thus endowed, the traditional cheese and bread dinners gave way to regular feasts of lamb and mutton plus vat-loads of Europe's finest wines and best beers.

In the Welsh town of Chepstow, around the year 1131, an Anglo-Norman Marcher lord called Walter de Clare invited a band of travelling Cistercians to consider setting up a monastery in his town. Chepstow is just a few hundred yards from the southernmost point of Offa's Dyke, close to a communicable river and not far from some important English market towns. De Clare's invitation was not unusual since the Anglo-Normans loved showing off how pious and important they were by dotting their holdings with large religious buildings.

When the Cistercian leadership in France heard about the Chepstow offer, they guessed Wales would be an excellent place for profitable sheep-farming. However, to adhere to St Benedict's guidelines, the monks arriving from France avoided Chepstow town – with all its profane diversions – to settle five miles upstream upon the River Wye. There, they raised their sheep, crafted homemade cheese and beers, and gradually built the fine abbey of Tintern.

Though Tintern Abbey has been in ruins now for centuries, it is still a lovely sight to behold. The abbey is positioned between two bends in the river and is shielded by elevations on both sides: Welsh hills in the west and English hills in the east. Trekking within the woodlands of either set of hills affords a graceful view of the abbey sitting aside the Wye, gently framed with overhanging sweet chestnut trees. Of course, sheep are part of the scene as well, flocking inside and outside the ruins, fluffy and peaceful. Alas, as pretty as it looks, the River Wye is not these days in the best of health for there is copious pollution running off into it from the thousands of modern farms lying along its course.

Back in the Middle Ages, the Cistercians were often nicknamed the White Monks. As the Welsh medievalist Catherine Johnson points out, this name came about because of the bright cream tint of their robes, which they themselves fashioned from the undyed wool shorn from their own fluffy white sheep.

As Tintern Abbey was being built, monasteries set up by the White Monks were popping up all over Europe – as though the Cistercian Order were a trendy franchise chain. Often the start-up funds would come from established monasteries or from a high-stationed monk hailing from a rich family. After they had been set up, though, Cistercian monasteries were expected to be self-sufficient, making their own food and paying their own expenses. In France, their business model revolved around viticulture but in Wales, it was sheep-farming.

However, even if the White Monks of Tintern could eat all the cheese and butter that their ewes could provide plus all the mutton and lamb they could raise, that still left an abundant surplus of wool every year. This they could sell within a continental network already set up by their sister abbeys and monasteries. In a few decades, the Cistercians of Tintern had become so wealthy they added covered walkways, ornamental gardens and then a grand new church emplaced within the abbey grounds.

Often, to get a big new project off the ground, the Cistercians would trade in futures with Flemish or Italian merchants, taking out huge advances whilst promising to supply their annual wool clip at a set price for the next twenty years. So important was this trade that the Cistercians had mercantile offices of their own set up in Cardiff and Bristol to monitor the wool's movements and to work out long-term agreements with the agents of the big buyers. Since they were a 'non-profit' religious organisation, at least on paper, the Cistercians were also granted easy access rights to merchant ships, trading ports and storage warehouses. As well, the Cistercians for the most part did not have to pay to cross bridges or to use river ferries – either in Britain or on the continent. These privileges cut down shipment costs markedly.

Occasionally, the Anglo-Norman kings of England stepped in as wool trade ambassadors, providing assurance to foreign buyers for the credibility of this or that abbey, before absolving all concerned of various taxes and duties. Also, as Catherine Johnson points out, because the Cistercians sold in bulk, wool traders liked dealing their wool. Doing so could save them many weeks of travel time for they could procure all the wool they needed in mere days from just a few abbeys.

As outlined above, the Cistercians were supposed to engage in daily labour. But as they grew more prosperous in Wales, they employed peasants and servants to do most of the manual work associated with sheep-farming. Most of the Cistercian abbeys were organised into granges. The granges could extend far and wide onto hilly pastoral terrain many hours' walk from the site of the abbey. Therefore, instead of forcing monks to traipse all the way to the pastures and then back again to pray in the chapel at set times, the abbots employed locals to work all day in the far-off fields. As well as this, a great proportion of monks usually came from well-off families. As such, they were not usually fond of all the messy labouring in the fields, much preferring other tasks like transcribing books and managing the accounts.

Some monks did work to counsel the poor and the sick but most were devoted full time to the businesses of the abbey. This meant they usually interacted with members of the priestly and merchant classes along with continually working out deals with agents of various kingdoms and duchies. Servants of God they may have been but by the twelfth century they were just as famous for being hardcore businessmen and international diplomats.

Often, the Cistercians also behaved like the mafia when their business interests were infringed upon. At Tintern, for example, once upon a time in the late twelfth century, the abbot stormed down to the abbey's weir with his monks to confront a couple of sheep-farmers who had been shifting their sheep over the Wye for years without ever paying the abbey's riverman. The abbot shouted and cursed at the farmers, demanding they pay up. One aggravated farmer responded by belting the abbot with his crook before a big ol' brawl erupted in the middle of the river, farmers throwing their fists about and monks doing the same with river stones. The monks came off second best but within days they had hired a group of thugs to accost the offending farmers and shake out the overdue river fees plus some annual tithes.

The entrepreneurial success of Tintern – and the popularity of its monks despite their stern approach to business – meant that a whole bunch of offshoot Cistercian monasteries were set up across Wales. First, Whitland Abbey was set up in Carmarthenshire in 1151, then Strata Florida in Ceredigion in 1164, along with Strata Marcella and Abbeycwmhir in Powys in the 1170s. Later in the century, more were founded: Llantarnam Abbey near Caerleon, Aberconwy Abbey in Gwynedd and Valle Crucis in Denbighshire. Though roofless and decayed today, each abbey is worth a visit, especially on an early autumn evening when mysterious fogs often flow over them to augment their Gothic ambience.

Those Cistercian abbeys that gained the support of local Welsh princes and gentry sometimes became hotspots of intellectual nationalism. Strata Florida and Valle Crucis were well-known examples of this. However, those abbeys set up in Marcher territories by Marcher lords, or under the patronage of the king of England, tended to bolster Anglo-Norman culture instead of Welsh culture. In fact, Anglo-Norman abbeys and monasteries in Wales did not recruit monks from Welsh communities, at all, instead bringing them in from England, Normandy or France.

One way that Cistercians reinvested their profits back into their sheep business was by improving the care of their flocks. Cistercian monks in Britain often took pains to build their flocks little mansions called sheepcotes. The sheep consigned to sheepcotes were attended to by a sophisticated hierarchy of sheepcote house masters and specialised labourers. Regular sheepcotes were mostly made from the branches of trees clumped in squares against hedgerows and roofed with fern fronds. Cistercian sheepcotes were much grander, with well-fashioned stone walls, thatched roofs and numerous arched doorways. I've been told a few of the finest have survived to be converted into modern-day guesthouses. Upon viewing one such sheepcote, it seems more likely, though, these are regular cottages just using the name to evoke warmth and snugness but I may be wrong.

Cistercian sheep also enjoyed superior health care since records show a considerable amount of tar was bought by flockmasters. This was mixed with grease to make sheep salve for scrapes and wounds. This attention to health and housing would very likely increase sheep fertility and decrease their mortality. Cistercian monks in Britain also took the art of sheep breeding to a new level to provide more profitable sheep. As pointed out by Yorkshire historian Alan Butler, the Fountains Abbey in Yorkshire bred a 'super sheep' whose fine wool was much in demand by medieval wool-buyers at home and abroad. As sheep-farming prospered under the stewardship of the Cistercian franchises, by the time of Llywelyn Fawr, who reigned as Prince of the Welsh in the 1220s and 1230s, sheep production had become the prominent wealth creator in the nation, especially in coastal south Wales. Still, there was a vast hilly interior where sheep-farming had yet to move beyond the level of subsistence. Indeed, some areas were still completely wild and untamed. This would change in the coming centuries.

Chapter 17

A LION SAVED BY SHEEP

EUROPE, 1186 TO 1199

If you were a Cistercian monk charged with bringing Welsh wool to Normandy in 1199, your cargo boat would have had to navigate the Bristol Channel and then the English Channel. After this, you'd have to sail upwards along the French coast to find the mouth of the River Seine. Some forty miles upriver, as you reached a wide curving bend near the village of Petit Andely, an imposing bank of limestone cliffs would come into view. Upon a stalwart mount on top of these cliffs was the Château Gaillard. This was perhaps the most formidable castle in Europe and probably the most innovative. It certainly was a splendid sight, constructed from the same gleaming white limestone as the cliff it stood above.

The Château Gaillard was designed and built by Richard I, king of England and ruler of the Angevin Empire. This was an empire that included England, the duchies of Normandy and Brittany, the county of Auvergne, plus most of the rest of the western half of France, as well as the eastern seaboard of Ireland and the Marcher lordships in Wales. At some point as well, Flanders also entered the empire, not as one of King Richard's domains but as an ally.

When he began drawing up the plans for Château Gaillard, Richard I had not long returned from a Crusade to the Holy Lands. In the Levant, he had vanquished Muslim armies and conquered the cities of Acre and Jaffa, feats that led to his alias Richard the Lionheart.

It was the Lionheart's plan that the Château Gaillard would be a grand strategic stronghold against the kingdom of France, whose border lay just a few miles away upriver. Indeed, the castle stood as a message to the rulers of all Europe that King Richard I's Angevin Empire was here to stay, right on their doorstep.

Returning to the cargo boat moving slowly up the Seine, I tested out just how impressive the castle might be upon a formative mind with the help of my co-traveller, Shelley. Dressed in medieval garb – him as Richard the Lionheart and me as a monk – we boarded a tourist barge in Rouen and proceeded slowly inland. Hanging on to the guard rails, we waited an hour for the castle to appear before us around one of the river's many twists and turns. The anticipation probably heightened his senses but nevertheless Shelley was suitably gobsmacked when the Lionheart's castle came into view.

Of course, the reason why we wanted to see this fine castle was that it owed just as much to sheep for its existence as it did to the Lionheart's strategic plans. To explain this, we must travel back a few more years in time to 1186, before the Lionheart became the King of England, to when his father, Henry II, wore that crown. That year, Saladin, Sultan of Syria, overran and conquered Jerusalem. In response, the Pope in Rome called upon the kings and Christians of Europe to band together and travel clear across the Mediterranean Sea to retake the Holy City. Henry II promised the Pope he would partake in the Crusade but only after he had raised a grand army – and a grand war chest to pay for it.

In Wales, Gerallt Cymro, the Archdeacon of Brecon, responded to the Pope's call by making a long march throughout the Welsh shires and kingdoms to recruit crusaders. This long march was often re-enacted by twentieth-century Welsh schoolchildren, but much less so these days. You might remember from Chapter 15 that Gerallt Cymro also roamed around Pembrokeshire trying to wrestle tithe payments away from Flemish mercenaries. Alas, his patchy success in that endeavour was matched by his failure to recruit Welsh crusaders – this despite spiritual threats and promises being issued left, right and centre from both the king of England and the Pope in Rome. Lords of Welsh descent, and even those of Anglo-Norman descent with holdings in Wales, generally refused to get involved in the Crusades. Some half-heartedly offered some part of their flock to Gerallt, telling him to go sell some sheep in England and then send the money to King Henry when he got to Jerusalem. The Flemish in Pembrokeshire did not even do this much, repeating their dubious claim that they had tax immunity granted by one or another king.

Though the Welsh evaded public involvement in the Crusades, Henry II still commandeered a massive amount of woollen cloth and silver coinage from his English subjects as well as wine money from his French lands. However, a crisis fell upon his reign before he could transform this immense war chest into a Crusade. Henry II's three sons, including Richard the Lionheart, started a war against him in Normandy and Brittany. All three of his sons were extremely angry that Henry II was liquidating assets from the lands they were due to inherit. Therefore, they conspired to take control of these lands prematurely before they were impoverished by their father's extreme fundraising efforts.

However, because Henry II had raised a significant war fund already, he diverted some of it to hire an outstanding band of Low Country mercenaries, including the Welsh Flemish, to trounce the combined armies of his sons. Yet he was so devastated by his sons' betrayal that he soon withered away and died of a broken heart. Or so it is said. In the end, he never managed to set out on Crusade.

Henry II's death saw his Angevin Empire – Marcher Wales and all – handed to Richard the Lionheart in 1189. Richard vowed to fulfil his father's goal to retake Jerusalem from Sultan Saladin. When the Lionheart was crowned in London as King Richard I, he found the kingdom's treasury still looked pretty full despite the monies spent against him when he'd fought his father.

However, before heading off into the Levant, the Lionheart wanted to be sure he had enough resources stacked behind him to guarantee success, so he levied his own peculiar tax upon Church estates in his kingdoms and duchies. This was undoubtedly an innovative endeavour but not very popular among those who had anything to do with the Church. Richard also sold off titles and offices to various wealthy and well-connected commoners. Then, in 1190, he set sail to the Holy City.

On the way, though, the Lionheart became sidetracked. He plunged his knights into a violent dynastic dispute in Sicily. As if this wasn't enough of a diversion, he then sailed eastward to overthrow the rulers of Cyprus before claiming the whole island as his own land. Richard's interventions in the Mediterranean upset several royal houses in mainland Europe, including King Philip of France and Leopold V, the Duke of Austria. Both Philip and Leopold were heading off on the Holy Crusade themselves but whilst joining with Richard on the battlefields of the Levant, they also worked behind his back plotting how to curtail the Lionheart's growing power and influence.

Eventually, Richard I and his Crusader knights alighted in the coastal deserts of Israel. Before they reached Jerusalem, though, news came in from Europe that King Philip had abandoned the Crusade, returned to France across the seas and was conspiring with Richard's younger brother to take over his territories in Normandy. The Lionheart hastily arranged a truce with Saladin, no mean feat in itself. He then hurriedly sailed back to Europe to confront both the French king and his own brother.

Alas, in the Adriatic Sea, the Lionheart's ship was caught up in a storm and washed ashore as a wreck in northern Italy. Richard and his small band of Angevin knights then had no choice but to walk across central Europe en route to his own lands on the Atlantic coast. However, many unfriendly realms lay in their way: Austria, France and the Holy Roman Empire. Because of this, the Lionheart and his knights had to disguise themselves as pilgrims.

Still, their aristocratic airs and royal bling betrayed their identities somewhere near Vienna, and they were apprehended by guards of the Duke of Austria. When the Duke informed the Holy Roman Emperor of his catch, the Emperor insisted on buying Richard from the Duke as his own prize prisoner. The Emperor then locked away the Lionheart in a castle on top of an isolated mountain before sending word of his capture to England. In the message, the Emperor offered to release

King Richard on payment of a ransom of 100,000 pounds of silver.

This was an enormous sum: twice the annual income of the kingdom. And not easily found whilst the king was locked up in a strange land. To make matters worse, the Lionheart's brother moved in to seize all of Richard's castles and manors in Normandy.

In England, Richard I's mother, the formidable Eleanor of Aquitaine, had been serving as England's regent ever since Richard sailed away on Crusade. Aware of the troubles in Normandy and fearful of rebellion in England, Eleanor knew she had to get Richard out of prison as soon as possible. Along with a team of eager tax collectors, Eleanor set about raising the ransom as quickly as possible via the extraordinary tax channels already set up by Richard and Henry II. The taxpayers of England and Wales – both rich and poor – were still smarting from previous Crusade taxes. Even so, Eleanor convinced most of them to hand over even more: some twenty-five per cent of their wealth. Most of this was offered up not in the form of silver but in kind, usually wool. In the end, Eleanor collected 50,000 sacks of wool, equivalent to the entire annual wool clip of England and Wales. This massive collection of wool, a king's ransom for sure, was baled up and hauled to the German lands of the Holy Roman Empire. Eleanor, in her seventies, travelled alongside this great woolly convoy to personally hand it over to the Emperor.

The Emperor at first quibbled with the form of the payment, suggesting he needed more. Still, Eleanor's deft diplomacy allowed the Lionheart to walk free after a few days' negotiation. King Richard then joined Eleanor and rushed off to England to show his subjects that he was still alive and still wearing the crown. However, apart from his mother, the Lionheart thanked absolutely no one in England and Wales for helping out with the ransom funds – least of all the sheep.

Within a matter of days, though, Richard was voyaging back across the Channel to secure his Norman lands – only looking back to England long enough to ensure the wool trade was sound enough to provide revenue in the future. In the ensuing months, he managed to push the French king clear out of Normandy, then subdue and subordinate his younger brother. As a final monument to his re-emergence in Europe, he then built the magnificent Château

Gaillard. As I tried to explain to Shelley on our river cruise, none of this would have been possible if fluffy sheep's wool from England and Wales had not rescued the Lionheart from prison.

Alas, as impregnable as the Château Gaillard might have been, the man who built it was killed by a lone archer. One day, whilst confronting a disloyal count in a small castle in Limousine, the king's guards alerted Richard to a young archer, a boy really, standing on top of the castle and firing off arrows in his direction. The king scoffed at the archer's audacity. But as Richard turned away, one of the arrows thrust into his neck. Richard I, still standing, pulled the arrow out with his own hands. Yet the wound grew gangrenous and within days he was dead.

With the demise of Richard the Lionheart, even the world's most fabulous castle could not stop France from overtaking Normandy and then threatening the entire Angevin Empire. As we shall see in forthcoming chapters, this provoked a rise in tensions between England and France that would lead to one of the longest-running wars in history.

Chapter 18

SHEEPLANDS OF THE MONGOL EMPIRE

EURASIA, 1206 TO 1368

On a cold December evening in 1241, Ogodei Khan, leader of the Mongols, son of Genghis Khan, was entertaining esteemed guests from Arabia in a gigantic yurt. As dancing girls whirled and twirled in sultry silk, Ogodei drank down pints of fermented milk. Lots of it. Each gulp was interrupted with a toast directed towards his accompanying cohort of diplomats and notaries. According to the macho ideals of medieval Mongol culture, it was incumbent upon Ogodei to get as drunk as possible in front of his guests without passing out. Since his guests were from the Muslim world, he probably did a better job of it than them – at least in the eyes of his own diplomats and generals. Eventually, Ogodei did pass out. The real problem, however, was that he never woke up again.

After consuming hardly anything but lamb, mutton and the milk of ewes and mares all his life, the tremendous amount of alcohol that Ogodei Khan had imbibed that night dissolved a load of fats from his body's reserves that went straight into his bloodstream and clogged his arteries – inducing cardiac arrest.

In the Mongol court, lamb and mutton were probably the last things suspected of causing Ogodei's death. Sheep's meat was thought to be healthy and therapeutic, mostly because Mongol sheep were encouraged to graze upon medicinal herbs. Suspicion was directed more toward Ogodei's Arabian guests, plus his sixty wives – any one of whom could have poisoned his food in retribution for this or that misdeed.

Meanwhile, on the other side of Eurasia, a group of Mongol armies were camped menacingly on the grasslands of Hungary and Poland, a stone's throw from various European capitals. The army was under the command of General Batu Khan, a nephew of Ogodei Khan and grandson of Genghis Khan. This army had just secured overwhelming victories against a sizeable Slavic force at the Polish border and also against a large Hungarian army at the Hungarian border. Batu Khan then sent Mongol parties out to terrorise the Germanic cities of Meissen and Vienna. These 'scare sorties' made it look like Batu Khan was readying his forces to conquer all of Europe. Batu Khan said as much when he trumpeted that the destiny of his army was to reach 'the ultimate sea', that is, the Atlantic Ocean. This would mean Mongol control over the entirety of Eurasia from ocean to ocean: from the Pacific to the Atlantic.

In the meantime, the townspeople of thirteenth-century Budapest certainly had cause to fear the Mongols. Batu Khan's army had ravaged the eastern European countryside so severely that the land was unable to produce any food for years. Worse still, the Mongol army had already slaughtered some half a million Hungarians, mostly non-combatants. Because the Mongol warriors were nomadic, they had neither the disposition nor the capability to take prisoners of war. They certainly had no dungeons or fortresses to lock people up in. However, many useful artisans, especially weavers and clothmakers, were enslaved in chains then force-marched back to Mongol provinces in Asia to make cloth and clothing either for the Mongol elite or the Mongol army.

Whilst the kings of Europe had galvanised their lands against Mongol attack by transforming wooden fortresses and stockades into embankments and castles made of cold hard stone, the Mongols' material of choice to help them craft their empire was much softer: felt. Felt is compressed sheep's wool. One of the primary uses of felt was to make yurts and gers. These Asiatic tents come in all shapes and sizes and they might be movable or permanent. As well as serving settled farmers – and settled royalty – yurts could be packed up and carried on horses by nomadic pastoralists and roving armies. The importance of felt to the Mongol Empire is reflected in the name of its founder, Genghis Khan, whose name translates into English as 'the ruler of all who dwell in felt tents'. Those that didn't live in felt tents, like the city dwellers of western Asia and Europe, were often regarded as decadent and servile, ripe for the conquering.

Thick-felted yurts were actually a staple for various Asian peoples long before the Mongol Empire arose. A 2,600-year-old bronze bowl engraved with a magnificent depiction of a yurt was recently unearthed from a prehistoric site in the Zagros Mountains. In fact, the first yurt probably did not arrive in Mongolia for another thousand years, brought by a series of nomads who moved their sheep north from Persia into the Eurasian steppes.

As well as using felt to fashion their homes, the Mongols also used woollen felt to produce clothing, floor coverings, furnishings, mattresses, baggage and vital little hold-all pocket-bags that kept their arrows and arrowheads safe and handy. Felt could also hold, cover or cushion just about anything that needed to be kept warm or protected, including the skulls of Mongol warriors, and their buttocks and feet as they rode or walked for thousands of miles through bitter winds and heavy weather. Without the sheep's wool to make all these yurts and gers and bags and cloaks etc, the Mongol Empire would never have gotten anywhere near Europe.

With felt so significantly useful and important, the Mongols had to keep great flocks of woolly sheep. Like the Mongols themselves, sheep are nomadic creatures – and self-insulated for the extreme weathers of the steppes. Indeed, it was their dependence upon sheep that constantly kept the Mongols entrenched in the nomadic lifestyle for they needed to keep the sheep moving over the landscape so as to graze new pastures every few days or weeks.

Sometimes, we think that nomads are living out some primitive early form of human existence long superseded by farming and fixed towns. However, on the Eurasian steppes, where grass grows across horizons in all directions, it makes more sense to allow the main economic asset of your civilisation – that is sheep – to roam wide and free and then to follow them around.

Mongolian breeds of sheep were particularly adapted to this challenging style of life, being stocky, sturdy and fast to fatten, with a dense, dark, shaggy wool. If given wide range, they could graze year-round on pastures lush or lean, without supplementary feeding, even under severe summery or wintery conditions and with only patchy greenery.

The Mongols also regarded sheep as an essential part of their armies. On long-term campaigns, sheep flocks often walked alongside the warriors, marching in unison as migrating conquerors of the world's grasslands. As well as offering their wool for felt, sheep provided Mongolian armies with milk and meat for food, lambskins for blankets, bones for tools and dung to burn as fuel – both to warm up the yurts and to cook food.

In most histories of the Mongols, the horse is usually the animal credited with helping forge their Eurasian empire. Wealthy Mongol warriors would keep three or four extra horses trotting alongside their mount as they moved with their army. The poorest soldiers, though, had no horses at all and usually had to walk. Given this mode of transportation, such soldiers were often delegated the role of 'war shepherds' or campaign drovers, moving the sheep along at the rear of the vast nomadic Mongol army. This was not a very glamorous role, perhaps, but nonetheless essential to keep the army functioning.

The Mongols were not the first nomads to create an empire over the Eurasian grasslands. The Huns did something similar in the fifth century AD, pushing Slavic and Germanic tribes westward as they brought their armies then pastoral flocks into Europe. Before the Huns, the Scythians undertook a similar project in the classical age, thrusting right up into eastern Europe. A few historians believe these civilisations might be distantly related to each other, either via culture or via bloodline. One thing that binds them together is their shepherding lifestyle.

Another commonality was their equine skills. The Mongolians, the

Huns and the Scythians were all great horse-riders. The functional usefulness of the horse – for transport and for battle – doesn't, however, diminish the significance of sheep to these civilisations. Indeed, equestrianism complemented shepherding, since horse-riding allowed the Huns and the Mongols to lead and follow their grazing sheep over pasturelands. Horse-riding also meant larger and larger flocks could be corralled and herded, thus greatly increasing the material wealth of the Mongols.

In addition, the Mongols' wool-craft skills enabled them to fashion special trousers that provided comfort and protection for many successive days of horse-riding. Also, part of the process of making felt suitable for building yurts was by using horses to draw giant clumps of wool across beds of stones.

Supported by legions of shepherds and horsemen, the Mongols made it all the way to the gates of Budapest by 1241. However, as they were preparing to attack, General Batu Khan received news of Ogodei Khan's death in the Mongol homeland. In the hope that he might be elected as the new leader of the Mongols, Batu Khan turned around and trudged the entire army, sheep included, back home to Mongolia. If sheep had helped propel the Mongol Empire to greatness by supporting their army and feeding their soldiers, they also saved Europe by giving Ogodei Khan a heart attack.

It took years for Batu Khan to finally get back to Mongolia. And then many more years before a new emperor was elected. In the end, it was not Batu Khan who became the new leader of the Mongols but his cousin Guyuk Khan. These two loathed each other and spent so much time fighting amongst themselves that the Mongols gave up on conquering Europe.

According to historians such as E. N. Anderson and John Masson Smith Jr, the fat-rich lamb diet of the Mongols not only saved Europe, it quite possibly also led to the decline of the entire Mongol Empire. Since the Khans refused to stop feasting upon lamb meat day after day and getting drunk on fermented milk night after night, they died a lot younger than their counterparts in the various Chinese kingdoms. Unlike the Mongols, Chinese emperors and warlords took almost all of their calories in the form of rice. So, while Chinese leaders ate plant-based diets to reign long into old age, Mongol Khans only ruled their empire for a comparatively short time before they suffered a coronary attack. The Mongol leaders thus forced their empire into frequent wars of succession whereby squabbling relatives crashed the empire into divisive civil wars. These slowly broke up the Mongol Empire. In turn, Chinese leaders reigned longer to create more stable states. Eventually, China's dynasties grew strong enough to expand and take over the troublesome Mongol homeland.

Chapter 19

THE WELSH PRINCE
vs THE ENGLISH KING

WALES, 1267 to 1307

Despite the dozens of castles that the Normans built in Wales – and despite all the English and Flemish merchants transplanted into Welsh lands – much of Anglo-Norman Wales was still very 'Welsh'. Suppose we painted in black upon a map of Wales all those areas controlled by England at the time of Richard the Lionheart's death. In that case, we'd see a small dark slither on the south coast and maybe some sooty patches up and down the Welsh side of Offa's Dyke. Many ancient Welsh dynasties and kingdoms were still alive and fortifying their ancestral lands with their own castles. From these, Welsh kings and warlords resisted or fought against further Anglo-Norman intrusion. However, the Welsh also fought each other with equal verve.

Most of the time, no one was pleased with their territorial standing: neither the Welsh kings, nor the Anglo-Norman monarchs, nor the Marcher lords squashed in between. Each pushed for more, either through negotiation and pact-making or via military takeover. However, gradually, haltingly, the successors to Richard the Lionheart had – by the mid-thirteenth century – brought south Wales under English control, both from a military perspective and a cultural one.

The northern and central Welsh kingdoms, though, had fallen under the rule of an ambitious and arrogant native Welsh king from Gwynedd called Llywelyn ap Gruffydd, also known as Llywelyn the Last. Whilst the English monarch, Henry III, was preoccupied with rebellious English barons, Llywelyn seized the opportunity to push against the Marcher lords – as well as against the weaker Welsh kingdoms. In these endeavours, he seemed successful for a while. By 1267, Llywelyn's dominion over Wales looked impressive when his own colours of red and gold were plotted out. All Wales northward of the Bannau Brycheiniog and the Preseli Hills was under his sovereignty or suzerainty.

Meanwhile, King Henry III was pretty much incapacitated as he forfeited control of Crown affairs to one particularly powerful warring baron named Simon de Montfort. Powerless to resist de Montfort's demands, Henry III had to sign a treaty acknowledging Llywelyn as the Prince of Wales. As part of the treaty, Llywelyn was duty-bound to pay a tribute to the English Crown, which he did not much like but acceded to. We should note, though, that despite Llywelyn's extensive reign over the Welsh and his grand title as Prince of Wales, many of his own underling kings and chieftains resented his overlordship of their lands.

In 1272, King Henry passed away, leaving the English throne to his gregarious son, Edward I, also known as Edward Longshanks. Now there were arrogant and aggressive rulers on either side of Offa's Dyke: each quick to take umbrage and each wildly stubborn. There was going to be a showdown. And the winner would be the one with the most sheep.

In Llywelyn's favour, he possessed the large Welsh isle of Anglesey, the breadbasket of Wales, plus various rights to exact taxes and tributes from his considerable Welsh domains. Llywelyn also had battle victories under his belt against English foes as well as Welsh. Whilst some of his Welsh vassals decried his arrogance, he could also count on others to support him against the hated English.

In times past, Llywelyn had forged a working relationship with

Simon de Montfort. With de Montfort backing him, Llywelyn managed to garner support from the Pope as the legitimate Prince of Wales. However, de Montfort died in battle in 1165. The de Montforts could still claim to be an important baronial family but their reputation was severely battered in England because of Simon's power-grab against Henry III.

In Edward I's favour, it was he who had battled Simon de Montfort in 1165 and it was his knights that had slain de Montfort. This victory forged a strong English royal house once more. Just as important, at this time England was becoming one of the wealthiest realms in Europe, at least per head of population. The kingdom had a strong and growing agricultural economy that offered food security for the majority of English subjects plus a dependable surplus. Thus, England had a steadily growing population of fit and healthy adults. This included men of fighting age that could swell the size of English armies – if the need arose. The English Crown was also growing richer as well via revenue garnered from foreign exports, more than half of which was wool. This, too, could be reinvested into military campaigns if necessary.

Edward I had also managed to get Llywelyn's brother, Dafydd ap Gruffydd, to defect to the English side. This could be a strategic advantage in any future Welsh dealings since Dafydd was familiar with the Prince of Wales's mindset and tactics. Dafydd's defection might also cause some Welsh warlords to waver in their support for Llywelyn.

Standing against Edward I, though, were the time-consuming demands of governing his inherited landholdings in western France, including quelling the odd revolt. Later, Edward would also begin a bloody campaign to subdue Scotland, when he'd assume his infamous nickname 'Hammer of the Scots'. However, that was decades in the future. For now, Edward was somewhat weary of crossing the Welsh mountains and then battling against the unpredictable Welsh as well as the unpredictable weather.

In 1275, King Edward sought a non-military way to subdue Llywelyn by journeying to Chester, the ancient market town in the borderlands between England and Wales. Here he summoned the Prince of Wales to offer him tribute. Llywelyn, however, thought the set of circumstances a tad suspect. This was precisely the sort of contrived situation that had seen previous Welsh leaders arrested and thrown into a dark dungeon for years on end. To avoid such a fate, Llywelyn stayed well away from Chester. He also sent a letter to Edward I declaring that the Welsh principality was strapped for cash right now but that a tribute might be possible, perhaps, in the future, maybe. This could have been true. Wales's economic surplus – including from the production of wool – was sometimes barely enough for Llywelyn to maintain his own royal household.

When Llywelyn's message arrived in Chester, Edward I was livid. The English king had been parading around Cheshire showing off about how magnificent he was and it was mightily embarrassing that the Prince of Wales had not turned up to the party. There was only one thing for Edward to do. He had to take on the Welsh mountains, invade the Prince of Wales's own ancestral territory and defeat the Welsh. To ensure success, though, he needed to make a proper declaration of war so a parliament would sanction a potent army.

Wars are costly undertakings, of course. Luckily for him, King Edward I convinced his first parliament in London to enact a customs grant on exported wool and sheep hides. This grant would directly send to the king's coffers the annual sum of around 10,000 pounds. This was an enormous amount for the thirteenth century. Later on, Edward I also took it upon himself to confiscate extra wool lying in the hands of foreign merchants and then resell it to make enormous profits. This crafty practice became infamous throughout the international wool trade. Edward was aware that merchants across the continent had sized him up as unjust and untrustworthy but he hardly cared.

With this wool money, Edward raised and equipped an army of 15,000 soldiers to deploy against the Prince of Wales. Half of these soldiers were recruited from south Wales where Llywelyn did not hold territory and where he was quite unpopular. By the summer of 1277, Edward I's forces began marching into north Wales. They did so in a decidedly menacing manner, attempting to frighten away any would-be Welsh rebels. Edward also pronounced Llywelyn disinherited of all lands that the English army marched through. This included all the assets standing upon the land – including all the sheep in Gwynedd.

Eventually, King Edward crossed the Menai Strait to set up camp in Anglesey. This meant Llywelyn found it difficult to procure food for his Welsh warriors. Backed into a corner in northern Wales, Llewelyn knew he would lose any battle fought against the English. Thus, he capitulated and signed a peace treaty. In the process, he handed over some of his lands to Edward I. Llywelyn's dominion over Wales had shrivelled to a small corner of Gwynedd west of the River Conwy.

Yet the Prince of Wales had not forsaken the idea of reclaiming his lost possessions. Five years later, in 1282, Llywelyn's estranged brother, Dafydd, had a falling out with the English to whom he had defected years before. Dafydd returned to Wales and sent messages of reconciliation to Llywelyn. Before Llywelyn could reply to his brother, Dafydd started a revolt against the English, leading an attack against the English-occupied Hawarden Castle in Flintshire and then besieging the newly built English castle of Rhuddlan in Denbighshire.

Llywelyn hesitated to join the revolt, fearing Edward I would invade Wales again. However, inspired by Dafydd's revolt, a rebellion spread across other parts of the country as various Welsh nobles mustered their warriors to attack Marcher strongholds. In the end, the Prince of Wales felt he had no choice. If the rebellion failed without him being a part of it, Edward would still come for him. And if the uprising succeeded without him, the Welsh warlords would seek to depose him. Thus, he joined the rebellion and started pouncing on English-run castles.

In the autumn of 1282, English forces stormed into Wales again, heading north once more to Anglesey. The stakes were even higher than before, both for the Welsh fighters and for the English king. Llywelyn's soldiers felt part of a national war against never-ending English intrusion, while Edward I had had enough of just stamping the Welsh into submission. This time he would conquer Wales and make it his own personal property. As such, King Edward sent two English armies into Wales, one in the north and one in the south. The English military stumbled initially, losing several battles. However, when Llywelyn's forces engaged a third English army organised by the Marcher lords, the Prince of Wales was lured to engage them, then ensnared in a trap and picked off by a solitary lancer.

With Llywelyn the Last dead and gone, Welsh resistance began to falter. Edward I then personally took charge of the northern army, successfully attacking Welsh-held castles there. When Dafydd ap Gruffydd was captured, all hope for victory was lost and the Welsh quit fighting. It is said that Edward felt so aggrieved by Dafydd's betrayal that the king invented a new form of execution, having Dafydd 'hung, drawn and quartered'.

This time, the king of England was not about to negotiate any new treaties. Wales, he thought, was now his. He even took the title of 'Prince of Wales' and gave it to his first-born son. This abuse became a long-standing tradition observed by English monarchs right up to the present day.

Edward I worked to secure his Welsh territories by quickly constructing a series of castles within them: the so-called Ring of Iron. These castles were grander than those built by Anglo-Norman Marcher lords 200 years before. And while the Anglo-Norman castles were built individually by various lords, all the castles of the Ring of Iron were commissioned and overseen by Edward I himself. Among them were the castles of Harlech, Aberystwyth, Caernarfon, Conwy, Flint, Builth and Beaumaris. Many of them stood for centuries, haunting the Welsh landscape.

King Edward's castle-building programme was wildly expensive. The 10,000 pounds per annum he secured from wool taxes was massive, but still not enough to pay for all the castles. Some individual castles would cost double that. But on the strength of the English tax statutes – which guaranteed a large income from the annual clip every year – he could entice wealthy bankers in Italy to lend him money. In the end, Edward I borrowed over 100,000 pounds to employ over 3,000 men to work on his encastellation project.

It is tempting to think that such a huge programme of castle-building would serve as a significant economic stimulus for the Welsh economy since it involved an unprecedented injection of funds into the country. Yet very few of those working on or in the castles would have been Welsh. They were mostly drawn from English and Flemish colonies in southern Wales and from distant parts of England. Even worse, Welsh peasants were sometimes evicted from the villages and

Above: The Standard of Ur, a rendering of daily life in the Mesopotamian city of Ur dating from the third millennium BC – with woolly sheep near the centre.

Below: The Little Shepherd Boy, an 1840 painting by Carlo Dalgas of a shepherd resting by a prehistoric dolmen.

Above: Ram-headed Khnum, a stone impression dating from the Greco–Roman period. Khnum was the prime creator God in ancient Egypt, revered for producing the rains that fed the Nile and for the primordial moulding of the human form.

Below: Welsh Landscape with Two Women Knitting, an 1860 painting by William Dyce. A mountain meadow might not seem a likely spot for communal Welsh knitting but those engaged in wool craft would have convened quite regularly in the small gardens of their cottages during good weather to use natural light as they knitted or spun wool.

Above: Highland Wanderers, a 1908 landscape painting depicting Scottish Blackface sheep in the mountains of Scotland, by William Watson.

Below: The Sheep Drive, an 1863 painting by John Linnell, probably depicting an actual scene in the North Downs of Surrey, England.

Above: Cader Idris from Kwmmer Abbey, an 1844 engraving of a Welsh landscape, by David Cox and William Radclyffe.

Below: The Emigrants, an 1844 painting by William Allsworth depicting Scottish settlers in New Zealand – with their sheep.

Above: Sheep gate in a dry stone wall, Eryri (Snowdonia), Wales. What is shown here is really a 'sheepscape'. Natural woodlands were felled many centuries previously – and their regrowth was thwarted to allow sheep to graze upon open pastures. Over the centuries, miles of dry stone walls were erected to manage the wide movement of highland flocks.

Below: Badger-faced mountain sheep. These sheep likely roamed the Welsh uplands ever since the Dark Ages, when it's probable that their badger pattern extended across their entire bodies. Later farmers then began selecting for sheep with a broad white fleece which had higher value in the international wool trade.

Above: Near Llanbedr, Barmouth, an 1872 Welsh landscape painting by Charles Thomas Burt. Here we see a trusty Welsh sheepdog helping to drove a flock across a stone bridge in the foothills of Eryri (Snowdonia).

Below: Tending Sheep, Betws-y-Coed, an 1849 Welsh landscape painting by David Cox. Like numerous artists painting as the Industrial Revolution enveloped Britain, Cox eagerly sought to escape his own smoky industrial city to capture idyllic Welsh scenes like this.

Above: A flock near Tintern Abbey, the Wye Valley, Wales. Tintern's Cistercian monks kept large wool-producing flocks here from 1131 until 1536, when the abbey was dissolved by Henry VIII.

Below: A Welsh mountain sheep on Llangynidr moors, Bannau Brycheiniog, Wales. Even before the Kingdom of Brycheiniog came into being, sheep farming would have been the mainstay of the Celtic economy since the dawn of the Iron Age.

Above: A flock in front of a Cotswold 'wool church', the Church of St James, Chipping Campden, England. Wool churches were far grander than their provincial settings would normally see – thanks to the stupendous wealth gained by local wool merchants.

Below: Mountain sheep in a woodland. Perhaps a sustainable future for Welsh sheep farming lies partly in working out how flocks might live within regenerating woodlands.

farmlands close to where the castles sprang up. This was undertaken not just to free up useful land but because the Welsh were perceived as something of a security threat.

Despite not really helping the Welsh locals economically, the resources expended were immense. The castles needed enormous loads of stone for the walls and great masses of lead for the roofs as well as lots of iron and timber. Some of these materials could be sourced locally in Wales but most were brought in from all parts of King Edward's various realms in the British Isles and France.

The labourers and craftsmen were assembled together amazingly quickly to push Edward's castles up into the Welsh sky as promptly as possible. Since it was such an important project for him, Edward I gathered the best master craftsmen from different parts of Europe to supervise and coordinate the work. He was also involved in the design of some of the castles. For instance, when it came to building Caernarfon Castle, Edward I insisted it replicate the famous Theodosian Wall of Constantinople with its polygonal towers and bands of contrasting coloured stone.

Some historians view the whole Ring of Iron as a net positive for Europe's medieval economy since it prompted a system of credit and cashflow between friendly states. This view is a tad rosy, though, since Edward I ended up defaulting upon many of his loans, sending bankers all over Europe into bankruptcy. The kingdom of England wasn't doing much better since the over-investment in Welsh castles meant the realm was, for a while, hard pressed to provide for its own basic upkeep. Incidentally, because the Edwardian castles are now managed by the Welsh Government, we could say that the Welsh eventually captured the castles originally designed to dominate them.

Back in the thirteenth century, Edward's castles served not only as military establishments but also as seats of civilian governance. This added to their status and influence within the Welsh landscape and also attracted new waves of English immigrants to set up in towns and villages nearby. As in earlier Anglo-Norman times, these English settlers were duty-bound to protect the castles overlooking their towns during times of trouble.

The Welsh were generally prohibited from inhabiting these new English towns and could only trade within them under strict restrictions. Of course, this situation led to simmering resentment for centuries since the Welsh were discriminated against in their own land. Some town officials were willing to overlook a merchant's Welshness if they hailed from a family of sound repute, or if they paid a 'special fee' to anglicise their name.

Within the new English towns, private wool-craft workshops were springing up in abundance. Each workshop scoured the nearby countryside for raw materials, readily buying up spun wool from the Welsh. This created an economic upswing for some fortunate locals.

Because the wool industry was booming all around England during Edward I's reign, when he took charge of Wales it was only natural that sheep-farming became a growing industry there as well. Not long after Edward had conquered Wales, a series of small ports was set up on the northern Welsh coasts near the new castles of Harlech, Conwy, Beaumaris and Caernarfon. These ports were created to supply the castles, mainly, but they were also used by traders to export wool back to England. This increase in trade kept many Welsh spinners and clothmakers in gainful employment for decades.

Sheep-farming and wool-spinning are generally thought of as rural activities. Yet in thirteenth- and fourteenth-century Wales, these industries provided impetus for the growth of many an urban centre. When William the Conqueror took an interest in Wales in 1067, he recorded the country as having no proper towns. By 1300, when Edward I's castle programme was complete, around a hundred towns had been established across Wales.

Those that did best out of the sheep boom of the Middle Ages, though, were the Marcher lords whose vast holdings in the countryside only increased after the Edwardian conquest. With all this land and with legions of shepherds working for them as bonded peasants, Marcher lords like the de Clares and the de Bohuns transformed their large flocks of sheep into enormous flocks of sheep; the lords themselves grew from being rich to being stinking rich.

As we saw in Chapter 15, the Marcher lords were generally haughty and tyrannical, most especially to their Welsh subjects. However, independent sheep-farmers and wool traders in Wales, both Welsh and English, would often choose to deal with the Marcher lords rather than go through one of the English towns or ports approved by the English king. Since the Marcher lords ruled over their territories like mini-monarchs, they could levy their own tax on all and any trade proceeding through their land. This tax was usually a one-off payment and – once handed over – would allow a sheep-farmer or wool trader access to various markets and riverports. A one-time fee paid to the Marcher lord would usually end up less expensive than the multiple taxes paid for entering a market town, then purchasing a trade licence, then crossing a river, then using port facilities, plus extra fees for just being Welsh. And since all rivers led to the sea, the trader could use the Marcher riverports to travel downstream and then off to a coastal town in England to sell the wool and wool-crafts at higher prices.

In Chapter 16, we learnt of another significant group of sheep-farming landlords operating in medieval Wales: the Cistercians. During the thirteenth and fourteenth centuries, many abbeys in Wales reinvested their profits into buying or making newfangled agricultural machines. At the time, a kind of medieval industrial revolution was washing over Europe, with an enormous flourish in the construction of big water-powered and wind-powered machines springing up in the landscape. In England and Wales, thousands of watermills were placed along rivers and streams, many to power the lifting and dropping of enormous wooden hammers onto wet woven wool. This was part of the fulling process and it mass-produced a softer, fluffier, warmer, more durable fabric that medieval consumers adored. Since fulling machines were costly to build and to maintain, only the biggest farming enterprises, like abbeys and the occasional prominent landowner, could invest in them. When they were up and running, groups of peasants and independent wool-crafters sought to hire a fulling mill just for a day to pummel their own wool. In this manner, fulling mills could attract additional income for the abbeys.

The Marcher lords, though, seem to have steered away from buying fulling machines. Most of them had profitable business concerns outside of Wales and they considered their Welsh land as a financial extraction zone rather than somewhere worthy of investment and development. Basically, Wales was a place for English overlords to earn easy money by taxing the local peasants and traders. This money was then reinvested in their foreign estates where the lords preferred to live. Sheep-farming fitted into this absentee landlord model because sheep could take care of themselves – and reproduce – with minimal human oversight.

Another wool machine that arrived in Wales in later medieval times was the spinning wheel. Such wheels greatly increased the speed of spinning since very long yarns could be continuously spun onto a bobbin without interruption. This method contrasts with that of the drop spindle used by spinners for aeons. Drop spindles had to be stopped every few moments, and the yarn regularly wound onto the spindle. Not so with a spinning wheel.

One more innovation soon to spread wildly in Wales was knitting. The art and craft of knitting came to Europe via Spain where it had been developed in the south by the Moors. Spanish artisans took to knitting with multiple needles and via this technique they made the stockings and leggings we commonly view in paintings from the Middle Ages. Knitting quickly became popular amongst village artisans since practical clothing could be made from basic equipment and raw materials.

In medieval England and Wales, entire families would often be involved in knitting. When all the other farm chores had been completed, family members could gather together on fine days to knit in unison just outside their dwelling. For Welsh villagers, it could also become a productive nightly social activity since knitters could share a candlelit room to knit together. Over time, certain knitting styles and patterns developed in specific areas of Wales, and modern-day artisanal knitters from Gwynedd to Ceredigion to Pembrokeshire try to replicate these today.

Nowadays, knitting is considered the domain of hobbyists and specialist craft shops. Yet, as I tried to explain to Shelley as we rode around Wales on a zippy twenty-first-century train, his grandma would busily work magic with needles whenever she sat still for a few moments, such was the necessity to provide the family with essential winter woollies.

Chapter 20
THE SHEEP OF AVALON

LLŶN, WALES, 1284

In north Wales, there runs out from Gwynedd's mountainous countryside a thirty-mile-long wedge-shaped peninsula called Llŷn. Devoid of any large towns, Llŷn stretches out ever thinner as you travel westward. It eventually tapers to a point in the Irish Sea. To get here, you will have to journey quite some while upon quiet rural roads that pass through small beautiful rustic towns parked against the coast. Near the last of these towns, you can stand astride upon a jutting jagged shoreside cliff and enjoy a marvellous view. You will likely be on your own, save for the odd intrepid birdwatcher perched upon a neighbouring cliff bank or fisherfolk waving from their vessels off the rocky coast. Probably, you will also meet lovely calm Llŷn sheep nearby with their bright, curious eyes, hornless heads and trademark black noses.

Standing here, watching the stark beauty of the splendid waves crashing against the rocks, you might feel far away from the rest of

Wales. And maybe the rest of the world. If it wasn't for the friendly faces of the sheep, you might lose yourself in loneliness. For those craving serenity, though, this place feels less desolate than secluded.

Yet beyond this remote point of this out-of-the-way peninsula, there is a place more isolated still. In fine weather, you'll be able to spot an island adrift some two miles out to sea in the heaving Atlantic waters. This windswept grassy isle is called Ynys Enlli. It is only a few miles in length, yet legend has it that 20,000 saints are buried in its soil. Amongst them are St Einion, St Dyfrig and St Deiniol. It must be said, though, archaeologists have yet to find any of their remains – and 20,000 seems like an awful lot of dead saints for an island so compact.

Because of its saintly aura, anybody who dies on the island has a free ticket to heaven – or so it is said. Though diminutive, Ynys Enlli has a mountain – a hill, really – some 500 feet tall. Yet its peak is often blanketed with wet rain clouds, which hover low in these maritime environs.

The best known of Ynys Enlli's saints was Cadfan. In Chapter 13 we saw that some sixth-century Britons like Gildas moved from Wales to Brittany to escape the expanding clutches of pagan Anglo-Saxons. However, not long later, Breton nobles felt so threatened by encroaching Frankish warlords, they sailed back to Wales. In St Cadfan's case, he ended up in Llŷn with a boatload of fellow Christians where he was granted the island of Ynys Enlli by a local Welsh chieftain.

The brooding remoteness of Ynys Enlli allowed the Breton clerics to take on a monkish lifestyle. They were alone in the universe with God and nature, detached from the vices of Dark Age society. On this naturally protected site, Cadfan and his monks constructed one of Wales's first proper religious dwellings: a small abbey. The abbey grew over the next centuries until it was sacked by Viking raiders arriving from across the Irish Sea. This assault led to Ynys Enlli being abandoned for a long time.

However, between the sacking of St Cadfan's Abbey and the Edwardian conquest of Wales, Ynys Enlli had become something of a pilgrimage site. Though perched in an obscure place, it assumed renown amongst devoted Christians and attracted small bands of monks and hermits. These pilgrims kept the Christian spirit of Ynys Enlli alive. Over time, the island's spiritual reputation was augmented by rumours of miracles and magic whereby illness was cured and old age reversed. In the High Middle Ages, curious lay people began gathering at the tip of the Llŷn Peninsula to gaze upon the magical isle. The most adventurous would then slide down the cliffs to a hidden cove to find a rickety wooden boat half-covered in kelp. Scooping out the seaweed, they'd cross the two-mile stretch of wild open sea to Ynys Enlli in hope of experiencing some of its magic.

In the thirteenth century, a new abbey was built on the island by Augustinian monks on top of the ruins of St Cadfan's Abbey. At this time as well, a tower was constructed, which still stands today. Augustinian monks across Britain customarily grew their own vegetables in the gardens of their abbeys, both to feed themselves and to offer to hungry locals. However, in Ynys Enlli, the soil was too windswept and barren to grow much of anything. Instead of a garden, the monks started a sheep-farm. Like the sheep of other offshore islands, probably only the hardiest and most gregarious of them survived, plus those sociable enough to huddle together to pull through the storms.

Over the centuries, the sheep of Ynys Enlli created their own well-trod trails across the island. These trails are ground into the island's earth even now, as Llŷn sheep still tread them. Llŷn sheep are known to be seriously tough but the ones on Ynys Enlli seem amicable and caring. If you approach a ewe in a non-threatening manner, as a curious medieval pilgrim probably would have, she'll look you in the eye for a moment then turn to gently guide you across the sheep tracks of the island. In a fluffy-soft game of 'follow-the-leader', the Llŷn sheep will chaperone you across the historical sites of the island: some ancient Celtic remains, remnants of the thirteenth-century abbey, a few lichen-covered cottages built in the 1700s, plus a nineteenth-century chapel.

If you let them, the sheep will also usher you up and down around the solitary mountain to view a shearwater bird sanctuary on the far side. From the top of the mountain, when the weather is clear, you can look back up along the curving spine of the Llŷn Peninsula, which is stretched out like a gigantic sleeping dragon. If you turn westward, you can also spot Ireland, on a clear day.

As your sheepish escort brings you back down, she'll lead you past a broken-down old lime kiln and then to the abbey tower. The last stop will be the island's tiny gift shop – no kidding – before she takes you back to a boat and bids you farewell to the mainland. Somehow across the world, sheep have earned a reputation for being passive followers. On this magical island, their role as leaders comes to the fore.

One of the medieval pilgrims who journeyed from mainland Gwynedd, through Llŷn, to Ynys Enlli was King Edward I. After vanquishing the Prince of Wales, Edward triumphantly toured the conquered nation in 1284 to get a sense of his new domain. The good people of Wales might think a little better of Edward I if they learnt of his pilgrimage to honour the native saints buried on Ynys Enlli. However, Ynys Enlli had drawn King Edward to its rocky shores for an entirely different reason.

In the thirteenth century, one of the most popular tales of the time was the legend of King Arthur. The legend was retold in books, plays and songs across Europe, and King Edward himself was a great fan. Many medieval writers, like the Welsh scholar Geoffrey of Monmouth, presented King Arthur not as legend but as an actual historical figure that united and saved Christian Britain from invading pagans. In Wales, King Arthur is generally believed to be Welsh and to have lived out his life mainly in post-Roman Wales, fighting off Anglo-Saxons as they pushed westward from England. Over years, Ynys Enlli became associated with the legend since it was held by some to be the mythical island of Avalon, the final resting place of King Arthur. Edward I visited Ynys Enlli not to honour Welsh saints but to appropriate the magical spirit of King Arthur for himself. In a way it worked since most people nowadays believe King Arthur to be an English legend rather than Welsh.

Despite this, Wales still celebrates its Arthurian legacy via many artworks and heritage sites spread around the nation. And nobody in Wales thinks that Arthur had anything to do with the English – apart from fighting against them.

Chapter 21
KINGDOM OF WOOL

WALES/EUROPE, 1327 TO 1377

By the fourteenth century, sheep in lowland Wales were being turned into veritable wool machines. From the pastoral lands owned by abbeys and aristocrats, huge flocks were gathered together at the beginning of summer, then shorn by peasants. The wool was then baled up and carted off to shipping ports such as Carmarthen and Cardiff. If the sailing was smooth, the wool would hit the wool markets of Flanders and Italy within a month. Though Welsh wool did not have the same repute as English wool, it was still the major export commodity and a great money-earner for landowners and farmers in Wales.

Welsh peasants and tenant farmers also often kept their own flocks. These may have been tiny: a solitary ewe and her lambs. These subsistence herds would be encouraged to graze upon what was called 'wasteland'. This was land left undivided into feudal strips and generally not blessed with rich soil or easy ploughing. Yet there was enough wild grass growing upon it for sheep to graze.

Sometimes small-time farmers could work cooperatively in their spare time to maintain shared flocks on rented land. For example, in the medieval lordship of Dyffryn Clwyd in Denbighshire, the lord's flock numbered almost 3,000 with the aggregated tenants' flocks nearly as many. A similar arrangement appeared on the lands of the Cistercian abbeys. For instance, Tintern Abbey rented out some of its granges to groups of tenant farmers to graze their collective sheep.

Another pattern of sheep-farming was sheep rental, whereby farmers would lease sheep from a large flock owner, maybe an abbot, just to produce wool. In this case, the lessee would keep the wool shorn off during the season and then return the sheep to their owner. If the sheep died by season's end, the lessee had to replace them at their own cost. Sometimes, arrangements could be made for the lessee to keep some proportion of the lambs born during the year, usually the black-wooled lambs, thereby allowing a peasant shepherd to start a flock of their own.

In decades when the wool trade was steadily growing year by year, entrepreneurial peasants might eventually find themselves with their own private flocks of 100 or more sheep. In some areas of Wales and England, such a flock when sold off together would allow tenant farmers to purchase their own land. In this way, they'd become freehold peasants, paying minimal taxes to some overlord. If they were very lucky, their new land would be located near a communication route leading straight to an English market town or to an English port, thus allowing them to enter the lucrative transnational wool trade.

Though such economic opportunities did exist in the Middle Ages, they were not common and even rarer when tenants were tied in feudal bondage to a landlord. A tenant who had managed to scrape together enough wool wealth to buy themselves out of bondage would still have to depend upon the good graces of their lord to allow the transaction to go ahead.

As the wool industry prospered all across Europe in the 1300s, there was also a growing domestic market in Wales for wool. This was not really due to the rising human population – which was growing only slowly – but because more and more workshops were being set up in the growing number of towns. As these workshops were set up, and the weavers and woolworkers within them became professionalised, the townspeople sought to protect themselves from outside competition. For instance, workshop administrants in Welsh towns like Ruthin, Tenby, Carmarthen and Haverfordwest conspired with their town officials to levy all sorts of arbitrary taxes and penalties upon those weaving outside the town's boundaries. This included thousands of rural wool-crafters working in their own homes and villages. Of course, those within the town limits were mostly English and those outside were mostly Welsh. So Welsh people could be forgiven for believing these taxes were levied to keep the Welsh in abjection. If villagers or farmsteads wanted to weave cloth to bring in a few coins, they would have had to account for these taxes – or evade them somehow.

Talking of tax burdens, many Welsh families usually needed an additional source of income to pay for them all. As well as spinning wool, keeping a few sheep was always a useful practice. If all else failed, a whole living sheep could be used as payment for rental arrears to an impatient landlord or overzealous tax collector. As well, landlords and sheriffs often dished out arbitrary penalties for minor transgressions ranging from premarital relations to the collection of mushrooms from wastelands to the consumption of wild rabbits squashed under a cart not one's own. It was always handy to keep some sheep in stock to pay off these penalties so worse forfeitures could be avoided.

Though dominated by a focus on wool, sheep-farming did also involve the sale of surplus meat from some parts of Marcher Wales if it could be quickly sent overland or downriver to an English market. However, most medieval British sheep were still quite small, certainly compared to cattle, and they generally stayed so until the eighteenth century, so they weren't seen as major meat commodities. Wool remained the real money-earner.

One figure who sought to take advantage of the continuing growth of the wool industry was the king of England. By 1327, this was Edward III, grandson of Edward I. King Edward III understood that wool remained the single most important source of wealth for the kingdom, which is why he ordered his Lord Chancellor to sit upon a sack of wool whenever Parliament met: a constant reminder to all that the nation's well-being rested upon wool. This same woolsack now cushions the seat of the Lord Speaker in the Upper House of the UK Parliament.

During his long reign, Edward III intervened numerous times to maximise the benefit of wool exports to his own royal house. Edward wore British woollens in public and chastised those who did not follow suit as unpatriotic. He also invited a new wave of clothmakers from Flanders to settle in Britain to add value to the wool industry. However, it is unclear if any new Flemish invitees ended up in Wales. As well as weavers, Edward sought wool dyers and fullers from Flanders, promising them they would be well cared for and boasting that Flemish clothmakers already settled in England feasted daily on bountiful fat English lamb.

Edward also personally chose the few towns in Wales and England that were allowed to export wool. This was so that he could conveniently count all the wool leaving the nation and easily extract export tariffs. He also mandated that the wool merchants in these towns had to pay for port operations out of their own pocket, including the construction and maintenance of all the docks, weirs, bridges, wharves, piers, cranes and customs houses. If they did not, Edward would revoke export privileges and give them to some other town.

So what did Edward III do with his kingdom's wool revenue? Did he spend it on new roads and waterways? Or on new cathedrals and castles? No. Instead, Edward III started one of the longest, bitterest, cruellest wars in human history: the Hundred Years' War against France. Actually, it lasted 116 years in all, thereby outlasting many generations of kings and queens in both realms. As the junior belligerent, England was probably only able to draw the fight out for so long because English and Welsh sheep loyally munched away eating grass to produce profitable wool every one of those 116 years.

So how did this long war get started? Ever since the death of Richard the Lionheart in 1199, there had been a lingering tension between England and France – a cold war in effect that was always threatening to boil over into all-out heated conflict. By the 1300s, Richard's Angevin Empire had long since decayed but the Lionheart's great-great-grandson Edward III still held land in Gascony, a south-western stretch of French land on the Bay of Biscay. This was quite a wealthy region because of its wine trade.

Edward III also enjoyed firm diplomatic relations with Flanders, which served as England's leading trading partner. Most of England's exported wool was sent there to be processed into cloth. So England generally – and Edward III specifically – depended on this international partnership for significant income.

In the 1330s, the king of France, Philip VI, was threatening to confiscate Edward's Gascon land and he warned Edward that he might also make a move on Flanders too. Apart from being an affront to Edward III's rightfully inherited property, these threats also endangered the all-important Anglo-Flemish wool trade.

In reaction, Edward III crashed over the Channel with an English army into Flanders and – in front of an adoring Flemish crowd – declared war on the French. With the help of Flemish mercenaries, paid for in part by the Anglo-Flemish wool trade, Edward moved south to invade France.

Much of the time, the French king assiduously avoided any face-to-face battles with the English, hoping Edward's armies would just return home when they ran out of food and funds. Since Edward III could not track down and engage the French in battle, he then started out on a reprehensible scorched-earth campaign. This tactic was known as a chevauchée, where English-led armies made devastating raids across the French countryside to systematically loot then destroy productive rural areas. Such onslaughts were led by well-heeled English knights adorned in glamorous shining armour and mounted on battle horses.

Supposedly, the knights were bound by codes of chivalry. Yet these codes were applied in a stratified manner. When one knight bested a rival knight – seizing him as he rode upon his armour-plated horse for example – the defeated knight was taken as an honoured guest until a ransom could be organised. Yet a simple peasant was offered no such grace, being slaughtered with brutal impunity. And it usually didn't matter if the peasant was battling with a pitchfork or just moving his sheep from a field of cabbages.

When medieval English armies crashed through the French countryside, they typically numbered about 10,000 individual warriors. This number comprised some 2,000 knights and some 8,000 or so archers. The archers were mainly peasants and labourers and moved about on foot. Over the course of a standard chevauchée, an invading English army would wander around the French countryside until they spotted a village lying tranquil and peaceful in the distance. Then, a band of around a hundred knights would peel off from the main army to ride into the village and kill anyone and anything they saw running away. They would also rip away any valuables that could be readily transported – such as jewellery and horses – before riding out again, leaving in their wake smouldering cottages, burning fields and dying villagers.

Thereafter, the English army's archers would drift into the burning village to scrape through the leftovers. The leftovers included food but also livestock. The archers could then shepherd a few bedraggled French sheep into a flock and entice them to follow them on the next sortie. A live sheep could be a valuable trading commodity for an archer in the French warzone. Or else, it could fuel a feast before a battle.

The aim of Edward III's chevauchée strategy was twofold: first, to degrade the resources of France so neither food nor taxable goods might be produced; and second, to sow fear amongst the French in the hopes of undermining the legitimacy of the king. This latter point assumes that the French would grow disloyal if their king could not protect them. However, it seems that whilst the Edwardian chevauchées effectively ruined the agricultural economy of vast swathes of France, they also united the rural French against the English army.

In response to Edward's brutal campaign, many French villagers and townspeople tried to quickly transform their settlements into makeshift fortresses to protect themselves. Alas, this in itself was economically devastating for French peasants for they were forced by the local mayors and landlords to donate all their possessions to fund the fortification, including their livestock. The French mayors sometimes used these donations to bribe English knights not to attack their town. Sometimes this worked. Sometimes it did not. Even when it worked, the villages and towns ended up destitute having sacrificed everything they owned, including their sheep.

In the 1340s and 1350s, French authors and artists regularly commented on the horror of the chevauchées. They could hardly not – such was the widespread chaos these caused in France. Scribes from the priestly classes, like the medieval literary figure Petrus Bercorius, linked the irreverent slaughter of sheep and the rape of shepherdesses with biblical stories about sacrificial lambs.

Though chevauchées were their prevalent tactic, English armies did occasionally confront mighty French armies face on to inflict defeat, such as at the famous battles of Sluys, Crecy, Poitiers and Agincourt. These English battle wins were the prime reason the French kings skulked away out of sight, unwilling to get into any more face-to-face fights. In such battles, the archers were a major contributor to victory. Many of the archers were peasants recruited from Wales and their Welsh longbows rained down so many arrows upon French knights that some would inevitably penetrate gaps in their armour. Impaled by Welsh arrows, the French knights would slide off their expensive battle horses into muddy fields. Squelching in the mud, they were easy pickings for advancing soldiers to finish them off with daggers. English monarchs like Edward III were initially uncertain of the attitude of their Welsh soldiery. Yet both they and the sheep of Wales ended up vital for English success in France.

Despite the financial firepower of English and Welsh wool, we should note that Edward III was such a profligate spender that his wool revenues were never enough to fully cover the expenses of the French military campaign. However, like his grandfather Edward I, Edward III managed to get various Italian banks to grant him enormous loans by convincing them they'd be paid back with future wool revenues. However, just like his grandfather again, Edward III ended up defaulting on these loans. This threw the Italian banking system into chaos once more – and then Europe into recession. Kings and princes around the continent roundly criticised Edward since they could no longer easily borrow money. Yet, Edward did not much care.

The wool merchants of Wales and England were also aggrieved because they never got paid in full for the wool they produced during the war, thus plunging many wool towns into economic precarity. And if the wool merchants were strapped for cash, they could hardly pay sheep-farmers and wool producers for their wool. Again, Edward III was not particularly concerned. His knightly war had cost those under him far more than it cost him.

Yet, even with the massive loads of loaned money piled on top of his annual royal wool revenue, Edward III still could not cover the cost of his French war. Indeed, much of the borrowed money was whittled away on grand celebrations in London to showcase Edward's battle wins. Alas though, these celebrations were premature; the Hundred Years' War had many twists and turns to go through yet.

Chapter 22

BLACK SHEPHERDS OF DEATH

WALES/EUROPE, 1348 TO 1453

In the eleventh year of the Hundred Years' War, when things were getting deeply desperate and deplorable in France, something arrived from the east to deepen the misery further. This something was a deadly pandemic that wiped out hundreds of millions across the world. Those that caught the disease knew very well they were about to die since their fingers turned black and great painful sores erupted in their armpits and groin. Variously named the Bubonic Plague, the Pestilence or the Great Mortality, its most gruesome title was the Black Death.

The Black Death first arrived in England and France during the summer of 1348, carried aboard Venetian ships that were ferrying luxury goods from the Orient. As well as unloading spices and silks, these same ships unloaded fleas carried in the fur of rats and in the hair of humans. These fleas were infected with *Yersinia pestis*, the plague bacteria. Before long, the fleas were jumping from rat to rat and human to human, spreading plague at rampaging speed. Its arrival in the French warzone meant many soldiers fell down dead without even fighting. The belligerents suffered so many losses that all sides decided to retreat to their strongholds. However, when the soldiers and knights returned home, they also took with them the bacteria that caused the Black Death.

Estimates vary but many historians believe up to half the population of France died from the Black Death and about a quarter of all people on the British Isles. This large difference in death rate between France and Britain might owe something to Edward's III invasion. Edward's scorched-earth campaign ravaged the French countryside so intensively that harvests were destroyed for years. This, in turn, invoked years of hunger and starvation that weakened the population, making them more vulnerable to the Plague.

When the Black Death dissipated a few years later, the landlords left alive pushed open the gates and doors of their castles and halls to find vast numbers of their tenant farmers dead or gone. They were left wondering if their farms could be worked at all and if rents could be paid.

With so many tenant farmers missing, a massive labour shortage ensued. In Wales – and across Europe – fields remained unploughed, unsown and unharvested for years after. Labourers were suddenly much in demand as landlords sought them out to make their land productive again. Because of this, many tenant farmers felt empowered to demand better rental agreements and farm workers higher pay. If such was not forthcoming, most felt strong enough to break their bondage and head off for a better life elsewhere.

King Edward III was not one who ever sided with the common people. He decreed that tenant bondage could not be broken at random and that labourers' wages must stay at pre-Plague levels. Mostly, these new laws were ignored. There were too few sheriffs and bailiffs left around to enforce them, anyhow. Many landlords were forced to accept the only way to rehabilitate their estates after the Black Death was to pay higher wages.

Landlords whose tenants and labourers had died or fled in large numbers often let sheep graze upon the abandoned fields of their estates. In this way, sheep-farming allowed some landowners to remain productive during the long stagnant period following the Plague.

Although agriculture across Europe suffered disruption during the Black Death, we might still find particular empathy for many small-time sheep-farmers in Wales since there was little let-up in the taxes and tithes they had to pay. Indeed, since Welsh landlords and Welsh churches were strapped for cash themselves, they got even tougher on those under their charge. This was particularly notable in the Welsh Marches where landlords sent out ruffian bailiffs to scare peasants into forking up their rents or else pay large penalties. They also took to spreading the word that runaway serfs and absconders would be hung up by their necks. Despite the threats, or because of them, there was a general exodus from farming lands in Wales with a corresponding rise in vacant fields and abandoned villages.

As we noticed in previous chapters, in the generations before the Black Death, new and prosperous market towns were popping up across Wales. These towns were hotspots of industrious activity and commercial exchange. The coinage circulating in medieval Wales increased from 30,000 pounds during the Lionheart's reign in the twelfth century to more than two million pounds when Edward III became king in the fourteenth century. Just after the Black Death, though, many of these towns – and the boisterous trade fairs held within them – were much reduced in size or forsaken altogether. The wool sector also suffered long term in the wake of the Black Death since many textile mills and wool workshops had to shut down due to the lack of trade. Although there were still great numbers of sheep producing wool, there were far fewer people around to buy woollen cloth. In the case of the mills, it took a whole century for them to return in good numbers to the Welsh landscape.

Although full economic recovery from the Black Death was exceedingly slow, as soon as the Plague had abated in Europe, Edward III reignited his war with France. In 1355, Edward's son, the Black Prince, embarked upon another scorched-earth campaign in French lands. The Black Prince earned his nickname not just because of the tint of his armour but because he was even crueller than his father. Many rural areas had not recovered from prior chevauchées, let alone the impact of the Black Death, so this third round of cruelty completely broke up some villages and communities. French geographers note that there are still population deserts in the French countryside today — devoid of towns, villages and farms — because they were wrecked by the combined force of the chevauchées and the Plague during the Hundred Years' War.

Since the Black Prince and his knightly comrades were on a renewed rampage, fearful French towns took to refurbishing their temporary fortifications in stone, many becoming walled cities. This pattern of construction continued for the rest of the Hundred Years' War. In later years, the French were also inspired into more offensive action by a young spinner named Joan of Arc. In 1429, Joan laid down her wool spindle to lead French armies to retake the cities of Orleans and Reims. This marked the beginning of the end for the English in France.

Eventually, English royals started fighting amongst themselves, and the war between England and France petered out. At its end, the English monarchy had lost their French lands altogether, save for the port of Calais.

Before the Hundred Years' War came to a conclusion, though, Wales had to suffer through further calamities. One particularly devastating crisis was the Glyndŵr revolt of 1400 to 1415. Owain Glyndŵr was a Welsh nobleman whose family had long been friendly with the English regime. That was until he lost a legal battle in an English parliament regarding a land dispute he was having with a neighbouring English lord. Returning to Wales more than a little miffed, he formed a militia that grew into an army then snowballed into a Welsh independence movement.

Many of Glyndŵr's followers were returned servicemen who had fought for English armies in France. Despite aiming their arrows at the French, they had long harboured their own grievances about English overlordship in Wales. Emulating English chevauchée tactics in France, Glyndŵr's rebel army ran and rode around Wales sacking and burning English-controlled castles and English-owned estates. They also went sacking and burning English-dominated towns in south Wales, murdering hundreds of innocent people. Most of these had lived in Wales all their lives, tracing their roots from settlers who had migrated to the area during Anglo-Norman times, hundreds of years before.

Though still regarded by many today as a national hero, Glyndŵr's raids and rampages managed to completely ruin almost half of all trade in Wales. Glyndŵr and his soldiers might have walked away with some small treasures, but the farmers and artisans who relied on peaceful trade were impoverished. Welsh historian John Davies suggests at least a generation passed before the economy began recovering. Since the English towns had many Welsh families residing within them, Glyndŵr also inflicted murder upon the people he claimed to be fighting for.

Because English armies were busy fighting in France, it took them a few years to muster up enough of a force to put down Glyndŵr's revolt. English lawmakers did throw out some oppressive new laws in Wales's direction during the revolt, banning Welshmen from buying land or assuming public office, but since England had lost control of Wales, these laws did not mean much. In the meantime, Glyndŵr formed alliances with England's foes: France and Scotland. He even managed to entice King Charles VI of France to send some French troops to Wales. After a few years, though, enough spare English soldiers could be rallied up and sent into the Principality to battle Glyndŵr's rebels and then drive them all into hiding. English soldiers then meted retribution against the Welsh countryside, causing even more harm to the average Welsh village.

As noted earlier, sheep were an important and expanding part of Welsh life in the Middle Ages, both at the subsistence level and in trade. Anyone with access to any land usually had a flock, however small. However, medieval Welsh sheep did not really compete all that well with English sheep on the international market. Welsh sheep and Welsh wool were routinely valued at a fraction of English sheep and English wool. Foreign merchants thought most Welsh sheep too scrawny and their wool too rough. The wet weather along with the remote location of many farms meant Welsh wool was liable to degrade before it was packed up and sent for export.

Ever since the Normans took over English estates in the eleventh century, sheep-farmers there had been breeding bigger and faster-growing sheep with finer and longer wool. In comparison, Welsh sheep-farming lagged somewhat. Only the large abbeys – and a couple of very wealthy Anglo-Welsh sheep-farmers − devoted the time and money to breeding better sheep or improving the processing of wool.

Of course, just because Welsh sheep didn't always make the grade on the international market does not mean they were unimportant in Wales. Welsh mountain sheep were perfectly adapted to survive the nation's heavy weather. Though the wool they produced wasn't ever fine enough to command premium prices in England or Europe, it was quite suitable for cottage workers to spin and weave at home into their own cloth. And given the ravages inflicted upon medieval Welsh farmers by the Black Death as well as by their own warlording nobles, it was mightily fortunate that Welsh sheep were standing stalwart in the rain and snow to help country folk through the rough times.

Chapter 23

DISCOVERY OF NEW SHEEPLANDS

EUROPE/AMERICA, 1483 TO 1600

Once upon a time in medieval Wales, a young prince called Madog ab Owain Gwynedd set to sea with a band of followers in a fleet of small ships. His father, the king of Gwynedd, had passed away the preceding year. However, murderous infighting between the king's dozen or more children left Madog facing numerous death threats. To stay alive, he took to the waves. He commanded his fleet across the stormy Irish Sea, then navigated around the Emerald Isle to avoid equally murderous Irish relatives before heading clear into the blue expanse of the Atlantic. A few months later, he hauled his ships up onto the beaches of Alabama in the Gulf of Mexico.

If you wander up and down the banks of the Alabama River today, it is possible you'll stumble across a few great cubic stones that resemble the ruins of a Welsh castle. Reputedly, Cherokee hunters in centuries past told early Spanish explorers that the stones had been placed there by white people generations before.

A bit further north, in Tennessee, eighteenth-century British explorers reported Native American villagers there as speaking in a language reminiscent of Welsh. They also noted these same villagers used round canoes fashioned in a similar manner to Welsh coracles. However, all these Native American villagers were wiped out by a terrible smallpox epidemic in the 1770s, meaning not one of them was left alive to be judged on how much Welsh they might have spoken.

During the nineteenth century, British antiquarians would wander up and down the rivers of Alabama and Tennessee looking for clear material evidence that Madog or his descendants had settled around there. They managed to scavage some stone tablets but none of them are compelling to modern archaeologists. Perhaps, one day in the future, some twelfth-century sheep bones will be dug up on the riverbanks to prompt a rethink of the evidence. Till then, the story is commemorated via a plaque set into a boulder on the shores of Alabama reading:

> In memory of Prince Madog: a Welsh explorer who landed
> on the shores of Mobile Bay in 1170 and left behind, with
> the Indians, the Welsh language.

Whether Madog's American adventures are an accurate tale or but a fancy, adventurers from Spain and Portugal would sail in his wake deep into the Atlantic Ocean some 300 years later. It did not take long before they discovered and colonised the Azores and the Canaries, a pair of island chains lying a thousand miles from Europe. However, when it comes to the Canary Islands, the Greeks and Phoenicians of the classical age had already set up trading posts there. Even before the Greeks and Phoenicians, African voyagers had founded settlements in the Canaries. These voyagers had transplanted a breed of hairless sheep from the Berber lands of Morocco sometime in the second millennium BC. By the time the Spanish colonised the Canaries, these sheep were still there, running wild in the rain shadow of the islands' rocky volcanoes.

These sheep were to play a crucial role in the first Spanish expeditions to America. Christopher Columbus and Amerigo Vespucci stopped here numerous times as they travelled to and from the Americas, resting their weary crews and letting them hunt the wild hairless sheep. Without this sheeply stopover in the Atlantic, getting to and from the Americas may have been impossible.

Whilst the hairy sheep of the Canaries provided a vital food source, it was really the woolly sheep of the Spanish central grasslands that propelled the European discovery of America. I say this because Columbus's initial trans-Atlantic voyage of 1492 was supported by Queen Isabella of Spain utilising three ships bought with profits from her vast wool business.

Despite this investment of wool money, Columbus's first voyage was not a commercial success. Columbus found precious little gold or silver and one of his three ships was wrecked when it ran aground in the Caribbean. Columbus ended up building a fort out of the ship's remains on the island it had crashed into. When he returned to Europe, Columbus told everyone he had left the ship intact in the New World to quell any complaints from his sponsor, Queen Isabella.

Yet Columbus was keen to travel again to the lands he had found, evermore determined to uncover treasures and to extract profit. This he would accomplish in ways both imaginative and despicable, involving skilful seamanship and navigation plus theft, fraud, abduction and enslavement.

Columbus's subsequent voyages were partly funded again via Queen Isabella's wool businesses. And sheep were included in the crew list as well, both woolly Spanish breeds and hairy Canary Island sheep. When the sheep landed in the islands of the Caribbean, they often ran feral. As did many of the sailors. This became a recurring pattern over the following decades since more European ships arrived with more unscrupulous adventurers and with more sheep, all setting ashore rather haphazardly.

In 1519, when Hernan Cortes set sail to explore Mexico – and to find gold – he took some newly-bred Churra sheep from Spain. As we've seen in previous chapters, sheep can significantly increase the chances of successful imperial conquest. Eventually, Cortes managed to subdue the entire Aztec Empire. However, most of his Churra escaped off into the mountains of Mexico.

Cortes's escaped sheep not only managed to survive in the wilderness of Mexico but flourished. They kept running wild for generations, with many flocking north until they strolled into the territory of the Navajo. The Navajo adopted and redomesticated the feral Churra, turning their scraggly wool into cloth. From the sixteenth century till the early twentieth, the Churra transformed into the Navajo-Churro, serving as the mainstay of their economy all the while.

Navajo folklore describes the coming of the first sheep as a gift from the heavens. However, the weaving skills of the Navajo were well developed before the arrival of the first Churra since they had been weaving Yucca fibre for centuries. They instantly turned to weave Churra wool in similar ways and just as quickly developed new techniques to create what is now the iconic Navajo wool style. The Navajo-Churro also provided meat and animal skins, plus sinew and guts for binds and string, and dung for fertilising crop gardens. Given the Churra's long march through the rough and arid landscapes of Mexico, they had become acclimatised to handling the patchy vegetation and seasonal grasses of Navajo territory.

During these years, Apache hunting bands occasionally moved across Navajo land. The Apache noted the value of sheep and the two nations often traded them with each other like a form of currency. However, because Navajo-Churro were so valuable, it was not long before Apache hunters took to raiding Navajo sheep when and where the opportunity arose. If they got caught in the act, battles between the two nations would break out.

In reality, though, the short-term fights between the Native American nations were insignificant compared to the long-term conflict they had to endure against the US government. Anglo-American prospectors and miners worked their way into Navajo and Apache lands in the eighteenth century whilst another larger wave of settlers attempted to take over more of the same lands in the nineteenth. During the second wave, a few disorderly companies of the US army took to bullying and harassing the Navajo to chase them away from their ancestral lands.

To compensate for their stolen land, Navajo warriors raided settler farms, confiscating tens of thousands of sheep. In retaliation an

American militia organised by an infamous 'Indian Hunter' called Kit Carson invaded Navajo territory to destroy their food-stores and field crops. The militia then captured any Navajo unable to run away, before force-marching them off to a faraway reservation. Despite severely straitened circumstances, the surviving Navajo still managed to carve out a viable existence, slowly growing up new Navajo-Churro flocks.

Sadly, in the twentieth century, another major threat to Navajo sheep-farming emerged. During the 1930s, the grasslands of America were being eroded fast by overgrazing. This was the time of the Dust Bowl, when giant dust storms blew away degraded soils from the land, creating desert-like landscapes and causing many sheep-farmers to lose their livelihoods as well. As part of their plan to allow the land to recover, the United States government culled a huge number of Navajo-Churro sheep. This ripped away the Navajos' economic base and pushed many families into poverty.

As significant as the Churra would become for the Navajo, by the time the two met in the sixteenth century, another world-dominating sheep had emerged in Spain. This was the mighty Merino. The Merino's luscious multi-layered coat made it the super sheep of the age. The fine quality of Merino wool quickly became the material of choice for clothmakers around Europe. Because of this, during the fifteenth and sixteenth centuries, the Spanish became the main wool trade rivals of England and Wales. It was Merino wool that had made Queen Isabella so grossly wealthy she felt confident to splash out on Christopher Columbus's speculative expeditions.

Columbus's re-discovery of America is often held to be a high point of the European Renaissance, ushering in a bright age of new technology and trade. However, given how much dislocation and degradation was inflicted upon the Native Americans – and the American landscape – we might declare 1492 as the dawn of the American Dark Ages. Whether a Renaissance or a Dark Age, without the riches offered by the advancing wool trade, Europeans might not have found or explored America for centuries to come.

The birthplace of the Renaissance is usually held to be Florence, Italy. Indeed, many incredible feats of art and science emerged in

Florence via figures like Leonardo da Vinci and Galileo Galilei. Much of this art and science was sponsored by the House of Medici, the wealthy family that governed Florence. The Medici were also financial agents. They lent such vast sums within Italy and abroad that they acted as the biggest bank in all Europe. Their banking concern was set up based upon riches gained and supported by their prior wool trading and clothmaking businesses: first and foremost, the Medici were a wool family.

The Medici made considerable loans to monarchs all over the continent, as well as to a succession of popes. In fact, the Medici also used their riches to install family members into royal and papal posts. Catherine de Medici, for example, was Queen of France from 1547 to 1559, whilst Giovanni de' Medici became Pope Leo X in 1513. Though the Medici are still honoured in Florence, even today, it is acknowledged that they employed every Machiavellian trick to maintain their political power, ranging from over-the-top promises and propaganda through to corruption and murder. Indeed, Machiavelli's infamous book, *The Prince*, was written in Florence partly as a reflection of the Medici style of rule.

Without the House of Medici, Florence would look and feel very different today. For instance, there would be no dome on the city's famous cathedral as that dome's construction was financed by the Medici. Other significant works sponsored by the Medici include the artistic innovations of Michelangelo, the scientific studies of Francesco Redi and the piano instruments of Bartolomeo Cristofori.

As well as giving Florence economic and intellectual impetus, wool-crafting acted as the major employer in the city. Of the 80,000 people in Florence in the fourteenth century, some 25,000 worked in the wool and cloth industry. And since the Medici were the city's prime wool family, this immediately gave them considerable influence.

Since the wool sector carried on being so commercially significant, Florentine wool businesses readily took up new innovations. For instance, Florentine chemists were sponsored to import oriental dyes then mix them up with their own concoctions to create new colours for clothmakers. As well, the clothmakers themselves worked at improving their spinning and weaving machines. One such innovation, imported from Arabia, was the treadle-operated spinning wheel, where the spinner would use a foot pedal to keep the wheel moving.

The addition of a treadle could speed up the spinning process both in the factory setting and in households. However, whereas factory owners in Europe's wool towns could afford to pay for their new pedal-powered spinning wheels, villagers and cottage workers could only afford to rent them. A big extra expense like this was a waste for those who spun wool only to create their own clothing. Yet for those who worked for the wool market, the treadles were often a necessity since wool traders demanded quicker production and more volumes of spun wool.

Another innovative practice was the mixing of wool with silk. Oriental silk was interweaved as the warp to a woollen weft. This glistening new silk wool created a fabric that was both functional and sturdy yet sumptuous and glamorous. The silk component, though, was very expensive, and when combined with high quality wool it became the preserve of the rich and powerful.

As well as being too expensive for the lower class to afford, there were also laws that stated such refined cloth could only be worn by those of a high station. If a peasant traded his entire flock to lavish himself with luxurious silk wool, he might well be accused of impersonating a high official and be thrown in jail. Or at least he'd have his fine attire confiscated to bring him down a notch or two. Such laws aimed to keep long-established hierarchies intact and in full social view.

Not everyone in Florence was impressed with the glimmering silky wool worn by the Medici, nor the great art and architecture they were associated with. The wool-craft labourers working for the Medici family were usually underpaid and often exploited. Sometimes, Florentine wool workers united in protest, demanding better wages or tax relief. One time, in 1378, they went much further, banding together to march to the city's central plaza. They then stormed the civic office and physically threw out the Medici from government. For four years the woolworkers ran the city themselves. Eventually, the Medici conspired with other elite families to wrestle their way back into government again. To do so, they resorted to various familiar Machiavellian strategies including hiring an army of violent thugs that menaced and murdered the woolworkers' families as they walked through the streets of Florence.

Before moving on from this chapter, I would also like to draw some attention to one particular scholar who reflected upon the Renaissance as a moment of human improvement and discovery: the English humanist Thomas More. For a while, More was appointed England's 'wool ambassador' to Flanders by King Henry VIII. This was a crucial post given the importance of the Anglo-Flemish wool trade. Whilst working in Flanders, More took time out from wheeling and dealing in the wool trade to write a book called *Utopia*, about a fantastic ideal nation just off the coast of America.

Utopia served as a great curiosity for the Renaissance literati before it went on to influence European thought for hundreds of years. More's book inspired thousands of small-scale communes across the world as well as imperial-scale Soviet Communism. In our own century, *Utopia* energises countless science fiction tales every year plus modern plans for a universal basic income. Yet if sheep had not worked to prop up trade between England and Flanders, Thomas More would never have been there, and the ideas of *Utopia* may never have been born.

Curiously, within the pages of *Utopia*, More critiques the overwhelming dominance of sheep in the English landscape. He suggests that wealthy landowners were too content to let farmworkers live in poverty as long as their highly valued sheep were thriving to produce valuable wool. Worse, though, More notes how many wealthy wool-hungry landowners were pushing poor small-time farmers off communal land, then enclosing that land with fences before stocking it with their own woolly sheep. The insatiable greed for wool, More suggested, was consuming English families, both rich and poor. Or as he puts it in *Utopia*, 'In England, sheep eat people'.

As the boundless flocks of pasture-hungry English sheep grew their wool, the accumulated wealth they provided was channelled into various large-scale ventures, such as the splendiferous wool churches of England. We shall step into them in the next chapter.

Chapter 24

SHEEPLANDS OF THE TUDORS

WALES AND ENGLAND, 1485 TO 1603

The immense medieval wool trade between England and the rest of Europe helped dozens of English wool families become filthy rich, including the House of de Bohun, the House of de la Pole and the House of de Vere. Most of them usually reinvested a large proportion of surplus monies into their wool business, including buying up more sheep-farms and various types of mills. Many also built themselves palatial castles or manor houses as well as purchasing various offices from the Crown.

In addition, these mega-rich wool barons funded the construction of grand churches near their estates and parishes to bring spiritual glory to themselves along with status and beauty to their land. These churches, built during the late fifteenth and early sixteenth centuries, are generally known as the wool churches. Despite their name, they were constructed and ornamented on such a scale they look more like cathedrals.

The artistry of the wool churches, with their ornate facades, stained-glass windows and gigantic square towers, still shower esteem upon their towns today. Even those tourists who don't really fancy grand architecture, like my young accomplice Shelley, can happily while away an hour trying to spot the many comedic grotesques and gargoyles lining the roof edges of a single wool church. (Evidently, the stonemasons of the late medieval period had a great sense of humour.)

Wool churches popped up all over England but were most concentrated in East Anglia and in the Cotswolds. The Cotswold wool churches were constructed out of the excellent local limestone. Like almost every other building premises in the area, the Cotswold wool churches cast a distinctive golden hue over the landscape.

The limestone bedrock of the Cotswolds also gives rise to a superb lush grass, making it an ideal place to raise woolly sheep. When the wool churches were built, these Cotswold sheep grazed in majestic flocks, and their wool was much prized by clothmakers in Italy. Later, in the eighteenth century, Cotswold sheep were dubbed Cotswold lions because of their enormous size and their mane-like fleeces.

Whilst the wool churches were rising high during early Tudor times, other kinds of religious architecture were soon destined to be torn down. In 1531, King Henry VIII made himself Head of the Church of England. He then began a grand reform of the Church, threatening to close down any monastery or abbey if it was proven to be morally corrupt. As part of this reformation, Henry passed a law that allowed him to seize all the assets of a closing monastery. This ensured that no more wool churches would be built since wealthy wool families did not want to waste their time and money trying to buy a ticket to heaven when their building project could attract the attention of the king's unpredictable reformation plans.

Within a few short years, Henry VIII's threats crystallised into a universal dissolution of almost every monastery and abbey in the nation. This included all those monasteries and abbeys specialising in sheep-farming and wool production. Henry had inspectors sent out to claim the farmland and flocks of the dissolving monasteries. So not only did the country's religious orders take a big hit but so did international trading. Meanwhile, the beautiful abbeys of medieval

England and Wales had their roofs and windows knocked in to ensure the monks would not want to return.

Monasteries and abbeys had been a characteristic feature of the English and Welsh countryside since the Norman conquest in the eleventh century. By Henry VIII's time, 800 or more were dotted around his realms. In Wales, just about every villager was less than an hour's saunter from a monastery. In fact, given the commercial and social operations around them, monasteries often served as proxy towns – propping up local communities with economic opportunities as well as spiritual nourishment. Monasteries and abbeys were also charged with distributing food and clothing to those who could not feed or clothe themselves, though Henry VIII seems to have thought they had long neglected this duty.

Given all this, Wales was affected particularly severely by the Dissolution since not only did the Welsh lose great architecture, locals around monasteries and abbeys may have lost their livelihoods and their only social safety net. Those Welsh monasteries that were forced to close included the great Cistercian wool abbeys: Neath, Basingwerk, Margam, Whitland, Strata Florida, Tintern and Valle Crucis, as well as Bardsey Abbey on the enchanted island of Ynys Enlli.

The beneficiaries of this process were the king and his nobles, the former selling the dissolved lands to the latter to quickly pump money into royal coffers. Many historians believe Henry VIII then went on to squander this new loot on showy royal events, plus a needless war in Europe, and then the building of a series of hugely expensive defensive castles on England's south coast.

As well as disrupting Welsh monastic traditions, Henry VIII was also responsible for officially annexing Wales into England via his Acts of Union. From then on, England and Wales would be one state, with the same laws governing all subjects. This unification was a double-edged sword for the Welsh. It finally entitled them to the rights of the English, including settling and trading within all the towns of Wales and being represented in the national parliament in London. It also finally eliminated the jurisdiction of the Welsh Marches, long run like mini-states by arrogant Marcher lords.

However, the Acts of Union washed away ancient rules and

customs, including some of the sensible and popular laws codified by the Welsh king Hywel Dda in the tenth century. The Acts of Union also mandated that all legal procedures and Crown activities be administered in English. So, whilst Welsh traders and craftspeople were free to set up shops and workshops in the towns of Wales, every Welshman and Welshwoman had to deal with bureaucracy and legal matters in English. This was nigh on impossible for most Welsh people, who spoke not a word of English at the time, meaning there was precious little chance for many to assert or defend their new rights. More important, perhaps, is that Wales's long claim to be a separate political and cultural entity from England – a whole different nation – took a painful blow when the Acts of Union were passed.

During the Tudor reign, the wool trade went through something of a slump. Or at least, it entered a phase of gradual declining importance compared to the kingdom's other revenue-making activities. Dissolving the monasteries and banning the abbeys didn't help the situation but this was not the only factor involved. England was facing rising competition in the wool trade from Spain as well as other European countries. On top of this, the one remaining English holding in France, the important wool port of Calais, was lost to a French attack. This ruined a very profitable entry point for English wool onto the continent.

Fortunes were shifting around in Wales at this time, too. Pembrokeshire was slowly losing its status to Powys as the premier county for Welsh wool and clothmaking. The steady rise in competition at home and abroad meant that some Pembrokeshire wool traders could only stay solvent by selling raw wool to foreign merchants rather than processing it into cloth and clothing in Pembrokeshire's wool towns. The town authorities of Tenby and Haverfordwest saw this happening and fretted they would lose their status as high-value components of the wool industry. To stave off the foreclosure of wool workshops, town officials in Pembrokeshire forbade the export of unwoven wool on pain of a large fine. Yet this strategy was to no avail in the long term. Cloth manufactured in England and Flanders was stepping up a level or two in quality and this step-wise improvement went unmatched in Pembrokeshire, even by the weaving experts of Flemish descent.

However, despite the decline of Pembrokeshire clothmaking, there was no fall in actual wool production. Sheep roamed the folding hilly meadows of Pembrokeshire in slowly increasing numbers. In summertime, the flocks were often held upon stretches of arable farmland left fallow so the sheep might fertilise the soil with their dung whilst grazing on surgent weeds. For the hillier parts of Pembrokeshire, this was an essential service to enrich the thin soil for future planting of crops.

Whilst Pembrokeshire's clothmaking businesses were dwindling in number, in Powys they were growing. Powys was particularly well placed to introduce water-powered wool mills near its towns since it was criss-crossed with gentle rivers. These rivers flowed down from the Cambrian Mountains whose ridges and valleys were at the same time being transformed into expansive sheep ranges. Some of these rivers also flowed near English towns and villages, which was extremely handy for getting wool products to market.

The new workshops set up in Powys during the Tudor period augmented the many thousands of villagers who spun and wove wool at home. Often those operating a cottage industry would take in raw wool from wool agents, spin it on rented spinning wheels and then send back both the finished wool and the wheel. Other families in Powys could sometimes do the same with their own wool, bought from the local farmers or shorn from their own flock. This spun wool was often a crucial side-earner for many a Welsh family, whilst also clothing Welsh people nationwide.

In Chapter 13, I suggested the Offa's Dyke Path as perfect for anyone seeking countryside idylls filled with verdant hills, all be-flocked with the fluffiest varieties of mountain sheep you have ever seen. When Shelley and I walked Offa's Dyke, we found one particularly beautiful spot just off the path on the outcrops of Llanymynech Rocks Nature Reserve. From here, we saw stretching one way the Cambrian Mountains of Powys and stretching the other the rolling green hills and riverside woods of rural Shropshire.

At this point I let slip to Shelley that an eighteenth-century canal cuts through the valley below, and upon this navigate colourful old narrowboats. Armed with this knowledge, Shelley negotiated to divert us away from our Welsh sheep journey so we could jump on a passing canal boat heading into England. 'We don't have to look at sheep stuff only, do we?' Shelley asked. I concurred.

I had the last laugh though since our narrowboat was adorned with paintings of heroic-looking mountain sheep and we floated past dozens of oak-lined sheep-farms. Also, at the end of the day, we ended up amongst the Tudor buildings of Shrewsbury, one of the world's wool capitals – at least in Tudor times. Further back in the past, Shrewsbury was once the capital of the Welsh kingdom of Powys. This was before King Offa wrestled it away into his Anglic kingdom in AD 778.

Shrewsbury's proximity was an important factor in the rise of Powys as the prime wool region of Wales in the Tudor period. The wool sheared from Welsh sheep and spun in Powys's workshops could easily be transported to Shrewsbury's specialised wool exchange. Shrewsbury's pre-eminence in wool trading was boosted by Queen Elizabeth I when she granted the Shrewsbury Drapers Company a monopoly to deal with all the wool coming into Shropshire. This suited her since it enabled the Crown to easily siphon off its share of wool profits.

As Queen of England and Wales, Elizabeth I was well acquainted with the importance of wool for the realm. However, she also acknowledged that throughout the Tudor period, English clothmaking had slowly become just as important, maybe even more so, compared to raw wool production. For this reason, Elizabeth sought to protect English clothmakers by restricting the export of raw wool. Supposedly, this meant more wool could be made available to clothmakers within the nation. In this way, she was really echoing a similar step that the Pembrokeshire wool towns of Haverfordwest and Tenby had tried to implement a generation before. Elizabeth I also pushed through a law declaring that every English subject of hers must on Sundays wear 'a cap of wool knit and dressed in England'.

Despite Elizabeth I's attention to the industry, the Spanish were, by her reign, now outcompeting England as the premier wool nation of Europe, especially with the rise of their much-prized wool weapon, the Merino. By then also, the Spanish had staged a political takeover of Flanders and its wealthy textile capitals of Ghent, Antwerp and Bruges. So, even when England could supply spun wool to Flanders, the Spanish Empire might yet earn much from the deal by being able to tax the sale of the final product.

As well as being important to the English Crown, wool continued to be crucial for the Welsh economy, making up two-thirds of Welsh exports during Tudor times. Though the Shrewsbury Drapers Company was based in England, the financial benefits of its trade percolated back to farmsteads and hamlets in Powys, each gaining coin for their wool surplus – and quite a bit extra if it was spun or woven. After leaving Shrewsbury, the final product was often exported to Europe via a special trade centre in London known as the 'Welch Hall'.

At the same time that Spain overtook England's wool dominance, it was also scoring rich rewards from its American conquest, especially gold. Queen Elizabeth sought to compete with Spain by encouraging English adventurers to sail to the New World to see what they could bring home. As part of this process, Elizabeth also sent Francis Drake to circumnavigate the world. As he did so, Drake accosted Spanish ships and looted the great hordes of gold and silver they were carrying. When news of this reached the Spanish king, he was much antagonised.

Around the same time, Elizabeth I was also stoking trouble for Spain in Flanders by supporting Flemish agitators. As a result, some textile producers in Flanders rebelled against their Spanish overlords by refusing to open their workshop doors when Spanish tax collectors came knocking. Others rebelled more brazenly by taking to the streets and harassing Spanish soldiers. Elizabeth also invited the best of Flanders' wool workers to abandon their Spanish overlords and set up shop in England. Some did trickle in but Flemish merchants trying to escape the Spanish usually headed to Amsterdam.

As well as egging on Flemish rebels, Elizabeth ramped up the granting of licences to English pirates to attack and commandeer Spanish ships in the Caribbean Sea. Eventually, Elizabeth I was giving Spain so much trouble that the Spanish king decided the best course of action would be an all-out invasion of England to get rid of her. He ordered an armada of 200 Spanish ships to head to Flanders where they would be loaded up with Spanish soldiers ready to assail England.

However, as the armada passed through the English Channel, it was harried by English ships, which was troublesome, and then by a great storm, which was devastating. None of the Spanish ships could safely enter Flemish ports and the invasion was hastily abandoned. Worse still, half the Spanish ships were then wrecked in another storm as they circumnavigated Britain to get back to Spain. Because the Spanish Armada failed so miserably, England's independence was assured for centuries to come.

—

Chapter 25

BRITISH WOOL AND AMERICAN FREEDOM

WALES/AMERICA, 1700s

In the early seventeenth century, English settlers in New England established their first flock of sheep in North America. The first woollen mill was subsequently built in Watertown, Massachusetts in 1662 to produce wool textiles for domestic clothing. In 1698, Americans began exporting woollen goods to England.

By the time England, Wales and Scotland were united as Great Britain, in 1707, the landed gentry there had grown perturbed by the potential for colonial settlers to use the vast space of America to create giant flocks of sheep that could produce massive amounts of wool and cloth. If this were allowed to happen, then sometime in the future – near or far – the profits of the British landed class would be undermined. The British elite were dependent on wool and wanted no competition when trading it.

Because of this threat, the wealthiest landowners in Britain connived with its wealthiest clothmakers to foment outrage against 'colonial ingrates' whenever wool or textiles from the American colonies were shipped ashore in British ports. After a succession of English monarchs had acted so publicly to protect the English wool trade, this competition from upstart commoners in a vassal colony was declared a national betrayal. It was believed colonists should just feel grateful for being granted land rights in America by the Crown and get on with growing their own food, not attacking their British homeland via trade. These arguments were, of course, ridiculously self-serving. Yet they led to the drafting of various laws curtailing the trans-Atlantic wool trade. One law was particularly menacing, stating that the export of wool from America was punishable by cutting off a person's right hand.

As drastic as they were, such laws were only partially effective. So, decades later, another set of rules banned the importation of sheep into the American colonies. This meant that American flocks could only grow very slowly and, as they did so, they were isolated from the best breeding opportunities afforded to English sheep-farmers. Farmers in the American colonies then had to smuggle in sheep from third nations to improve their flocks. Wool processing in America was also made subject to burdensome restrictions.

This frustrated desire to own large flocks of sheep and to freely produce woollen textiles added to the growing American resentment of British control. Indeed, the obstruction by Britain of the venerable relationship between sheep and humanity was a vital part of the lead-up to the American Revolution: so much so that spinning and weaving were considered patriotic activities in the eighteenth century. After the Revolution, Presidents Washington and Jefferson were inaugurated in patriotic suits made of American wool. Both presidents also raised sheep in a highly visible way: George Washington at Mount Vernon and Thomas Jefferson at his Monticello estate.

Regrettably, wool was not only part and parcel of American freedom but also part and parcel of American slavery. In this, there was also a Welsh link. Slave owners in the West Indies and the American colonies slowly came to admit that slaves were more productive if they were clothed. This might seem like common sense but any commercial endeavour depraved enough to rely on slavery would also be inclined to cut down non-essential costs to an absolute minimum – whatever the human suffering it might inflict.

The standard set of clothing covering the backs of American slaves came from unprocessed coarse woollens. During the seventeenth and eighteenth centuries, these were most often produced in the wool workshops of Powys and were known as Welsh plains. As historian Chris Evans points out, slaves in the New World would seldom have known of Wales but they knew of the Welsh plains they were given to wear. Welsh plains destined for the backs of African slaves were sent to Bristol and loaded upon the same ships plying the slave routes between Africa and America. Sometimes Welsh plains were also used as a trading commodity in African kingdoms to buy slaves from African slave traders.

As the number of slaves in America grew, so did the Welsh cloth industry in Powys. Thusly, some villages in the county transformed into significant wool-craft centres, like Welshpool and Trefeglwys, as Powys cottage workers moved into workshops and workshops transformed into factories. In this case, the average wool worker may indeed have owed their job to the slave trade. However, they hardly became rich, toiling every daylight hour to make enough money to feed and clothe themselves. Sometimes, specialist wool workers, like master weavers, could earn more than the average workshop wage. However, the only people making enormous profits were the factory shareholders, some wool merchants, plus the largest landowners, mostly English, whose flocks produced the wool.

Step by step – and against the wishes of those in England and Wales profiting from the trade – Great Britain and the world slowly moved away from slavery. During this transformation, Welsh workshops and factories in Powys shifted their production of Welsh plains to producing Welsh flannels. Indeed, some Welsh towns became famous flannel towns, like Newtown, Hay-on-Wye and Llanidloes. Flannel is a woollen textile that has been brushed to a soft fluffy feel. This type of garment had been made in Welsh households for centuries but was then taken up enthusiastically by factories as the demand for Welsh plains subsided.

Unfortunately, the growing number of large factories often pushed cottage workers out of the textile trade since factory-made cloth could be produced at lower cost and sold at a lower price. The failing cottage workers then went to work in those same factories as they sought a stable income. As we shall see in later chapters, this changing situation gave rise to a working class who both submitted to and then revolted against the transforming workplace of the ever-enlarging wool factory.

Chapter 26

CLEARANCES AND ENCLOSURES

SCOTLAND AND WALES, 1750 TO 1850

Scotland, like Wales, is a nation of mountains. From the peaks and lochs of the Grampians to the riverside woodlands in Sutherland, these mountains and their interconnected valleys make up the Scottish Highlands. Nowadays, woolly sheep of all kinds roam their slopes, including the shaggy-haired Scottish Highland sheep with their thick and curling horns and the cold-loving Greyface with their distinctive speckles. Though the Scottish Highlands are dotted with plenty of sheep today, this has not always been the case.

Medieval Scotland was a society dominated by clans: kinfolk claiming historic attachment to each other and to a specific geographical area. In Scotland, the chieftains of the Highland clans long asserted their patrilineal rights as lords, leaders and protectors of their fellow clanspeople. The chieftains demanded their clansmen fight with them at times of conflict and war. In return, when their clanspeople needed help, the chieftains would step in to provide it. This relationship was highly stratified and the power distributed unequally but still the chieftains were strongly obliged to care for each clan member.

In 1746, Highland chieftains deployed their clansmen to fight to enthrone Bonnie Prince Charlie as king of Great Britain. However, the Highlanders were routed by the British army at the Battle of Culloden. Subsequently, the chieftains and their clansmen were forced to disband, disperse or hide. The British government then worked to disempower the whole clan system. As part of this process, the tartan woollens shown off by rebellious clansmen were banned from public view, as was the playing of traditional Highland bagpipes. Those caught asserting clan symbols like these would be subject to 'transportation' – enslaved at penal colonies in faraway territories of the growing British Empire.

By the second half of the eighteenth century, the clan system was in tatters, and a new capitalist world was emerging. Surviving clan chieftains transformed from being clan leaders with moral authority into commercial landlords empowered by the laws of the state and by the free market. This transformation meant the Highland elite lost their traditional social status within the Highlands but it would enable them to climb up the social ladder of Great Britain – if only they could convert their large tracts of land into serious money-making ventures.

As we've seen in previous chapters, sheep-farming was usually an assured business for large landowners in the British uplands. Flocks were generally at home in the hills and quite self-reliant. And since Great Britain was often at war with someone or other in the world – most often France – there was a steady demand for Scottish wool to make soldiers' and sailors' uniforms. Even if the wool prices flopped in any one year (when a peace treaty was signed, for instance), the sheep could still be sold as mutton to the burgeoning Glasgow population.

However, to enable sheep-farming, the chieftains-cum-landlords had to make alternative arrangements for their tenant farmers. These farmers had been growing crops on strips of tenanted land for many generations. Some landlords tried to find their tenants new strips of land in other areas. However, this new land was usually squashed between a rocky cliff-face falling from a high Scottish mountain and another rocky cliff-face falling into the sea. Such land sported poor soils and was splattered with salty sea spray so it could hardly make for good crop farming.

Traditionally, rural landlords liked to keep their tenants hanging around in some part of their holdings just in case they were needed for farm projects like building walls or hedgerows. However, from the late eighteenth century onwards, most Highland landlords didn't really credit their tenants with much economic value − so they tried to get rid of them. Some tenants were given free tickets to relocate to far-flung British colonies whilst others were given tiny patches of sea-washed land and told to go fishing or scavage for kelp. Many landlords didn't even do this much, kicking tenant families out of their homes and threatening hangers-on with violent eviction. The displacements became so widespread, they were dubbed the Highland Clearances: a time when sheep colonised the Highlands to push away the Highlanders themselves.

Many tenant farmers felt utterly betrayed by this traumatising process. They had grown up convinced of their inalienable right to strips of land their families had farmed since medieval times and that their landlords had a customary duty to continue the tenancies. However, as the agricultural sector became fully commercialised, long-established customs and connections were abandoned. To force tenants away forever, some landlords had houses, cottages, crofts and villages burnt to the ground. Youthful tenants with excess energy were invited to enlist in the British army − where they could pursue a life of aggressive bullying of their own.

Scottish and Anglo-Scottish landlords found it increasingly easy to ignore age-old Highland customs for they were increasingly absent from Highland life anyway. Many sought to make money then spend it elsewhere. Highland landlords unable to turn a profit usually had to sell up their inherited land just to stay out of debt. In this way, Highland estates sometimes ended up in the hands of wealthy lowlanders or English investors, neither of whom understood the concerns of tenant farmers.

One English landlord with holdings in Scotland − and who

became a notorious symbol of the Highland Clearances – was George Leveson-Gower, the Duke of Sutherland. Leveson-Gower was the richest man in England, inheriting estates left, right and centre from wealthy relatives across the nation. Not content with being called 'the leviathan of wealth', the Duke of Sutherland wanted more. Taking advantage of new laws he had helped pass through parliament, the Duke sent his own Scottish tenants packing with hardly a thought for their future.

Leveson-Gower replaced them with a new breed of highly productive sheep called the Cheviot. The Cheviot were specifically bred for Scotland's harsh seasons. They were hardy creatures that could nibble away on stunted grass, converting it rapidly and efficiently into just enough meat and wool to reliably extract a profit. Just before he died, Leveson-Gower had a statue of himself commissioned for one part of his vast Scottish holdings. It is still standing now but the story the locals tell is that it is a favourite place for canine companions to relieve themselves.

One witness to the Scottish Clearances was a five-year-old boy named John Mackenzie. John's father was a tenant farmer in the remote community of Croik in the Northwest Highlands. John's father had a penchant for agricultural experimentation, pushing himself and his fellow farmers to become more productive. He also demanded much of his son. John was sent to a school many miles from Croik where his teacher drilled into him the values of fairness and democracy – this at a time when Britain was only very weakly democratic. When school was out, John's learning continued at home, his father teaching him about new farming techniques so their crop output might improve.

Every Sunday, John Mackenzie was awoken long before dawn and marched by his father sixteen miles to the nearest Free Church of Scotland. Sunday services were actually offered much nearer by the established Church of Scotland but the ministers preaching them were selected by Anglo-Scottish aristocrats. John's father was sick of hearing the word of God filtered through the morals of the elite.

One Sunday morning in May 1845, just before he entered the church, John spied tenant farmers from the nearby Glencalvie estate huddled together in the overgrown garden of the graveyard.

Laid about between the Glencalvie families were bedraggled old luggage cases, knocked-about trunks and a scant bunch of household furnishings. Evidently, they had been forced out of their home a few days before and could find nowhere else to stay.

This image would be ingrained into John's memory for the rest of his life. As far as John could tell, the Glencalvie residents were evicted without dignity. Yet at least they managed to escape the violence that had accompanied some of the other Clearances. It was not uncommon for landlords to assemble intimidating hoodlums to empty out entire villages and to stand guard for a few days so the evictees wouldn't return. There were various regulations stating that landowners had to consult with the tenants about the eviction process but these were manipulated or ignored. After some arbitrary deadline, whose date was seldom made public, the tenants' right to negotiate was nullified.

John's father could see the writing on the wall. Before any ruffians turned up unannounced one morning, he went to the landlord's estate manager to try to negotiate his family's migration to a coastal plot of land in Galloway – also owned by his landlord. There, he took in a small flock of Cheviot sheep arriving from England and transformed himself into a shepherd, trying to make the best of changing circumstances.

As John grew up, he became aware that his family's new land in Galloway was just too small to make a go of it commercially. After some years their rent fell into arrears. At the same time though, it was clear his landlord was doing very well as he extracted money from the land via wool and lamb. Whilst tenants rented smaller and smaller patches of land, the landlords themselves were building larger and larger mansions.

For John's family, things slowly became harder over the years. In the 1850s, a potato blight brought from Ireland hit the area with devastating consequences. Not only did John's family find it hard to pay the rent but they also couldn't even grow their own food. When he reached adulthood, John felt his best option to escape deepening impoverishment was emigration. Leaving his family behind, he took free passage to the other side of the world, finding himself in New

Zealand. We'll return to his story in Chapter 28, as we follow the rise of sheeplands in Oceania.

The practice of enclosing fields and pastures – then clearing off peasant farmers – did not originate in the Scottish Highlands. Really, the Highlands were one of the last holdouts against such enclosures and evictions. As we saw in Chapter 23, Thomas More observed the same sort of phenomenon in Tudor England where fields once tilled by tenant farmers or grazed by villagers were cordoned off for exclusive use by the landlord's own flocks of sheep. In this way, many communal grazing areas long shared by villagers were monopolised into the hands of one family. In England and Wales, enclosure plans had to pass through parliamentary or court approval. However, the parliament and the courts were extra friendly to the whole enclosure idea because most parliamentarians and judges were from big land-owning families.

Welsh lands were also enclosed during the Tudor period, in the manner observed by More. However, the process didn't really gather steam until centuries later – at about the same time as the Highland Clearances in Scotland. As historian John Chapman explains, in the late eighteenth and early nineteenth centuries, some seventy-five enclosure laws were tabled in the English parliament regarding Welsh lands, covering some 200,000 acres. These enclosures were most often directed at wasteland. By this, it was meant land not permanently worked by either a tenant or a landowner but which was only temporarily grazed communally by small-time livestock herders. Some of this land was of questionable productivity, being a little swampy, too hilly or partially wooded. A lot of it, though, was just the irregularly spaced plots squashed between larger farms. Generally, this was not very useful or valuable unless you were a subsistence farmer; then it was vital.

When wasteland such as this was enclosed – in other words privatised – it wrestled away the capacity for thousands upon thousands of small-time or part-time farmers to sustain themselves. In their stead, the big landowners quickly gained exclusive access to develop industrial-sized flocks. After such enclosures, big farmers could legally demand that small-time farmers stay well away from their fields. In some areas, many miles of new drystone walls were erected so as to clearly demarcate where small-time farmers could no longer venture.

After achieving exclusive rights, the resale value of the land was also pushed up since the landowners could sell the land deeds as a complete package covering an entire landscape rather than a mix of broken-up portions. Because of this, as soon as land was enclosed, land speculators from London began sniffing around looking to make a killing. This often pushed up the price of land further, well beyond the means of Welsh rural families who aspired to own their own patch.

Whilst Scottish Highlanders didn't muster up effective resistance to the Clearances, small-time sheep-farmers of Wales had a little more success. Welsh locals regularly took to disputing enclosures in their local courts and also publicly protested over the innate unfairness of the process. In 1809, riotous farmers assembled outside courthouses in Gwynedd whenever enclosure cases were convened. A few years later, their counterparts did the same in Ceredigion. Sometimes these protests were successful because small-time farmers managed to secure rights to graze alternative wastelands. Sometimes they also managed to wrestle away some form of compensation from the landlords. However, this usually didn't amount to much in monetary terms and was never enough for them to buy their own land.

Moving back to the Scottish Highlands, a few generations after sheep had displaced Highlanders, the sheep themselves were displaced by an even more exclusive creature: deer. As wool prices dropped and cheap meat from the colonies flooded into British ports, the sheep were kicked out and the land restocked with deer to serve the hunting fetishes of wealthy Londoners. Previously, the Highland Clearances had been promoted by the Duke of Sutherland as 'agricultural improvement', necessary to feed and clothe all Great Britain. However, when the Duke's beloved sheep became unprofitable, they were readily replaced with an animal that offered Britain little but sport for the rich.

Chapter 27

THE WELSH DROVER

HARLECH, WALES to LONDON, ENGLAND, c. 1770

The landscape of Gwynedd is dominated by wondrous mountains that the locals call Eryri, yet most Britons know as Snowdonia. Towards the southern part of Snowdonia is a circular array of folded peaks called the Harlech Dome, which by some accounts is the oldest known geological rock formation in the world. The imposing Harlech Castle is perched upon a knolly crag near the westernmost edge of the Harlech Dome. From here, the castle maintains watch across a narrow strip of coastal land and then over the dark expanse of the Irish Sea. Harlech was one of the castles built by Edward I between 1276 and 1295 to defend English interests in Wales. However, it ended up being a holdout for several rebellious Welsh leaders, including Owain Glyndŵr in the 1400s.

By the late eighteenth century, the castle was in ruins. Still, its ominous visage on a craggy outcrop began to attract curious travellers from England, especially artists and poets lured by its dark romantic appeal.

One fresh and breezy afternoon, Shelley and I found ourselves perched high within the castle. Looking out through crumbling arch windows, we imagined for a moment what a late-eighteenth-

170

century painter would have seen from the same spot. If they'd gazed seaward across the village of Harlech, they might have been treated to the sight and sound of another timeless fixture of this landscape: the sheep drove.

The drove would first be observed as an indistinct ball of dust working along a dirt pathway from fields in the north. As the dust-ball moved slowly closer to the foot of the knoll, it would be possible to spot individual sheep then hear their individual bleats, plus the shouts and whistles of the drover and the barking of his sheepdog. Channelled between a hedgerow and a cliff bank, the flowing flock would trundle as a slow-streaming river of wool draped in grimy mist.

During the 1700s, Britain was passing through what historians call a second Agricultural Revolution. It comes in 'second' when compared with the first Agricultural Revolution outlined in the first chapters of this book when Stone Age hunter-gatherers transformed into settled farmers. During this second Agricultural Revolution, there was a steep rise in food production throughout Britain. This rise outran the simultaneous increase in the island's population. This meant there was usually enough food for everyone, accompanied by much larger profits to be had in the farming sector. During the period there was also a gradual migration of workers from the countryside into the towns. The Enclosures in Highland Scotland might be considered part and parcel of the second Agricultural Revolution as might the rise of commercial sheep-farming in the Welsh Cambrians. In both nations, sheep were becoming just as much valued for their meat as their wool. This meant there were increased opportunities to trade in greater and greater numbers of live sheep if only these sheep could be moved to the markets of the bigger cities, such as London and Glasgow.

Of course, there were no steam trains or sheep trucks at this time. Flocks had to be moved around on foot. Thus, the venerable tradition of droving – moving whole flocks long distances on foot – grew in significance around this time. Welsh sheep from Gwynedd, Ceredigion, Pembrokeshire and Powys were driven eastward over the border into England then on to London. For middle-class Londoners, Welsh lamb was renowned as the sweetest. This fame was underpinned as various Hanoverian royals habitually ordered Welsh lamb be laid upon their dinner table. The source of the sweetness was often ascribed to the heathers and herbs that Welsh sheep grazed upon in the Cambrian uplands.

The sheep of Britain usually travelled from one part of the realm to another via the many drovers' roads or droveways. These sheep roads criss-crossed the country through lands owned by the Crown and lands owned by the Church, as well as through private lands and wastelands. In many parts of rural Wales and England, they acted as significant paths for transport and communication, especially where the highways were few and far between. They also traversed the difficult landforms of Wales where few horse-drawn carts and carriages would dare to go.

Drovers with a track record of successfully conveying flocks usually became respected businessmen. Their persistent travelling, though, meant they were not able to attend Sunday services as much as settled country folk might like. Because of this, when a drover died, it was customary to bury them with a handful of wool so that the angels at the Pearly Gates could identify them as sheep herders and forgive them their many absences from church or chapel.

Anyway, returning to our dusty eighteenth-century flock migrating under Harlech Castle, they may have walked in from the nearby coastal valleys of Snowdonia just a day's trek away, or maybe they walked the thirty miles from the spectacular cliff-tops along the Llŷn Peninsula. The journey from Llŷn to Harlech would have been pleasant in good weather but dangerous and arduous if rainy. In the wet, every hill would be shrouded in mist, the droveways muddied and the streams overflowing.

In good conditions, the sheep would need no guidance, confidently following a path carved by measureless numbers of animals over many centuries. In bad conditions, though, the sheep would need to be gently guided – or smartly cajoled – into following a set route by the shouts and whistles of the drover or the nip of a sheepdog.

From Harlech, the plan would be to take the sheep around the Harlech Dome, then meander slowly eastward across Merioneth to Powys until the flock hit the market towns of the English midlands. From these towns, such as Shrewsbury and Oswestry, they would then

– as often as not – make the journey to Smithfield Market in London. Such a journey from Harlech to London would cut across more than 250 miles of countryside at a good average rate of ten miles a day.

Given that wet weather was bound to curtail progress at some point, an experienced drover could do this in about four weeks with hundreds of head of sheep under his crook. Of course, the goal was for the sheep to arrive at the English markets in about the same condition as they left their Welsh pastures. Some sheep would lose some fat but typically make up for it by building up their muscle mass as they journeyed.

So, let's follow one particular drover on this journey from Harlech to London, around the year 1770. We will call him Wil and imagine him an experienced drover. Wil is really an amalgam character of real-life drovers from various time periods identified by the likes of historians such as Philip Gwyn Hughes, Twm Elias, Fay Godwin and Shirley Toulson.

Rising bright and early to move his sheep along the next stage of the journey, Wil aims to push his flock all the way to the bustling market town of Dolgellau in Merioneth. To get there before sundown, Wil needs to navigate a bewildering range of terrain: gentle meadows, rocky mountainsides, thick forests and open woodlands, as well as heathland and bogland, plus a hazardous old slate quarry as well.

There are two options for travelling from Harlech to Dolgellau. The first is a long winding lowland path that mostly hugs the coast, including the edges of Mawddach estuary. This measures maybe a dozen miles or so. The second is a shorter route but takes the sheep directly across the hills and mountains of the Harlech Dome.

Either path can be followed on foot by walkers today and because they sweep through such stunning and varying landscapes, they attract many daytrippers. In the nineteenth century, the English poet John Ruskin noted that the coastal trail was the 'most beautiful walk in the world'. This compliment cannot be taken lightly since Ruskin is one of Britain's most famous art critics and one of history's outstanding walkers, regularly clocking up to twenty miles every day of the year.

Our drover Wil, though, is more interested in the weather than the beauty of the landscape. If rain is on the cards, or snow, Wil must learn

of it as soon as possible so as to choose where to push his flock. This
is especially important should he take his sheep across the mountain
route. If he does, Wil must also estimate where the best pastures might
lie and whether they may have been grazed by flocks driven through
already. He would also have to guess whether the wooden footbridges
were intact and the streams fordable. Still, this might only reveal itself
once his flocks come up against the first crossing.

Taking a chance on the mountain route, Wil's sheep would press
first into a gentle boulder-strewn grassy rise cloaked with mist, then
around a ridge and through a copse into the next valley. Though
showered all the time by rain, this would be no problem for the
sheep, so thick is their wool and stalwart their manner. Yet if
waterways are swollen, the sheep's undercarriages are likely to get
wet – which is not that bad – but also muddy as they ascend the
banks on the other side. A mud-covered sheep might not look their
best at Dolgellau market.

As Wil drives his flock toward Dolgellau, they move between the trees
of the Coed y Brenin forest on the slopes of Cader Idris mountain.
Here, each valley of this highland forest has its own character: some
strewn with jagged boulders, others with stunted pines, yet others
resplendent with tall birch trees and plunging waterfalls. This might
be a tad on the wild side for most drovers but our Wil enjoys the
protection the trees offer from the wind. Walking through the woods,
his sheep can graze heartily around the eerie ruins of Cymer Abbey,
pulled apart by Henry VIII's dissolution, before crossing the ever-
sturdy limestone bridge of Llanelltyd village. On the edge of the
village, roadside marker stones between the stone cottages indicate a
well-trod path onwards to other towns.

By the mid-eighteenth century, villages like Llanelltyd, in the
shadow of Cader Idris, were filled with busy spinners and weavers
– typically girls and women. Their finished work would then be
brought to market in Dolgellau, marking the town as a local centre
for both wool and sheep.

As Wil brought his sheep into Dolgellau, he would look for a trio of
Scots Pines standing tall above a stone building. These trees, which
could be seen from far and wide, were the well-known signal in the

Welsh landscape that a drovers' inn stood close by, complete with layover fields. Here, the sheep and their shepherds could munch to their heart's content then enjoy a comfy rest.

Drovers in this part of Wales would hope to arrive in Dolgellau during the days of a county fair to profitably sell a few sheep. Also, a drover might adopt a few more sheep loaned to him by local farmers for sale in England. Sometimes the farmers would set a preferred price tag, and sometimes they'd let the drover make the call.

At the county fair, Wil would size up good deals and share information about the state of the trade. Nowadays, Dolgellau's narrow stone streets bustle mostly with hill-walkers and mountain-bikers seeking rest and refreshment. The mountains perched behind the town are often enveloped in preternatural morning fogs that cast the entire town in a mysterious glow. However, they are equally photogenic on a sun-drenched afternoon when the bright light plays among their ridges and furrows. The mountain-bikers that ride there these days invariably strap a camera to their bike to capture these changing moods.

After a few days of the sheep munching grass at Dolgellau, Wil would whistle at his dog to bring the sheep together and move off. The next stopover is the town of Bala ten miles north-east. To get there, the sheep and their drover would sometimes bypass the wool-spinning villages of Merioneth, edging instead along the dramatic folds of rock making up Snowdonia's foothills. At times though, there was no choice but to move the flock through the cramped main street in order to use the village bridge to cross a river.

Most drovers had at least a few hundred sheep under their charge but often many more. Some needed to hire an entire posse of shepherds to keep the sheep in line. The shopkeepers and tradespeople of a village would sometimes welcome a flock of loud dusty sheep moving through since they could sell supplies to the drovers and shepherds. Other villagers panicked at the sight of an approaching flock, rushing outside to retrieve anything they did not want covered in a thick layer of dust: linens drying on a line, woven blankets stretching on tenterhooks or young children playing in the garden.

As well as worried villagers, Welsh drovers further back in time – say the 1500s – would have had to look out for wolves. Wolfpacks tended to follow a flock all day to be able to pounce on a stray at nightfall. By the 1770s, though, wolves were a distant memory. The last wolf in Wales was trapped and stuffed about a century before then. However, with the wolves gone, feral dogs replaced them, scouring the countryside looking for easy prey.

Another problem that drovers faced and that seemed to worsen year by year was road tolls. To raise the funds needed to maintain the main thoroughways between towns, travellers were charged as they crossed between specially erected tollgates. Livestock was also charged at a rate per head. Whilst some drovers factored the expense of tolls into their business, others tried to avoid paying by travelling on minor roads or ancient pathways usually only known to themselves and local farmers. Very occasionally, a new tollgate would suddenly emerge on such a droveway as well, prompting outrage from the drover. Unless the tollgate keeper was willing to compromise, they would risk an uncomfortable confrontation, including a near stampede of unstoppable sheep or cattle bursting through and wrecking the gates.

Once our drover Wil arrives in the wool town of Bala, he and his flock would find a lovely field overlooking Llyn Tegid, the largest natural lake in Wales. The sheep could then recharge overnight before continuing their journey either to the town of Wrexham – on the Welsh side of the border – or to Shrewsbury or Oswestry on the English side. Bala, Wrexham, Shrewsbury and Oswestry were all proper wool towns at this point in history, so Wil has the option of renting out his flock to shearers in the morning and accepting them back – minus their wool – in the evening. The shearers then could sell the wool to a range of middlemen before it was spun and woven in cottages near Bala or Wrexham or sent off to the woollen mills of Powys.

Some of these wool towns also served as cattle-stock towns. As a rule, the sheep drovers worked on foot, walking all the way across the country. However, cattle drovers were plying similar routes on horseback. A rowdy activity for all at a county fair was when cattle drovers raced their horses against one another around the edge of the town. Bets were invariably laid but Wil is long enough in the tooth just to enjoy the mere spectacle of the races without gambling. Apart from lost monies, the wagers deals would often end up in raging fist fights.

In the eighteenth and nineteenth centuries, a trusted drover might find extra employment as a guide for wealthy English tourists visiting Snowdonia. Wil needn't have been very talkative or even very friendly to secure such a role, for the main task would be just to keep the tourists from being robbed. Travelling across Britain during this time was risky since highwaymen – the pirates of the roadways – plied their trade by accosting lonely travellers in isolated places. The inns were sometimes very unsafe as well, since innkeepers might conspire with robbers to steal from guests as they slept. Bearing firearms was against the law across Great Britain but licensed drovers were exempt so that they might protect their sheep from wild dogs as they travelled. Highwaymen probably knew it would be risky to try their luck against a drover.

Drovers also possessed formidable local knowledge of country roadways and how they were affected by the changing seasons. Thus, whilst keeping robbers at bay, our Wil could also keep English voyagers from slipping down a collapsing riverbank.

As the sun grew shallow in the sky, Wil might pass through or around Wrexham, keen to spy a trio of Scots Pines. Although, if his next destination was one of the market towns of Shropshire, Wil would have to be on the lookout for three yew trees instead since this was the customary signal for an English drovers' inn. Once in Shropshire, our drover would assiduously size up trading opportunities. If the price was right, Wil would offload some sheep here instead of driving them all to London. The London earnings were better but the droveways and roadways more crowded, so it would be best to get the flock down to the best manageable number.

Though most sheep were usually easily driven in the right direction, especially with the assistance of a faithful sheepdog, some homesick sheep just wanted to turn around and walk back home. If a shepherd was not careful, some sheep would up-sticks from a layover field before the sun came up to escape back to Wales. Indeed, there were times when a Welsh drover would return from a long journey to find missing sheep grazing happily in the field where they were born. The same sheep would then be corralled into a subsequent flock and driven back to England – only to take flight once again. Some of these homesick sheep had actually been sold to English farmers before making their escape. Countryside folklore recounts how one clever Welsh drover managed to sell the same sheep to the same Englishman three or four times.

Whilst homesick sheep may have puzzled drovers, another ovine behaviour was more problematic. Sometimes sheep like to take shortcuts and sidetracks through holes in walls and hedges as they glimpse an excellent fresh grassy field. If the errant sheep is not caught by a sheepdog in time, dozens of their fellow sheep might follow and start grazing on pastures and crops. If they were caught by the caretaker of the field, some form of compensation would be demanded. An irate crop farmer might expect disproportionate reimbursement for his partially ruined field. A stressed-out drover would shout out in riposte that he would pay for repairing the hole in the wall and no more. Perhaps we should note again that very many of the beautiful stone walls and hedgerows that adorn the British landscape have been crafted over many years not to keep livestock confined to a particular farm but to keep migrating sheep out.

After shedding his sheep's wool in Shropshire, Wil would then process through the droveways and highways of Staffordshire, Warwickshire, Oxfordshire, Buckinghamshire, Middlesex and right into London. The closer the sheep got to London, the tighter the country lanes and the more crowded the town streets. Wil would also come across herds of other kinds of livestock. As well as drovers of sheep and cattle, there were also swine drovers, turkey drovers and geese drovers. Occasionally, there would also be drovers of Welsh ponies, a miniature horse running half-wild in the hills of Wales.

Sometimes, England could seem like an alien nation to rural people from Wales. The English had a different language, a different landscape and different rules. For experienced drovers, it was both a land of opportunity but also challenges. The pastures might have been lusher and the selling prices higher yet there were tricksters and con artists at each corner, including chancy strangers asking for customs to be paid when a Welsh flock passed over an English bridge.

English townspeople were also sometimes assaulted by brusquely trotting Welsh sheep. Drovers knew they couldn't keep every creature in line all of the time and they sometimes valued the well-being of their sheep much more than they did passers-by. The crowded craziness of the drove would climax in Smithfield when Wil would have to somehow keep his flock from merging with all others whilst offering them up for auction in the chaotic cacophony of the market. The fairs and markets in Wales and Shropshire were usually conducted with some degree of order and ease. In Smithfield, though, things were much more intense, the agents competing against each other in shouting matches over huge bleating flocks of agitated livestock.

The trick for a drover to profit from this bedlam was to discern the good buyers from the troublesome ones, with the general aim to find someone unlikely to change the deal's conditions after an agreement was shaken on. Some agents would refuse to honour the total amount by claiming some sheep to be underweight or a bit mangy.

In any regard, when the transactions were done, the drovers were generally flush with money and freed from the burden of caring for the flock. The wise drovers would quickly disburse their shepherd's pay, buy a few sausages for their dogs, chat to other drovers about business for a bit, then smartly head back home to Wales laden with the cash. The incautious ones, though, would stick around in London and maybe waste a significant portion of their pay on all the various temptations of the city.

Walking home to Wales through the countryside with a bag full of money could also be risky. Drovers often sought to convert their stash of coins into cheques or signed banknotes issued by special drovers' banks, such as the Black Sheep Bank of Aberystwyth and Tregaron. Such rural banks were set up by some highly successful Welsh drovers and they were much trusted within the livestock industry. When our drover Wil made it back to Wales, this is where he would consign his profits.

Wil would then have to distribute all the sales monies back to the farmers whose sheep he had successfully driven to market. As well, because Wil was so well travelled, he was prevailed upon to retell important national affairs. In this way, country people would learn about the wars the nation was entangled in, the latest intrigues affecting the monarchy, and stories about distant colonies and the opportunities they offered.

Regarding the latter, many young Welsh people were intrigued by romantic tales about the New World and the South Seas: some, so much so, they dared to leave their homeland farms and set sail for pastures new. As we shall see in following chapters, these Welsh travellers often brought their woolly friends along, for the pastures new could probably stand some grazing.

Chapter 28

SHEEPLANDS OF THE ANTIPODES

OCEANIA, 1773 TO 1893

As British sea power grew stronger during the eighteenth century, Britain's imperial conquests in distant regions of the world also grew more assertive. Captain James Cook, for instance, was commissioned by the Board of Admiralty to travel to the other side of the world to search for new land in the vast South Pacific. When he got there, Cook ended up planting the British flag in the ground of Aotearoa/ New Zealand.

When Captain Cook returned to London, the Admiralty was impressed by Cook's discovery of dozens of Pacific Islands but wondered why he hadn't come across the Great Southern Land. This imagined continent was regarded as necessarily existing in the South Seas to counterbalance all the continents in the northern hemisphere. Therefore, the Admiralty sent Cook back out again to the furthest reaches of the South Seas to discover this continent – or prove once and for all that it didn't exist. As part of the trip, Captain Cook came up with the idea of transplanting sheep from a British colony in South Africa to New Zealand, where they could run wild and free and hopefully breed naturally. This would mean any future colonists settling in New Zealand would already have flocks of feral sheep to hunt or to draw upon as they set up new farms.

As well as the sheep, Cook's two ships *Resolution* and *Adventure* included a team of highly talented botanical investigators. The botanists were tasked with recording the agricultural potential of all the lands they visited, and an assessment of New Zealand's floral character was a major part of this task.

As far as we know, James Cook sailed further south than any other navigator as he crossed the southern zones of the Pacific Ocean. Many times, he sighted then skirted the icy shores of the Antarctic. Although it was continental in scale, Captain Cook proffered that Antarctica was not equivalent to the landmasses of the northern hemisphere nor at all habitable. After his botanists failed to find any plant life in Antarctica, Cook made for New Zealand again, arriving in 1776. At this point, he put ashore the sheep he had picked up from South Africa.

However, despite his expedition brimming with plant experts, the British could not halt the sheep from grazing New Zealand's poisonous plants. As Cook's log puts it:

> Last night, the ewes and the rams I had with so much care and trouble brought to this place expired. We did suppose them poisoned by eating some native plant. Thus, all my fine hopes of stocking the country with a breed of sheep were blasted momentarily.

The offending plant was probably the tutu. Honey made from the dew of this plant can kill even humans. Despite this inauspicious beginning for New Zealand's first sheep, the botanists kept writing in their journals how perfect the climate and soils were for British-style agriculture, including sheep-farming.

Decades before a colony was founded in New Zealand, however, the British were sending settlers to its Tasman Sea neighbour, Australia. Many of these settlers were penal convicts, sent to help establish Britain's first colonies in Oceania. Colonial planners in London entertained the idea of setting up sheep-farms to support the earliest settlers but they never got around to implementing the plan.

At the time, the world's most sought-after wool sheep continued to be the Merino, the super sheep of the Spanish Empire. However, the Merino was still an embargoed commodity when Britain first began settling Australia. The only woolled sheep readily available in significant numbers were fat-tailed breeds like those picked up by Captain Cook from the Cape Region in South Africa. These Cape sheep were hardy enough to survive the dry lands of Australia and they also produced enough mutton and coarse wool to feed and clothe the convicts and settlers. Yet they were never competitive in the international wool market.

When Napoleon Bonaparte invaded and took over Spain in 1808, this blew apart the restrictions on the trading of live Merino sheep. Soon after, two prominent British settlers in New South Wales imported as many Merinos into Australia as they could get their hands on. These two were John Macarthur, an army captain and colonial paymaster, and Samuel Marsden, an Anglican priest. On their own farms in New South Wales, the two began intermixing Merinos with Cape sheep to give rise to Australian Merinos. These new sheep were good wool producers but also adapted to Australia's dry grasslands.

Though Australia's new British colonies were laden with convicted criminals, the people in charge were probably more corrupt than the convicts. This certainly applied to John Macarthur. Macarthur hailed from a small-time mercantile family that ran a textile business in Plymouth, England. Whilst everyone else in the family seemed satisfied with this moderate success, he despaired of his low station as a tailor in the family workshop. In search of a grander life, Macarthur joined the British army and was stationed as a lieutenant to manage a large group of convicts in a new penal colony near Sydney.

Macarthur used this position to import cheap rum from the British colony of Bengal and then resell it at inflated prices to fellow soldiers, to settlers and to the convicts. Because there was a shortage of coinage in early New South Wales, he also paid his labourers with rum. As you might imagine when rum serves as a main form of currency, problems of drunkenness, gambling, prostitution and brawling became rife. Macarthur took advantage of this wild rum economy to work himself into official colonial posts and then give himself and his family profitable government contracts. For example, the contract to provide convict labour with clothing was given to his brother back in Plymouth.

After he'd spent quite a few years enriching himself via corruption and rum-running, Macarthur decided to diversify into farming Australian Merino sheep. Since he had used his colonial posts to acquire vast tracts of grassland in New South Wales, he surmised he could probably produce enough wool to sell it profitably on the London market. At some point, Macarthur took some samples of his Australian Merino wool back to London to show it off. There, he strolled around London's most illustrious clubs and shops, promoting his wool as the best in the world. He also dished out bribes to editors of London's most fashionable magazines as well as to a few politicians, all to get influential people talking about his wool.

Whilst John Macarthur worked tirelessly to promote his wool in England, his wife Elizabeth was working hard running the family sheep-farm and assembling great bales of saleable wool. John Macarthur then did a deal to hire a returning convict ship at a marked-down rate to cheaply transport the bales to England. Using such tactics, Macarthur's wool trading returned profits even higher than his rum-running and he was able to expand his sheep-farms across New South Wales.

The other major wool pioneer of Oceania was Samuel Marsden. Marsden was less a rogue entrepreneur and more an overly severe and self-important churchman – yet still every bit as ambitious as Macarthur. Marsden didn't try to scam the convict labour under his charge, as Macarthur did. Instead, he liked to whip them. This was especially the case if they were Irish, Scottish or Welsh prisoners convicted of some small act against the British establishment. In Australia, Marsden's nickname was the Flogging Parson. In the early 1800s, Marsden channelled his punishing form of Christianity into setting up a series of missionary settlements in New Zealand. One of these had a model sheep-farm attached to it, with sheep he imported from Australia. As well as preaching the Christian message to the native Māori, Marsden lectured that they could secure their future by farming sheep. Though few Māori took up the challenge, those that did were often quite successful.

When Captain Cook and his botanists first arrived in New Zealand, they were happy to note the islands were heavily forested with plenty of tall tree species, like the kauri and kahikatea. Cook suggested that one of the benefits to be gained from settling New Zealand would be that the Admiralty would have a ready supply of masts for their ever-growing fleet of ships. This was not trivial since Britain had long ago felled most of her old growth forests, forcing the navy to import pretty much all their timber from Baltic nations.

However, half a century later, it wasn't the Admiralty colonising the islands of New Zealand but private farmers. Farmers don't need forests, they need grasslands and fields, so when pioneers like Samuel Marsden set up farms, they had to get rid of the trees. In Britain, it took 6,000 years for sheep to leave the forests in ruin. In New Zealand, it took just over a century. New Zealand is a celebrated sheep nation but it has come at the price of a deforested landscape where less than thirty per cent of the native forests survive.

It should be mentioned though that large sections of New Zealand's forests had been burnt away by various Māori tribes before the first sheep-farm was ever set up. This burning activity transformed many of New Zealand's rainforests into tussock grasslands. In the 1850s, this is where many British farmers first set their sheep to graze. In the process, though, native grasses were eventually overrun by introduced grasses brought from Britain. Some of these introductions were on purpose but some were accidental. Seeds regularly travel as stowaways all across the world in the hooves and hair of livestock and this seems to have happened many times when farmers moved from Britain to New Zealand. Because of this, New Zealand's landscape was radically transformed during initial European settlement.

The process whereby New Zealand vegetation was displaced and rendered a fragmented copy of Britain is nowadays held by some as a case of ecological imperialism. As it happened, though, it was not recognised as being anything negative. Instead, it was labelled 'land improvement'. However, by the late 1800s, New Zealand newspapers were already lamenting the diminishing quality of New Zealand's grasslands, native or otherwise. As in other settler lands across the globe, overgrazing often became a problem within a few decades, causing widespread floral loss and the erosion of productive soils.

In the decades before such overgrazing came to the fore, sheep-farming boomed as the predominant enterprise in New Zealand. By 1853 there were half a million sheep in the country, and by 1863, three million. One of the British immigrants that arrived in New Zealand to take care of these sheep was the twenty-one-year-old John Mackenzie, who we met in Chapter 26 during the Highland Clearances. Mackenzie took up a shepherding job in the tussock grasslands of New Zealand's South Island. Like Scotland, there was an array of mountains and valleys cascading in many directions so – at least visually – the South Island seemed reminiscent of his homeland.

At this time, New Zealand's population was very small; far fewer people lived there than sheep. This meant labourers were scarce enough to draw good wages from employers, as was the case with Mackenzie. After a few short years, he had saved up enough money to purchase his own land: some seventy-six acres. This was quite a vast area and those back in his native Scotland could only dream of owning such a stretch of territory after so few years. Upon it, he set about farming sheep.

During most of the nineteenth century, wool was seen as the ideal commodity for those British colonies perched at the far end of the world. As New Zealand historian Robert Peden explains:

> Wool could easily be stored and shipped, and there was a strong demand for it in the expanding textile industries of Britain, Europe and North America. In 1856 wool grown on the South Island grasslands became the country's most valuable export.

Because of this, small-time freehold farmers like John Mackenzie seemed to have a good future.

As Mackenzie developed his sheep-farm, his stature in the community rose. He was elected to various community boards before running for office to become a member of parliament, firstly as an independent then for the Liberal Party.

In the 1850s, New Zealand farmers had banked all their time and resources into cultivating one product: the wool of the Merino. Almost all the wool that New Zealand farms could produce was sent to the hungry textile factories of industrialised Britain. However, in the 1870s, the price of wool began to fall. And surprisingly, Merino wool was plummeting faster than other wool types. Why was this? In Britain, the woollen textile factories had adopted new steam-powered rolling machines that stretched and prepared wool faster than ever, mainly to make worsted cloth. But these machines only worked well on short solid fibres, not the long fibres of the Merino. Thus, such mills rejected Merino wool.

In Britain, if sheep-farmers could not sell wool, then they could usually still secure a return from their sheep by selling their meat. However, New Zealand, being young and uncrowded, did not have enough human mouths to eat up the millions of sheep on its farms. Therefore, by the 1870s, New Zealand had a glut of unprofitable and unsaleable sheep. Many farmers resorted to slaughtering their entire flock and melting them down to sell tallow, which was then the only profitable product they could extract from their Merino sheep. Other farmers did worse, some driving their flocks off cliffs into the sea just to get rid of them or butchering them to feed pigs. The farmers knew they would have to change sheep breeds – to the tough-wooled Romney for example – if they were to re-enter the British wool trade but this would take years.

Back in Britain, the teeming populations of cities like London, Glasgow, Birmingham and Manchester had all become habituated to inexpensive lamb and mutton for their evening meals. Yet any meat sent from New Zealand would go rotten during the hundred-day voyage clear across the tropics to the ports of Britain. Meat packers in Argentina and Australia had managed to send beef and lamb all the way to Europe packed in containers of ice. However, too much of the meat arrived in a bad condition so the endeavours drew a loss rather than a profit.

Eventually, in the early 1880s, a team of New Zealand pastoralists consorted with a team of British shippers to buy a brand-new off-the-shelf refrigeration unit from the Scottish Bell-Coleman Mechanical Refrigeration Company. The Company had barely fabricated their first ever refrigerator into an actual working form before it was disassembled, shipped off to New Zealand, then immediately reassembled on a sailing ship called the *Dunedin*. Laden with thousands of fresh sheep carcasses, the crewmen fired up the refrigerator and headed back to sea, aiming to unload them near London's Smithfield market.

However, over the course of the journey, numerous technical problems cropped up. For instance, leaks in the cold store let cold air escape whilst the coal-fired boilers set the sails on fire. To fix these problems, some of the crew nearly froze to death plugging up leaks in the cold store whilst others nearly burnt to death putting out the fire. Still though, after ninety-eight days, the *Dunedin* arrived in London, and the cargo – still frozen – was conveyed to Smithfield. Of the carcasses presented to the wholesalers, only one had to be condemned. A fair few then ended up on the tables of London's fashionable restaurants and salons. The reviews over the following days were gushing, with many saying it was on a par with anything from the Welsh hills.

By the 1880s the social background of New Zealand agriculture had become quite unfair. Two-thirds of New Zealand's farmland was owned by one per cent of its registered residents. Many of this one per cent were actually based in England. Whilst big landowners could make big profits, New Zealand's smallholders strove daily just to keep their farms in financial order. The smallholders bemoaned the fact that New Zealand's pattern of land ownership was increasingly mimicking the disparities of the Old Country. For settlers who migrated to New Zealand on the promise of opportunities not available in Britain, this was a betrayal of what had brought them in the first place.

One person that wanted to address this situation head-on was John Mackenzie. By now, Mackenzie had served as an MP for a dozen years or so and had assumed the role of the Liberal Party's

Shadow Minister of Agriculture. Mackenzie still exuded the spirit of democracy and fairness drummed into him as a youngster in Scotland. He campaigned on a platform of land reform whereby the monstrously large farms would be taken over by the state then split up and sold at reasonable prices to smallholders.

In the late nineteenth century, New Zealand was moving rapidly towards becoming a full-fledged democracy. Soon, every adult man and every adult woman would be empowered to cast a vote. This was about to tear away the decision-making power from the big landowners and redistribute it amongst the general public. Bolstered by John Mackenzie's land reform ideas, his Liberal Party was swept into power during the 1893 general election. Before long, family-level farmers were placing down payments on the broken-up plots of large estates. With the help of these family farmers, the sheep population of New Zealand rose from around seventeen million in 1893 to a staggering seventy million by 1983.

Chapter 29

WOOL AND THE INDUSTRIAL REVOLUTION

BRITAIN, 1789 TO 1860

The nineteenth century brimmed and boiled with revolutions and rebellions, and sheep were caught up in many of them. The most famous of these radical shake-ups was the one most drawn out in time – the Industrial Revolution. In the early 1800s, machine-driven factories were coming of age where inventive mechanics mingled with aggressive entrepreneurs to build factories that could churn out products quickly and cheaply. Though sheep might seem far removed from anything mechanical, our woolly friends actually provided much of the initial impetus for the Industrial Revolution.

Usually, the cotton textile industry of middle and northern England is celebrated as paving the way for the Industrial Revolution in Britain. Certainly, the cotton cloth made in Lancashire factories ended up dominating the global textile market. Yet, as historian Alan Butler explains, cotton only developed into a massive industry in

English towns like Manchester and Bolton because a woollen textile industry already existed there previously. This meant that textile business networks were already in place as well as an abundance of skilled textile workers. Often sheep are seen as symbolic of a pastoral idyll. Yet, at the beginning of the nineteenth century, their wool had a big part to play in the onset of mass production and the industrial transformation of the world.

However, the growth of the mechanised factory system plunged small-scale cottage industries into crisis. Across England – and decades later in Wales – spinning machines variously called spinning jennies and spinning mules, and then also steam-powered weaving machines, were all set up in big factories. Altogether they outcompeted cottage-based spinners and handloom-weavers. The middlemen of the textiles industry began to drop the Powys villagers and spinners from their trading networks altogether. In some villages, this pushed families into destitution. Sometimes the only way out was for rural people to move to the towns – and the Welsh to England – to look for factory work.

Large wool factories did slowly come to Wales a little later in the 1830s and 1840s. Welsh industrialists and politicians then cajoled the government to set up railway networks that connected Welsh towns with English markets. However, as soon as these railways were up and running, they brought in inexpensive cloth made in the mighty factories of England. Welsh consumers then took to buying the cheaper English fabric rather than that made in Wales.

Despite the problems inflicted upon rural Welsh livelihoods, the economic power of the machine-driven factory in the textile sector was plain for all to see. Consequently, it was emulated in countless other industries in Britain and across the world.

Whilst cotton was to become the world's prime fabric midway through the nineteenth century, we should note that cotton did not always directly compete with wool. Whilst cotton cloth was preferred in hot climes and hotter seasons, woollen cloth was still valued in cooler climes and wintry seasons. And in the temperate zones of northern Europe and North America, most people in the nineteenth century chose to wear one layer of cotton under one layer of wool as their usual attire. Also, the technological and industrial innovations made within the wool industry were applied to the cotton industry and vice versa, so for many decades the two fabrics often worked in ways to encourage each other's profitability.

It must be admitted, though, that despite its ongoing commercial viability as an independent textile product, wool was becoming less important as a product for Britain's economy as a whole. By 1860, wool had been pushed back into fifth place in English trade behind iron, machinery, coal and cotton.

Ultimately, the mechanisation of the British textile trade was hugely successful and transformative. Yet, it did not proceed without resistance. One morning in the spring of 1789, Ned Ludd, a young stockinger – a weaver of stockings – walked the pleasant roads of rural Leicestershire to a small workshop in the village of Anstey. For seven long years, Ned had been an apprentice to a grumpy old master weaver earning nothing but his dinner and a paltry stipend. Today, though, was his first day after qualifying as a fully-fledged tradesman: the first day of actual paid work.

Upon opening the door, he saw a massive wooden weaving machine standing in his workspace. The machine clunked and jabbed as woven wool folded into a tray. Dumbfounded, Ned hardly noticed the workshop owner calling from across the room. 'We have no work for you any more, Ned,' said the owner. 'A new machine has arrived.' Ned gazed at the noisy machine as the reality of the situation seeped into his head.

Usually, the workshop was packed with five other weavers. But he saw none today – only a young girl untangling threads from the machine. When the workshop owner slipped out of the back door to attend to other business, Ned Ludd picked up a mallet and set about smashing the machine to smithereens. When he was finished, the girl was wide-eyed and looking on. 'Tell 'em it was Ludd,' Ned told her. And he ran away down the road.

These were revolutionary times in more ways than one. As the Industrial Revolution was just gaining steam in England, the French Revolution had set the guillotine upon the French monarchy. Over the next decade or two, a military dictator, Napoleon Bonaparte, crowned himself Emperor of the French and then set about overthrowing monarchies all over Europe, replacing them with members of his own family. In reaction, the aristocrats making up the British government set about quelling the rise of revolutionary activities – both in Britain and in Europe. For his part, Ned Ludd knew he wouldn't be able to show his face back in Anstey again, so he adopted a new name, joined the British Expeditionary Forces, then went off to Europe to shoot at the French. He would not return for many years.

In 1812, Britain also went to war against the United States whilst still entrenched in the European war against Napoleon. Wars can be good or bad for sheep-farming and the wool trade. Mobilised armies require food and uniforms, so mutton and wool can be readily sold at guaranteed prices. However, international trading is often abruptly impaired, which is a serious problem if a significant number of buyers are abroad.

To circumvent the economic disruption of the wars, industrial entrepreneurs around England were planting machines into workshops and factories to cut down labour costs. One spring day in 1812, a Yorkshire factory owner installed weaving machines into his West Riding workshop. The next day he inspected the workshop to see all the devices had been attacked and busted up. According to neighbours, the saboteurs ran off into the night yelling 'Tell 'em it was Ludd!'

In the months that followed, workers assembled in all the textile towns of northern England demanding no more machines be sent into the textile manufactories and that compensation must be made to those already replaced by machines. These demands came with a warning that every weaving machine in the nation would be put out of commission if the factory owners refused to negotiate. These demands and warnings were printed in various newspapers and signed by 'Capt. Ludd'. The warnings sent shivers down the backs of aristocrats and industrialists throughout the country. So much so, that Parliament quickly convened to pass a law prescribing the death sentence to anybody convicted of breaking a machine.

Meanwhile, the machine-breaking protests spread across the wool-craft and cotton-craft workshops of Yorkshire, Nottinghamshire and Lancashire. Those involved called themselves Luddites. In response, the government sent 12,000 army troops to the Midlands and the north of England to find the rebellious machine-smashers. Assembling such a large number of troops was no mean feat given the British army was engaged in wars against both Napoleon and the United States. Despite gunning down some innocent protesters, the military never managed to catch any Luddites in the act. And in fact, errant soldiery caused much more local crime than the Luddites ever did.

In 1813, government officials rushed to set up a mass trial in Yorkshire but many of those accused had to be set free by local magistrates for lack of evidence. However, a couple of men were found guilty of grievous harm to a machine and sentenced to death, with their female conspirers sent to Australian penal colonies.

Although the British establishment declared war against Luddism, the protesters did find one sympathiser from the elite classes in the form of the superstar poet of the era, Lord Byron. As a peer in the House of Lords, Byron was obliged to turn up in the Upper House of Parliament to vote on matters of state. One of his first speeches in this venue was an eloquent statement against the death penalty for Luddites. From this speech, he later crafted his *Song for The Luddites*:

> As the Liberty lads o'er the sea
> Bought their freedom, and cheaply, with blood,
> So we, boys, we
> Will die fighting, or live free,
> And down with all kings but King Ludd!

> When the web that we weave is complete,
> And the shuttle exchanged for the sword,
> We will fling the winding sheet
> O'er the despot at our feet,
> And dye it deep in the gore he has poured.

> Though black as his heart its hue,
> Since his veins are corrupted to mud,
> Yet this is the dew
> Which the tree shall renew
> Of Liberty, planted by Ludd!

There is no record regarding the fate of Captain Ludd. Maybe he died fighting in Europe or was caught and hanged under another name. Many now believe Ludd was just a mythic figure invented by the Luddites to send the paranoid leaders of the British army on a wild goose chase across the countryside in search of a ringleader who did not exist. He certainly made the soldiers nervous, though. According to the writer Richard Conniff, there were reports of many British infantrymen seeing the dreaded captain out of the corner of their eye standing menacingly with a pike in his hand.

Some Welsh history-buffs suggest the name Ned Ludd was borrowed from the writings of the medieval Welsh scholar Geoffrey of Monmouth, who listed Ludd as a Celtic king who founded London in pre-Roman times. Supposedly, King Ludd's remains are interred at Ludgate, the westernmost part of London's ancient Roman wall.

Nowadays, the term Luddite often gets thrown around as a criticism of those fearful of new technical things. Those fondest of using it this way are usually modern industrialists who want to foist some dubious new technology upon a suspicious community. However, we should note that the letters signed 'Capt. Ludd' record in black and white that the Luddites were not 'against all machines', just those brought in by greedy factory owners to replace workers.

Eventually, Wales would become an important cog in the Industrial Revolution since the engines of steam-powered factories, and of steamships and steam trains, needed lots of coal to keep them moving. The south Wales coalfields opened in the second half of the nineteenth century as a response to this demand and quickly became a massive industry of global significance. Coal mining also helped invigorate the Welsh woollen industry since mineworkers were migrating from across Britain into the south Wales valleys. They and their families had to be clothed and their beds blanketed. In a reprise of an earlier industrial revolution in medieval times, water-powered woollen mills began reopening on Wales's southern waterways in order to process wool once more.

Chapter 30
THE CHARTIST REVOLT

GWYNEDD AND POWYS, WALES, 1812 to 1839

I have yet to fully explain this to Shelley, my trusty co-explorer of modern sheeplands, but he shares his name with one of the most inventive yet rebellious minds in British history, the poet Percy Bysshe Shelley. This nineteenth-century Shelley caught the travel bug whilst young with a special desire for the classical sites of the Mediterranean. However, with the Napoleonic Wars still raging in Europe, Shelley initially had to make do with explorations in the Welsh uplands. He grew to be intrigued and then inspired by the Welsh landscape, yet sometimes bewildered by the people that lived there.

By the time he came to live in Wales, Percy Bysshe Shelley had already become a radical figure. The University of Oxford had thrown him out because he had pinned atheistic pamphlets all around the colleges. The Home Office was tailing him because he had posted seditious leaflets in Cornish towns decrying British Rule in Ireland. He also wrote pamphlets on vegetarianism and handed them out to influential businessmen in the meat industry before private security ran him away. Whoever suggests poetic writing is a meaningless sideshow to real life must reckon with its ability to provoke the rich and the powerful.

In 1812, Shelley arrived in a small settlement in Gwynedd called Tremadog. Along with Porthmadog, its sister town on the sea, Tremadog was a planned settlement brought into being by an enthusiastic Anglo-Welsh landscaper called William Madocks. Madocks had converted a nearby estuary into farmland to raise sheep. He hoped this would help ensure some economic future for his settlements. In the burgeoning Industrial Age new land could be reclaimed more easily from the sea, in this case by draining the estuary and building walls to stave off the tides. Madocks also put in train lines and tramways to the quarries in the Snowdonia mountains nearby. These lines have since become the tracks of the well-known Ffestiniog Railway. Whilst supervising these constructions, Madocks also built himself a beautiful modern wooden bungalow in Tremadog, now a heritage-listed building named Plas Tan yr Allt. However, since Madocks was wheeling and dealing in London most of the time, he rented out this bungalow to Shelley.

Shelley cut a strange figure in Tremadog. He mooched around in the local pubs antagonising the English quarry managers, mouthing off how badly they treated their Welsh workers. After one night's drinking, he stumbled back to Plas Tan yr Allt, crossing fields laid about with several sickly sheep. The following day, a few sheep lay dead and the farmers accused Shelley of shooting them in the head to put them out of their misery. The next time he went to the pub, Shelley got into another argument and loudly lambasted landowners for growing rich by enslaving and abusing both innocent fluffy beasts and impoverished locals.

Eventually, someone got so annoyed by Shelley's uninvited rants that they decided to scare him away. Late one night, a couple of hired thugs turned up at Plas Tan yr Allt in the middle of the night to rattle its doors, break its windows and then shoot off a pistol into the house. Shelley was so perturbed that he fled Tremadog at daybreak.

This might be seen as a victory for the Tremadog elite but they did not know that while residing in the town, Shelley had penned the first draft of his famous political poem *Queen Mab*. This poem would come back to haunt the British establishment in the future.

Over the next decade, Shelley lived a short but creative life, composing what would become some of the most celebrated poetry of the Romantic era. In 1816, he married Mary Wollstonecraft Shelley, the writer of *Frankenstein*, and together they travelled through post-Napoleonic Europe. The couple lived for a time in a Swiss villa with Lord Byron, the supporter of the Luddites whose poem we read in the last chapter.

Living his life fearlessly, Shelley drowned at sea in a storm whilst sailing in a two-man yacht race against Lord Byron. Unlike Byron, Shelley never achieved fame or fortune during his lifetime but as the nineteenth century progressed, his political poetry became admired amongst the literati and then adored by activists. Various progressive journalists were particularly drawn to his poetry. After they quoted from *Queen Mab* a few times, the poem began to be recited aloud at activist meetings and public demonstrations across Britain. This was a time when poets commanded the same sort of social influence as folk singers like Bob Dylan did in the 1960s or Hollywood movie stars like Sean Penn and Emma Watson do today.

In the years 1838 and 1839, a specific form of political radicalism burst out across British society. Inspired by ideas like those in Shelley's poetry, the founders of this new popular movement wrote up a very elegant vision of Britain's future within one short document: the People's Charter. The main demand of the Charter was universal suffrage: that everybody should have the right to vote via secret ballot in general elections, as well as the right to stand for election. At the time, only landowners or the wealthy held these rights. Those that went along with the ideas of the People's Charter – whether they were activists or not – were called Chartists.

Not coincidentally, I am writing these words in a notebook while in a restaurant called The Chartist in the fetching old Welsh wool town of Llanidloes. My companion, again, is young Shelley. Though it is a bit hard for me to keep tabs on him as I write because he has slunk off somewhere, playing with an enormous friendly ginger cat called Llew. The Chartist shares a stylish old red-bricked building with a pub called The Trewythen, whose facade glows prettily with white Romanesque columns on the town's main road. The artwork on the interior wall of The Trewythen relates the story of Llanidloes' own Chartists along with their historic entanglement with this very building.

Llanidloes is in Powys, whose eastern side is set hard against the English border but whose western heartland comprises the green Welsh desert of the Cambrian Mountains. As we have learnt by now, the high pastured hills and riverine valleys of Powys make for great sheep country. Each range of hills or mountains seems to have its own speciality sheep breed: the Black Welsh, the Beulah Speckle-Face, and the Kerry Hill are some examples.

Within the valleys, there are many pretty villages and towns dotted about – including a series of delightful old wool towns named for their springs: Builth Wells, Llandrindod Wells and Llanwrtyd Wells. From the sixteenth century until the nineteenth, the wool-craft undertaken within these towns helped make Powys a vital focus of the wool trade. As we noted in earlier chapters, many of the stone houses of this area had an archetypal cottage industry going on inside, mostly spinning and weaving wool. By the 1830s, though, the weaving sector was upscaling and shifting into the workshops of towns like Llanidloes, which had more than twenty weaving manufactories by this time. As the Ned Ludd story showed, weavers would train for years before being let loose to weave cloth on sophisticated looms. These hand-operated looms of the nineteenth century were exceedingly difficult to master. If you want a practical demonstration of this, you can try your hand at weaving a few lines at the Newtown Textile Museum in Powys or the weaving rooms at the National Wool Museum in Carmarthenshire. Like young Shelley and me, you will come away with a new-found admiration for the technical complexity of artisanal weaving.

The problem for workshops in Welsh towns like Llanidloes was that by now the colossal textile factories in England were churning out clothes and selling them cheaply in markets across Britain – indeed, across the whole world. It was becoming nigh on impossible for the smaller non-mechanised workshops of Llanidloes to compete. There were a few firms that received the crucial investment to fully mechanise, but most languished and went out of business, sending skilled artisans into poorly paid factory jobs elsewhere.

Sometimes, the largest factories required new workers to offer up their whole family – children and all – into the firm's employ. The family was then housed in nearby dormitories built by the factory owner. However, these accommodations were often cramped and overcrowded and the rent for living in them was deducted directly from workers' wages.

The workday schedule would keep workers labouring away for twelve hours or more, tending to noisy, clunking, dangerous machines. Because working families had no time to visit the local market, the firm would also provide the workers with food and clothing. However, it would do so at exorbitant prices that left workers with little or no spare cash. Those workers who bought from other suppliers were usually sacked. Because of these oppressive conditions, skilled wool-crafters that took up a job offer in the new factories often rued the day they did so.

Against this background, many disaffected artisans and their apprentices in Llanidloes had joined the Chartists to agitate for a right to vote. They believed that universal suffrage would create a government much more attuned to the needs of workers, rather than just those endowed with wealth or titles. In the spring of 1839, as Chartism erupted across industrial towns all over Britain, three Llanidloes craftsmen held a quiet outdoor meeting on an old stone bridge traversing Afon Hafren, the River Severn. These three were Abraham Owen, a veteran weaver, Lewis Humphreys, a shoemaker, and Thomas Jerman, a carpenter.

Though the meeting was very low-key, it still attracted the ire of the town's mayor and magistrate, a wealthy landowner named Thomas Marsh. Marsh violently opposed the working class being allowed to vote in general elections. Like others in the establishment, he referred to Chartists as revolutionaries and publicly announced he would not tolerate their activity in Llanidloes. He even paid some of his own tenants to inform on those expressing Chartist sympathies. Marsh conspired with acquaintances to entice the London Metropolitan Police to send men to arrest the three Chartists and to halt further meetings. Much to Marsh's dismay, the Met's superintendent sent only three policemen to Llanidloes. Nonetheless, when they arrived, Marsh directed them to arrest the three Chartists. The London constables dutifully obeyed, apprehending the three Welsh workers: the weaver, the shoemaker and the carpenter.

There was no jail in Llanidloes, however, so Owen, Humphreys and Jerman were held in a room in The Trewythen. The three were much amused – if a little indignant – about their arrest because it was not illegal to be a Chartist or to advocate for democracy. Mayor Marsh, though, was familiar with the tricks of the legal process and he guessed he could probably charge the Llanidloes Chartists with inciting rebellion.

When news of Owen, Humphreys and Jerman's imprisonment in The Trewythen spread amongst the general townspeople, a grand assembly of workers and supporters marched down to the hotel to demand their release. Poking their heads out of the upstairs windows, the imprisoned Chartists shouted out that they were being guarded by just three men inside a regular room behind a single locked door. Knowing their mayor was probably using every minute to fashion trumped-up charges against the three prisoners, the crowd outside was galvanised into action, storming The Trewythen. Shoving the hapless policemen aside, they broke the locks, released the prisoners and took over the whole hotel. They then announced an impromptu town meeting was to be held about the role of Chartism in Llanidloes, inviting all disenfranchised townspeople to join them.

Mayor Marsh was aghast. He shot off messages about an insurrection underway 'in *his* town' to authorities in Cardiff and London, instructing that a battalion of troops had better be sent quickly to quell it. He also cajoled tenants working his own lands to act as Special Constables – threatening them with eviction if they didn't obey. Armed with clubs and farm equipment, these Specials surrounded The Trewythen. There was the odd scuffle between individual Chartists and individual Specials with a few broken windows and broken noses. However, most of the Specials were not really concerned about the whole affair – being long-time friends with the Chartists – so they disappeared back home before it got dark. The Chartists in The Trewythen, about one hundred of them by now, then took charge of the whole town whilst Marsh fled across the border to England to wait for army troops to be sent in.

The next day the Chartists woke up in the hotel to find everything in the town was quiet. So they relaxed in The Trewythen, waiting for the troops to come. They did not. The next day it was the same. And the next. And so it went on for five days. During this time, Llanidloes was secured and policed by the Chartists themselves, making sure there was no riotous activity or looting. There was a lot of singing and dancing, though, as the beer in The Trewythen flowed freely. And there were a lot of political discussions, too, held in open town hall fashion. Those present calculated that only eighty-six of the 4,000 men residing in Llanidloes were allowed to vote. All eighty-six were big landowners or wealthy merchants or the owner-operators of large factories. None of the Chartists thought this fair.

When journalists in the big cities got news of the Llanidloes revolt, many reflected the Chartist sympathies of the moment with headlines celebrating Llanidloes's 'Five Days of Freedom'. For many of the Llanidloes workers, these five days felt like a festival of liberty where they were finally in charge of their own lives and their own community.

Eventually troops did show up from England, along with cavalrymen. By then, though, the Chartists had already chosen to surrender the town without a fight and they walked quietly back to their homes. Over the next few weeks, Marsh rounded up and arrested all the men and women he had personally identified as being part of the Days of Freedom. Most were sentenced to a year in prison but Owen, the weaver, Humphreys, the shoemaker, and Jerman, the carpenter, were sent to an Australian penal colony, never to return.

Back in The Chartist, as my mind washed back from the nineteenth century to the twenty-first, I ordered another cup of tea and spotted little Shelley splattered from head to toe with icing sugar and sprinkles. Coming down from a sugar high, he had fallen asleep on a comfy armchair with Llew. I looked at the paintings above him. The scenes felt very material and imminent – and a tad humbling. The Chartists of Llanidloes had left a legacy of courage and defiance: Percy Bysshe Shelley's words writ real and large in a daring Welsh wool town.

The revolt by the weavers and artisans of Llanidloes was a prelude to bigger things. Later in the same year, 4,000 people marched from the south Wales valleys to Newport. Just like the mayor of Llanidloes, Newport's mayor did not welcome Chartists in his town. Indeed, he ordered the army to halt their progress by any means. In the end, jittery soldiers opened fire upon a band of particularly rowdy Chartists, killing a dozen of them and injuring more than fifty. For their part, the Chartists only managed to put a bullet in one man, shooting the mayor in the groin: he lived on though. By the end of the gunfight, some 10,000 Chartists had assembled in the middle of the city. Yet to avoid more bloodshed, they agreed to abandon their demonstration and returned home.

Though the Chartist rebellions of Llanidloes and Newport did not succeed in changing the election laws, over the coming years and all over the industrial centres of Britain, hundreds of thousands of Chartists gathered to demonstrate their desire for reform. In the summer of 1842, more than three million Britons had signed the People's Charter. The signatures were then all brought to London and delivered to Parliament as a petition. During these heady days of Chartism, Percy Bysshe Shelley's poems were republished in sympathetic magazines of the day – inspiring hearts and minds all over Britain to press the cause.

By 1848, more than six million Britons – from all walks of life – had signed another petition. The upper classes began trembling in their seats as the winds of change started to cast a gale. If the Tremadog elite did scare off Shelley in the early nineteenth century, then he returned decades later to haunt them – at an industrial scale.

Chapter 31

DAUGHTERS OF REBECCA

CARMARTHENSHIRE, WALES, 1839 to 1844

The flannel-makers of Llanidloes were not the only section of Welsh society partaking in revolts in the mid-nineteenth century. The farmers of Carmarthenshire were also protesting. As we discovered a few chapters ago, many of the roads of Wales were maintained via fees collected at roadside tollgates. These were generally managed by private companies called turnpike trusts. Despite being legally bound to use the toll revenues to sustain the nation's roadways, many such roadways were degraded and decayed, and frequently ridden with obstacles – from mud pools to potholes and from rockslides to fallen trees.

Roadways were especially dilapidated in Carmarthenshire. Most farmers there suspected the funds raised from the tolls were being used for purposes other than road maintenance: notably to pay off bribes to the owners of the land where the tollgates were set up. The farmers also bitterly resented a whole series of new tollgates that popped up in the county in the 1830s. The county town of Carmarthen was surrounded by a fortress of one dozen tollgates. Many of these were sneakily designed to catch out those who had avoided the established tollgates by heading across traditional droving routes around them.

The tollgates did not only affect sheep-farmers and sheep drovers but farmers and labourers of all kinds. Perhaps the tollgate fees could easily be factored into standard operating costs if you owned a large-scale farming estate. However, if you were a small-time farmer or labourer, who needed to get to the market or bring new resources or stock to your small farm, the tollgates sliced heavily into family income. In order to graze sheep on unclaimed wasteland, small-hold farmers and independent shepherds were increasingly obliged to pass through one or more tollgates, both on their outward bound journey and then back again journeying homeward. Making such payments multiple times a day would ruin the whole point of raising a flock by letting it graze for free on wasteland. Those farmers who needed lime to fertilise their fields were also aggrieved since they had to pass many tollgates on their way to the lime quarries and then to their fields. With so many farmers discontented and distressed, something had to be done.

Banding together on moorland near the village of Efailwen, a group of Carmarthenshire farmers held a public meeting to 'consider the necessity of a tollgate at Efailwen'. After vigorous discussion, the consensus was the gate was unnecessary. The farmers then pulled on masks and wigs, cloaked themselves with white petticoats, and set off to the tollgate. Some were on horseback brandishing pistols, and others walked alongside with pitchforks. When they arrived at the tollgate, they stopped. Then they yelled out a verse from the Bible at the bemused tollgate keeper:

> And they blessed Rebecca and said unto her, thou art our sister, be thou the mother of thousands of millions and let thy seed possess the gates of those who hate them.

Obscure to some, this passage from the Bible was uttered in the Welsh tongue commonly enough as a hopeful refrain against injustice:

> A hwy a fendithiasant Rebeca, ac a ddywedasant wrthi, 'Ti yw ein chwaer, bydd yn fam i filoedd o filiynau, a bydded i'th ddisgynyddion feddiannu pyrth y rhai sy'n eu casáu.'

Because of the reference to Rebecca, the tollgate smashers called themselves Daughters of Rebecca. They then smashed the gates as the keeper ran away.

Quite why they were wearing wigs and petticoats was a mystery to some. However, as well as allowing them to disguise their identity, it may have allowed them to appear less aggressive as they approached the tollgate. Also, in this part of Wales, it was customary for those dispensing mob justice against some local scoundrel to dress up in women's garb, especially when confronting snitches or philanderers.

The Efailwen tollgate operator saw the mess of the smashed gate the following morning but he quickly arranged to rebuild it in order to start making money again. A few nights later, the Daughters of Rebecca pulled it down once more, along with a few other tollgates into the bargain. The owner of all these tollgates was an impatient Englishman named Thomas Bullin. His sole entrepreneurial activity was to accumulate turnpike licences by dubious means, then fleece those that passed by his tollgates.

Bemoaning his lost revenue, Bullin inquired of a Carmarthen magistrate what action would be taken against the offenders. Unfortunately for Bullin, the magistrate seemed more sympathetic to the plight of the Daughters of Rebecca than with violations wrought on the Englishman's property. For now, Bullin gave up rebuilding his smashed tollgates.

As well as being aggrieved by the tollgates, the Daughters of Rebecca were angered by another tax they were forced to pay, the tithes of the local Anglican Church. As Carmarthenshire farmers were generally not Anglicans – preferring to attend the non-conformist Welsh chapels – none of them thought it right they must hand over a tenth of their income to the Church of England. By this time, tithes had to be paid in cash. You could not just rock up to the church minister with a bleating lamb as in medieval times. The Daughters of Rebecca would occasionally write angry letters to Anglican clergy based in Wales declaring they had no money for English tithes. However, they never assaulted Anglican churches as they did the tollgates.

We can suppose that the Daughters of Rebecca might have been overjoyed to see the Efailwen tollgates gone for good. Yet tollgates all over the rest of Carmarthenshire and into neighbouring Pembrokeshire were still exacting their tolls and attracting ire. Not only that but the revenue Welsh farmers could garner from selling their produce during the 1830s, including sheep and wool, was wavering wildly up and down, though usually down more than up. This put them under great financial pressure. When farmers and labourers met in chapels and pubs, their conversations inevitably turned to the dire economy. Many were extremely anxious about slipping up on rental payments and worried what might happen if they couldn't feed their families.

At this time, the spectre that haunted Britain's working classes was the hated workhouse. In 1834, the British government declared that any able-bodied person seeking welfare for themselves or their family would be confined to a state-sponsored workhouse, a giant prison-like institution set at the edge of most major towns. Often referred to as 'The Poorhouse', the inmates – as they were called – would only be housed and fed if they worked all day at menial tasks, such as cracking rocks or untwining old rope.

The absurd conservative morals of the day demanded that the conditions inside the workhouse be made deliberately inhumane so that only the desperate and starving would seek welfare. On knocking on the door of a workhouse, families were immediately split up – wives from husbands, children from parents, siblings from siblings – and sent to other sides of the compound or to workhouses in other towns. If families were lucky, they would be allowed to meet up once a week for Sunday services. It was a cruel and humiliating system from which those incarcerated found it difficult to emerge. In the case of Carmarthen, the local workhouse was a dour brick monolith perched overlooking the River Tywi, a site of stigma and severity.

Prior to 1834, instead of paying taxes to fund an inhumane workhouse, rural Welsh communities, including landlords, would generally offer food and goods to the poor, usually via local chapels or churches but sometimes directly if those in need were neighbours. Often, the better landlords would also provide temporary employment to hard-up farmers, getting them to rebuild bridges or plant hedgerows upon their estates, for example. Welfare was thus tied to the practicalities of toughing out the rough times rather than a pecuniary measure to discourage social leeching. Whilst some in Carmarthenshire endeavoured to carry on this tradition of local aid – often just to keep good people out of the workhouses – the community resources to provide such help were sapped by the busting economy of the 1830s and by the rising workhouse taxes many were asked to pay.

Carmarthenshire's rural precarity became even worse in the early 1840s when the price of sheep, wheat, cattle and dairy dropped simultaneously. Amidst all this, the tollgates were putting their prices up. One summer day in 1843, the Daughters of Rebecca donned their petticoats and wigs once more and went about from town to town and village to village smashing tollgates county-wide. Then when they were done smashing tollgates, they marched to Carmarthen. Here, they planned a raucous public meeting to 'consider the necessity of a workhouse in the town of Carmarthen'.

To lend some joy to the proceedings, a musical band and some acrobats were hired. When a giant conch shell dubbed Cragen Beca, the Shell of Rebecca, was blown by one of the musicians, it acted as an invitation for the crowd to march to the workhouse. While deemed by those in it a procession, really it was a protest against the nation's workhouse laws.

At the head of the procession were the Daughters of Rebecca riding their giant draught horses. Because most of them were well-established small-time farmers, they were granted respect as 'fathers of the land'. Their presence guaranteed the protests would be joined by 'mothers of the town' and a hundred festive children as well. As part of their merry protest, the Daughters of Rebecca bashed open the workhouse to set the inmates free. As well as being gifted hot soup and bread, the inmates were serenaded with respectful songs by their liberators.

By this point, some of Carmarthen's officials were getting mighty panicky. Whilst the Daughters of Rebecca themselves were in a festive mood, the town's council feared public property was being destroyed. Messages were sent out from the town seeking assistance but the police and the army were busy coursing the countryside for tollgate wreckers. As a *London Times* reporter wrote at the time:

Although the Dragoons are in the saddle every night, scouring the country here and there, they are always in the wrong place. The work of outrage continues not only undiminished but with increased audacity. This is the state of things here, and there will not be a single gate in the country if a different mode is not adopted to end it. The government are pouring in troops. A detachment of artillery is marching by way of Brecon; a detachment of artillery is marching to Carmarthen by way of Swansea; the whole of the fourth Regiment of Light Dragoons are to be stationed in South Wales; three companies of the 75th Infantry are to arrive in Carmarthen within the next two or three days; the Yeomanry are kept on permanent duty, and every military appliance of the government is exercised. Yet, no single tollgate outrage has been stayed nor has a single Rebecca protester been captured. They laugh at the display of power by the government.

However, the luck of the Rebecca protesters was about to run out. Just by coincidence, the Army Dragoons had decided to pass through Carmarthen on the afternoon of the workhouse protest. When mounted officers spotted the boisterous crowd, they charged through on their horses, scattering both revelling inmates and celebrating protesters as well as the draught horses left grazing nearby by the farmers. The captain of the Dragoons paused the charge just for a moment to read aloud the riot act. However, rather than quelling a riot, this warning provoked panic since some protesters feared they would soon be shot at. The revellers caught inside the workhouse busted open windows in a hurry to jump through and escape whilst others ran screaming into the nearby streets and fields.

Luckily, the blood that poured that day came only as civilians trampled upon broken glass and over broken fences, not via bullets and bayonets. That night, the fields of Carmarthen were filled with wandering draught horses, their owners too afraid to reclaim them lest they be arrested. Over the next few weeks, some Daughters of Rebecca were apprehended on their own farms or in pubs and inns.

The policing authorities did not find it easy to get any one Rebecca protester convicted, though, since Carmarthenshire magistrates believed the tollgate managers were dishonest swindlers. To make the charges stick, government prosecutors had to haul the protesters in locked wagons to courts outside the county.

Though some reactionary newspapers labelled them 'rioters', enough journalists opined that the Rebecca grievances seemed reasonable enough. Because of this, a parliamentary enquiry was set up to explore the causes and consequences of the riots. Eventually, the tollgate system was found to be corrupt and in need of overhaul. The reviled private tollgate trusts were ordered dissolved in favour of public road boards that were instructed to take account of the entire rural economy.

Whilst it felt revolutionary to some, the Rebecca Riots might be classified as a rebellion rather than a revolution. The precise focus on tollgates proved to be quite successful in ameliorating the acute financial pressure piled on Carmarthenshire farmers – at least for a few years. Unfortunately, the much-hated workhouses carried on intimidating and humiliating poor families for another century.

Chapter 32

THE WELSH SHEEPLAND OF PATAGONIA

WALES/ARGENTINA, 1862 TO 1902

Wales had suffered for hundreds of years as a colony of England, since the dark days of the Anglo-Norman Marcher lords. Yet in the mid-nineteenth century, some Welsh thinkers came to believe some form of outward Welsh colonialism could remedy ongoing English domination at home. Certainly, the economic opportunities offered by life in the New World and in the Antipodes were enticing for many Welsh people. The promise of land ownership was particularly attractive.

For Merioneth clergyman Michael Daniel Jones, the settlement of Welsh people in a Welsh colony abroad would not only lead to economic empowerment but to a cultural flourishing as well. Jones, like other Welsh nationalists, feared that Welsh culture was fast being subsumed in Wales by English culture. Some in Wales even fretted the language was doomed to extinction. As something of an insurance policy, Jones aspired to forge a distant 'New Wales' so that Welshness could prosper far removed from the encroachments of the English. At this time, British colonialism was at its height and

211

usually involved the treacherous takeover of independent lands and kingdoms. Jones did not dismiss colonialism as a wholly troubling enterprise, though. He embraced the common idea of the age that colonial expansion was giving England both prosperity and cultural stamina. If the Welsh could emulate this, Jones thought, they could prosper in a similar manner.

The idea excited two other nationalist friends of Jones: Thomas Love Jones-Parry and Lewis Jones. Though the three shared the same name and they all hailed from Gwynedd, they were not related. They did, however, share a common interest in the literary arts of Wales and in Welsh politics. Jones-Parry, for example, was an aristocratic Welsh politician who often used the bardic name of Elphin. Lewis Jones, for his part, was a publisher and printer based in Anglesey.

As the self-selected management team, this trio of Joneses worked out the finances for setting up a Welsh colony and of selecting where abroad it might be founded. The Joneses pondered the idea of locating the settlement in a British territory such as Australia or Canada but far enough away from English-dominated towns that it would remain culturally independent. However, if they did this, the Welsh settlement would be subject to British law and British protection and could probably only prosper by working through British trade, meaning it would likely be swamped by English customs and the English language at some point in the future. Michael Daniel Jones had trained to be a minister in the American state of Ohio and had frequently visited a Welsh settlement set up there earlier in the century. Jones noticed the settlers had become relatively wealthy at a personal level but they had just about abandoned their Welshness for the Anglo-American culture they were embedded within.

For reasons such as this, the Joneses looked to Patagonia with its vast unsettled grasslands (unsettled, that is, if we ignore the Native Americans for a moment). Patagonia was nominally administered by the independent Argentine government, so, in 1862, Thomas Love Jones-Parry and Lewis Jones sailed from Britain to Argentina to explore if they might start up a Welsh Patagonian colony. When they visited the capital, Buenos Aires, they found that the Argentine Ministry of Lands was most receptive to the idea. The Ministry believed that Argentina would only grow to be a strong nation-state if European immigrants were encouraged to settle the scarcely populated regions and carve out some sort of agricultural success.

At this time, Argentina was quibbling with Chile regarding who owned the vast arid Patagonian grasslands in the eastern rain shadow of the Andes. The Ministry of Land was particularly keen to settle this area with migrants loyal to Argentina since it would strengthen the nation's claim to it.

The Minister of Lands advised Lewis Jones and Jones-Parry to sail far south beyond the Valdes Peninsula to the central coast of Patagonia. However, as they rounded the peninsula, a storm swept over their ship, the *Candelaria*, forcing them to seek shelter in the Golfo Nuevo of northern Patagonia. The geographic features of the coast of Golfo Nuevo bore no names on the maps, so Jones-Parry took the liberty of naming the spot they landed upon after his Welsh estate: Port Madryn. Nowadays, Puerto Madryn is an important city of 100,000 people but then it was not much more than a stony slip of land pierced by a rocky river lined with a few raggedy trees.

When Jones and Jones-Parry returned to Wales, they told everyone what a beautiful site they had stumbled upon. Maybe the few days they had taken refuge in Puerto Madryn coincided with a flush of flowers after the stormy downpour or maybe their bardic enthusiasm just got the better of them. They also relayed to Welsh speakers back home that the Argentine Congress had granted the Joneses land rights and promised gifts of 3,000 sheep for the fledgling colony plus a store of grain seed.

By 1865, Parry-Jones was ready to despatch the first Welsh colonists to Patagonia. He hired a converted tea clipper, the *Mimosa*, from the Liverpool docks before selling 150 tickets to Welsh pioneers who dared to stake out a future in faraway South America. Of course, the major attraction for these adventurous Welsh was not the vision of a New Wales but the abundant free land offered by the Argentine authorities. With the Red Dragon of Wales as their masthead, the *Mimosa* set sail from Britain and arrived in Puerto Madryn in the southern winter.

Whilst the Joneses promised a Welsh-like landscape – green, wet and fertile – what the pioneers actually found was windswept pampas, quite barren and dry. Precious little food could be extracted from the wilderness and no forests grew to provide wood for the building of homes. The few stunted trees were quickly felled for firewood and never grew back. Most of the settlers' first homes were mud-houses moulded from riverbank clay.

The settlers began their new farming lives in Patagonia by broadcasting seed on the dry soil, hoping they would get a crop. A mediocre crop did pop out from the riverside earth a few months later but it was almost entirely washed away when the river flooded. Another issue was that the promised sheep and grain seed didn't arrive from Buenos Aires. Unbeknownst to the settlers, Argentina had just declared war with their neighbours Paraguay. Any extra food managed by the government was sent to troops heading north, not Welsh settlers in the south. Because of these problems, it was not long before hunger and starvation threatened the fledgling settlement.

In desperation, the settlers sent word to the British ambassador in Buenos Aires, begging for help. A shipload of emergency supplies was sent from the British Falklands but that was only a temporary solution. Eventually, a year later, in 1866, the Argentine government donated 800 pounds to the Welsh settlement specifically to buy their own sheep. This was much welcomed by the despairing Welsh colonists yet it bought less than half the sheep they were contractually promised. The settlers were also barred from eating most of the sheep so that the stock might increase year by year. The Argentines didn't care so much about the hunger of Welsh immigrants as they did about the long-term economic future of the territory.

The thing that everybody seemed to overlook was that none of the Welsh colonists were sheep-farmers – or farmers at all. They were carpenters and cobblers and coalminers and brickmakers and tailors. Over the next year, due to their lack of shepherding experience, the flocks became feral and disappeared into the parched pasturelands. Unlike Wales, Patagonia was not carved up by a network of stone walls or hedgerows to corral livestock. With the sheep dispersed across Patagonia never to return, the colony had to rely on potato farming. Alas, when the seasonal floods arrived again, the potato crop was decimated, as were the mud-houses the Welsh had been living in.

Luckily, traders from the native Tehuelche tribe had noticed how badly the settlers were doing with their farming. In what was a friendly gesture towards potential trading partners, they showed the Welsh how to hunt rheas and guinea pigs. These new skills enabled the settler families to avoid starvation.

As well as learning from the Tehuelche, the Welsh also learnt from their own failures. One observant colonist, Rachel Jenkins, noted that seasonal floodwaters might be diverted via small canals to irrigate their crops a little way from the river. When she demonstrated the feasibility of this process, the colonists quickly transformed arid land into fertile fields – especially as the floods brought nutrient-laden silt from the Andes to nourish the soil.

Although some of the Welsh pioneers were growing disenchanted with Patagonia, Lewis Jones was still plugging away at the project both in South America and in Europe. He busily lobbied both the Argentine government and British entrepreneurs to invest in the area. By the 1880s, Jones had enticed the Argentines to grant a railway licence for the area. He then flaunted the licence in the boardroom of a British railway company and before long, tracks were being lain between Puerto Madryn and Welsh settlements in the Patagonian interior.

At about the same time, another boatload of Welsh colonists arrived on the scene, some 500 of them. These new immigrants brought new stocks of sheep and also the know-how to care for them. With the new railway installed, the new sheep-farmers also had the means to haul both meat and wool back out to ships docked in Puerto Madryn. Most of the meat was destined for Buenos Aires but the wool was exported to Britain and North America.

The sheep industry across all the farmlands of Patagonia was very modest at first, with sheep numbering only in the hundreds by 1875. However, the numbers grew well in the 1880s until there were some 60,000 sheep being farmed there by the 1890s. Sheep-farming then grew at a staggering pace early in the twentieth century such that Patagonia became a globally significant 'sheepland'. The number of sheep reached a peak of around twenty-two million in the 1950s.

The dryness of the landscape, though, made Patagonia sensitive to overstocking, even in the nineteenth century. When the flock numbers crept upward, wild pastures found it hard to recover after their grazing. In fact, sheep-farming quickly transformed some grasslands of Patagonia into degraded desert-like settings. The denuded nature of the landscape, though, was usually blamed by the farmers not on overgrazing but on lack of rainfall.

Despite this overstocking, the Argentine government was happy to see sheep helping them tame and settle the inland areas of Patagonia – all the way to the foothills of the Andes. Alas, this process was only made possible because Argentina also led a cruel military campaign to evict indigenous tribes from the region, including the congenial Tehuelche whom the Welsh had been trading with. This campaign was dubbed the 'conquest of the desert' at the time. Here, 'desert' does not really refer to the arid character of the landscape but an area supposedly deserted of people. Many of the tribes that suffered at the hands of this conquest were displaced into rugged areas in the dry valleys of the Andes, often to real deserts. In order to survive, they sometimes rustled sheep from European settlers on the plains, thereby increasing the tensions between the two groups.

We should note that Welsh farmers did not get Patagonia all to themselves. Once the indigenous tribes were displaced, wealthy Spanish-speaking sheep-farmers sent giant flocks from the north of the country to the pampas in the south. There was often conflict between the bigger Argentine sheep ranchers and the smaller Welsh family farms, since both had to fight to secure grazing.

During their first decades in Patagonia, the Welsh settlers founded and developed several towns that are still doing well today, including Trelew, Rawson, Gaiman and Dolavon, as well as Puerto Madryn. Initially, these towns were largely self-governing with all adults having the right to vote on town affairs. However, the Welsh towns lost their autonomy as they grew more integrated with the Argentine political system. By 1902, the Patagonian provinces came under the direct control of the central Argentine government.

At this point, Welsh pioneers began to feel pressured from a cultural perspective, since the government dictated Patagonian schools must conduct all classes in Spanish. Some Welsh settlers noted how the Argentines were acting in Patagonia in a manner similar to the

English in Wales. Many of the Welsh Patagonians decided it was not worth carrying on struggling to survive economically year after year if they weren't allowed to be in control of the towns and schools they had created. When an offer came to resettle in Canada, half the Welsh in Patagonia got on a boat and sailed away.

The other fifty per cent though weathered overbearing Argentine officials with the support of their sheep flocks and they survived to give rise to a sustainable Welsh-language community. If you visit the old Welsh Argentine towns today, you'll still find a few thousand Welsh speakers there, the descendants of those first settlers that arrived on the *Mimosa*.

Chapter 33

WARS OF THE RANGES

THE AMERICAN WEST, 1870 TO 1930

In the mid-nineteenth century, the United States fought a war against Mexico and won. This vastly extended the USA's already considerable western territories. American settlers then brought great sheep flocks and cattle herds into these territories – to the plains and plateaus of the American West.

It was supposed that the sheep would graze in the higher, rugged lands, and the cattle could have everything else. Or at least this is what the cowboys thought. The sheep-farmers and shepherds, on the other hand, usually took to moving their sheep from the highlands into lower areas for winter grazing, mostly on public land. Sometimes shepherds had secured grazing rights by purchasing a licence but usually they did not. Regardless, they had to get their flocks to grazeable low land during the winters or else their sheep would starve.

Up until the end of the 1800s, much of the American West was pretty much a frontier zone for most Euro-American settlers. The farmers and ranchers there had to battle social isolation, unpredictable environs and some unfriendly Native Americans determined to defend their hunting grounds. The farmers also fought against each other. The government of each American territory or state was usually far away across distant mountain ranges, and the federal government in Washington DC was even further removed. Therefore, rights were usually asserted and enforced via coercion and violence as much as by the rule of law.

The public land of the American West was supposedly open equally to all. However, the cattlemen took advantage of the remoteness of the western ranges to fence off their preferred pastures to keep competitors out. Still, fences are hardly impenetrable to hungry sheep and desperate shepherds. With a twist of a pair of shears, barbed-wire fences can be forced open and woolly sheep can run straight to fresh pastures, impervious to the odd barb.

In the later part of the nineteenth century, shepherds whose flocks trampled on pastures claimed by cowboys were sometimes sent home bruised and battered after being punched, kicked and pistol-whipped, their flocks in turn sent scattering into the hills. A number of times, rowdy cowboys raided shepherd camps in the dead of night, shooting shepherds dead as they reached for their rifles. The cowboys then marched the unattended sheep off the edge of rocky bluffs to ensure they'd never compete against cattle. In 1894, near Rifle, Colorado, 4,000 sheep were sent over the edge of the cliffs of Parachute Creek. This piece of cowboy terror made the national newspapers with the conflict between cowboys and shepherds being dubbed the Range Wars. During the Range Wars, shepherds and their flocks were not considered by cowboys as mere competitors but mortal enemies.

Into this Wild West came the Welsh sheep-farmer John G. Edwards, or Jack to all who knew him. Hailing from Merioneth, Edwards had arrived in the American West in the 1870s, recently married. He and his wife decided to invest her inheritance in setting up sheep ranches in the high plateaus of Oregon and Wyoming. Since sheep are much cheaper than cattle, it seemed a good choice. And the high plateaus of Oregon and Wyoming resembled somewhat the landscape of Merioneth.

After he had set up his sheep-farms as going concerns, Edwards also set up some vital services for his fellow frontier homesteaders. For instance, in Oregon's Hay Creek Valley, he established the first general store as well as the first post office and the first school. Also, he was happy to hire homesteaders for various extra jobs so they could ride out the tough early years without quitting for some other place.

With time and commitment, the Hay Creek Valley community grew – as did Edwards's own sheep business. Eventually, he became the biggest wool producer in the state. Whilst cowboys might claim the American West as the domain of cattle, Edwards transformed Oregon and Wyoming into lands of sheep. His repute became such that everybody in the West referred to Edwards as the Sheep King of America.

As part of his business, Edwards would send great flocks down from his Wyoming ranches to the Colorado plains, where they would graze for a time on public land before being shepherded to livestock railcars to be auctioned off in markets across America. When Edwards managed to get his flocks to market, he would usually make a killing. However, the cowboys of Colorado had long warned him to halt his flocks from chowing down on the pastures of Colorado's public lands. Since his sheep were so numerous, they grazed out pastures the cowboys thought rightfully theirs. Over the years, various Colorado cattlemen had tried to intimidate and rough up Edwards's shepherds and also assault his sheep. Sometimes this would scare the shepherds so much they headed straight back out of Colorado without having put a single sheep on a railcar. This annoyed Edwards no end, since it not only dented his earnings, it was an insult to the liberties and rights of honest American business.

One year, Edwards decided to get involved in the droving of his own flocks into Colorado. He hired an armed guard and then headed off south from Wyoming with his shepherds and an enormous flock of 50,000 sheep. News of the southbound flock travelled fast. The cattlemen of northern Colorado hastily assembled in a hotel bar to publicly pass resolutions that forbade out-of-state shepherds from bringing their flocks into Colorado. Although these resolutions had no legal standing whatsoever, they were published in the cowboy-friendly newspapers of the West. A showdown was on the way.

According to reports in the press, Edwards's 50,000 sheep were going to be met by a posse of 1,000 Colorado cowboys. Edwards believed this was just bluster to deter his advance so he ignored it.

However, a much smaller posse of a few dozen or so cowboys – calling themselves the Sheepshooters – did catch up with Edwards and his immense flock. Arriving on horseback, each man was masked and wielded multiple rifles. Putting on a fearsome show, they personally confronted Edwards, ordering him to turn back to Wyoming. Edwards's armed guard had lost his bottle, cowering behind the shepherds and unwilling to risk personal harm for the sake of sheep. In the face of such odds, Edwards chose to back down. He ordered his shepherds to withdraw the flock and headed back to Wyoming.

After a few years, the Welshman decided to give the Colorado route another chance. This time, he hired a dozen gunslingers and set forth with another massive flock of sheep. By the time he was at the Colorado state line, the Sheepshooters accosted him once more, this time in greater numbers: some fifty armed riders. Edwards boldly insisted on his right to the public land of Colorado. The cowboys were far from impressed. They circled around his gunslingers and levelled their rifles at them. Outnumbered, most of the gunslingers demurred to the Sheepshooters. Those that kept their rifles raised did so for self-preservation not sheep-preservation. The Sheepshooters then made a showy performance of riding up to Edwards as he sat on his horse, then tearing him down to the ground. They dismounted and slipped a makeshift noose around his neck. The gunslingers knew that someone would probably be killed if any shooting started so they yelled at their boss to cooperate.

The cowboys demanded that Edwards turn his giant flock about or be hanged until he was dead. Still he refused, believing they were bluffing. The Sheepshooters bound his hands and legs, blindfolded him and dragged him to a nearby tree to throw the rope over a branch. Three cowboys jerked the rope and Edwards's head was strained upwards. For a few seconds his feet left the ground menacingly before the cowboys let their rope slacken. The gunslingers looked on aghast but each one had three rifles aimed toward them so they did not move.

Again, the cowboys yelled at Edwards to turn the flock around. Again, he refused. The Sheepshooters jerked the rope again. With the noose tight around his neck, Edwards swung aloft with his legs flailing. It was only when he grew blue in the face and lost consciousness that he was let down.

Edwards was alive but completely incapacitated. Waving their guns about at the gunslingers and the shepherds, the Sheepshooters warned them they had better leave Colorado immediately or be hung out like their boss. The shepherds and gunslingers then packed their unconscious boss upon a horse and rode out of Colorado. After this ordeal, Edwards decided to make do by grazing his sheep just north of the border.

When a railroad was lined up to connect Wyoming to the Pacific coast of Oregon, it seemed like Edwards's sheep business might become highly profitable again. However, by this time, federal land agents were telling him he had far too many sheep for the land and that he would have to downsize to comply with newly-passed regulations. Because the railroads had enticed investors into the area, the Welshman took the opportunity to quickly sell off his entire flock at a grand profit.

Edwards then settled into a very long retirement on the coast of Oregon, devoting himself to the lucrative hobby of breeding new types of sheep. By crossing Merino sheep with Rambouillet sheep, and then crossing their offspring with Delaine sheep, Edwards ended up breeding a colossal new kind of sheep weighing in at 200 pounds a head. This new breed, the Baldwin, became world famous for a time, with extensive numbers sold abroad to Australia and Argentina. The biggest one-off sale of Baldwin sheep, though, was to the newly established Soviet Union where the state bought 10,000 Baldwins and distributed them across nationalised farms on the Russian steppes. However, the rural people there were traditional wheat farmers not sheep-farmers. As such, they merely 'harvested' the Baldwins as they received them rather than breeding them for future flocks.

Like Jack Edwards, the Range Wars lived on long into the twentieth century with Wild West skirmishes always threatening to break out. The government in Washington DC knew they had to do something to bring law and order to the open ranges of the Western states, so in the 1930s they charged the Forest Service with drawing up grazing allotments for each farmer or homesteader. Backed up by patrolling officers, this regime of regulation put paid to the Range Wars. However, it also meant there would be far fewer shepherds and far fewer cowboys in the American West from then on.

Chapter 34

GLOBAL SHEEPLANDS

AFRICA/ASIA, 1870s TO THE PRESENT

As we saw in Chapter 6, Egypt had sheep-farmers long before it became the land of the Pharaohs. As for the rest of Africa, it seems various early African and Arab peoples imported and then relayed a kind of hairy fat-tailed sheep from Arabia across the Red Sea and then all the way down the length of the continent until – thousands of years later – the sheep ended up with the Khoisan people of South Africa's Cape region, around 600 BC.

When Dutch settlers arrived in southern Africa another few thousand years later in the seventeenth century, they referred to the descendants of these ancient sheep as Cape sheep and then interbred them with European breeds. The resulting hybrids were productive wool producers yet well adapted to the arid African savannah. Come the early nineteenth century, Dutch farmers in southern Africa got their hands on the coveted Merino and quickly cross-bred them with the Cape sheep. These Merino-Cape hybrids were then sold to Dutch traders heading to Java in the East Indies.

Java had long had sheep of its own: some brought in by Chinese entrepreneurs, some by Hindi merchants, some by Arab traders –

223

all during the Middle Ages. But the Merino-Cape sheep that the Dutch imported were something new. In the 1870s, Dutch settlers in West Java gifted some Merino-Cape hybrids to the Javanese regents there. In one regency, Garut, a mountainous part of West Java, these Merino-Cape sheep were then cross-bred with local breeds whose ancestors had arrived in Java centuries earlier.

This grand series of journeys from various parts of the world – and the subsequent mixing of sheep genes – then gave rise to a peculiar breed called the Garut fighting sheep. Whilst the number of sheep in Java currently exceeds that of Wales, at some twelve million in total, most modern Java sheep serve as subsistence livestock, living within small villages. They generally provide milk every few days and meat for special events. The sheep also serve as a kind of living savings account, quickly sold or exchanged when needs require. The Garut fighting sheep, however, serves a different purpose. It has become an elite 'sports sheep'.

Imagine venturing into a modern Javanese village in the Garut regency on market day. In this case, you will possibly encounter a cacophonous cascade of cheers, singing and dancing – all set against a backdrop of energetic traditional music played live by a gamelan band or sometimes blaring through loudspeakers set up on an adjacent pick-up truck. All this noise is peripheral, however, to the main attraction. Within a sizeable straw-floored fighting ring, Garut rams are paraded around by Javanese shepherds. Their heads, horns and saddles are adorned with ribbons, tassels, sashes and blankets. They are then released to re-enact the behaviour of their wild ancestors, rising onto their hind limbs before crashing their mighty horns against each other. Despite the loud music and cheering, you can still hear the cracking thud of one ram's horns on another.

The rams never suffer any harm, their shepherds say, except injured egos when they lose. The reason for this is that their horns and skulls are permeated by air pockets and their brains are padded with fat. Despite this, the trainers and owners carefully look over the entire body of their rams after each fight, patching up scrapes and sprains. It is said this breed of sheep intuitively enjoys banging their head against all manner of things: trees, gate posts or other sheep's horns.

To win, a ram must collect points in various categories: the vigour of its stance, the boldness of its attack, the splendour of its horns and the curly lushness of its woolly coat. Thus, these competitions are half-sport, half-beauty contest. The fighting usually takes place at a farmers' market to enable the Garut fighting sheep to be traded. Usually, they can easily fetch prices higher than dairy sheep. Of course, a win will push their value even higher. Often, though, the breeders are reluctant to sell their champions. Instead, they may just loan them out for breeding purposes.

Some fans of Garut fighting sheep dismiss the idea that their favourite sheep have ever been interbred with African or European breeds. Some even state the fighting sheep is even older than the Garut regency itself, living in Java since time immemorial. To look at some specimens, it might be true. Many have a unique look: jet-black facial features and superheavy curling horns strutting out from hyper-alert faces. However, other Garut fighting sheep exhibit lush fine wool as though they have Merino blood pulsing within them.

Though the lineage of the Garut fighting sheep might be ambiguous, some Asian sheep have been far more precisely bred by scientists for use in specific Asian settings. A prime example from the twentieth century comes during the Japanese occupation of Inner Mongolia and Manchuria during the 1930s. In Chapter 18, we saw just how useful sheep were to the Mongols during the Middle Ages. However, imperial experts from Japan looked at the sheep of modern Mongolian nomads and thought them too small, too primitive and too unproductive. As historian Sakura Christmas points out, Japan's occupying scientists: 'sought to create new hybrid species of sheep with finer wool, whose profitable fleece would transform what they saw as a declining nomadic borderland into a sedentary, productive part of the Japanese empire.'

As noted in previous chapters, imperialism is a very expensive pursuit. If there are no mineral resources to easily extract, living resources need to be fostered and exploited. In the twentieth century, sheep were one such living resource, and quite amenable to improvement by modern science and technology. Thus Japanese-run farm stations with scientific sheep breeds popped up all over the grassland zones of

Manchuria. The Japanese authorities then encouraged – or ordered – the Mongols to settle within these farm stations. These forced settlements went by the unnerving title of concentration villages.

When the Japanese were expelled out of Mongolia toward the end of World War II, you might think that Mongolian shepherds would have been left in peace to return to their traditional nomadic way of life. Unfortunately, within a few years, China's new Communist government came to rule over Inner Mongolia and Manchuria and they forced many Mongolians off the land altogether and out of pastoral sheep-farming. The Chinese State then compelled the nomad farmers to settle down in one of the many new planned towns popping up all over the region.

From ancient Mesopotamia until the Industrial Revolution, sheep were common co-creators of empires. However, as the example above shows, shepherds were usually more pushed around by empires than active creators in them. Even in areas where imperial power has faded and where nation-states are weak, today's sheep-farmers sometimes still get pushed around and displaced.

One example of this relates to the traditional sheep-farmers working in the Western Sahel region in Africa. On the borderlands where Mali and Niger meet, small-time sheep-farmers graze their flocks of dryland sheep as lively business concerns. With attentive shepherding and good planning, entire villages in the Sahel's grasslands and shrublands can raise just enough sheep for their own daily needs plus a surplus. These surplus sheep can then be cashed in at distant markets like those at Timbuktu in Mali and at Niamey in Niger.

To sustain this lively sheep economy, two requirements must be met. Firstly, there must be just enough rainfall or waterflow to keep some dryland grasses alive at various points along the long route from village to town market. Secondly, there must be peace.

Unfortunately, the rise of the Jihadist movement in the Sahel in the early twenty-first century meant that sheep began disappearing from the landscape. Bands of terrorists would sweep through villages in the Western Sahel confiscating anything of value, including – and most especially – the sheep. After several years of carefully nurturing a small flock, shepherds might be accosted by soldiers wielding Kalashnikov machine guns. Within moments, their sheep disappear into dust on the back of a truck. Bandits have been an episodic problem in the Sahel for centuries. The modern-day Jihadists, though, run livestock banditry as an organised crime syndicate, thereby wrecking the sheep economy of the Western Sahel far worse than average thievery.

As well as threatening villages, the Jihadist groups are a major headache for the fragile governments of Mali and Niger. The terrorists steal government property and attack bridges and airports. Worst of all, they seduce and cajole poor villagers, including those they have impoverished, into joining with them against the government. To counter the Jihadists, the Mali government hired mercenaries from the Wagner Group, a private army connected to the Putin regime in Russia. In the early 2020s, the Wagner Group went on a series of rampaging sorties across Mali, hounding villages thought to be collaborating with the Jihadists.

Unfortunately, Wagner mercenaries did worse than just stealing some sheep. They arrived at villages in armoured trucks with mortars and incendiaries, reportedly burning out farmsteads and slaughtering both shepherds and sheep. No Jihadists were ever caught in these terrible raids, yet the villagers suffered horribly. For a time, this shepherd-slaughtering war temporarily abated somewhat but only because the Wagner Group had been redeployed into the Russia–Ukraine war.

As bad as this twenty-first-century sheep slaughtering is, we might note that there are plenty of examples of similar stories from history. In Chapter 21, we noted how fourteenth-century French flocks were targeted and destroyed by the chevauchées of King Edward III. Likewise, in Chapter 33, we saw how nineteenth-century militia attacked indigenous sheep-farmers in the American West. In both these cases, it took many decades before this violence waned. Hopefully, the fighting in Mali and Niger will dissipate sooner rather than later so the shepherds and sheep of the Sahel can also prosper.

Whilst millions of shepherds and small-time farmers from the Sahel to Indonesia rely upon sheep for their daily needs, the fastest growing commercial land of sheep appears to be China. China has a national flock of 200 million and growing. Most of this huge number belong to industrial-scale sheep-farms, where the sheep are bred intensively for their meat. The government is encouraging this boom because they believe an enlarged sheep flock will help China to become self-reliant regarding food production. However, rather than ranging at will across the grasslands and steppes, these sheep are usually housed within vast covered factories, somewhat reminiscent of livestock batteries that many other countries are trying to phase out.

While China's unique form of communist-tinted capitalism is trying to grow sheep in factories, the sheep themselves might be working against this. In July 2021, the superintendent of police in Hong Kong displayed to the media three illustrated children's books whose main characters were sheep – not because the superintendent was fond of sheep, but because the sheep characters within the books were deemed seditious. The books were written and illustrated by a team of speech therapists and, via various storylines, they had the sheep working together creatively to repel a pack of wolves menacing their town. Though such storylines hark back to folktales of old, the ultra-sensitive Chinese authorities concluded the sheep are supposed to represent the free people of democratic Hong Kong and their enemy – the reviled fearsome wolves – are a stand-in for the Chinese government.

During the long trial, fans and supporters of the accused creators held up cardboard cut-out faces of the book's sheep characters outside the courtroom. That is until they were forced by police to disperse when the trial lurched towards a conclusion. The judge, appointed by the Communist Party, convicted the books' creators of harming the Chinese State and sent them all to prison. As well, anybody caught with the offending sheep books in hand is subject to arrest. Despite this, or more probably because of it, the symbol of sheep as agitators for freedom and fairness grows month by month in Hong Kong. For the record, my fellow sheep expert, Shelley, reviewed the three sheep books with an apolitical mind and gave them all the thumbs up.

Chapter 35

A GREEN SHEEPLAND

WALES, 1973 to the FUTURE

Early on the morning of 26 April 1986, the technicians in charge of Reactor Four at the Chernobyl nuclear plant in Soviet Ukraine were frantically working their control panel. They had been ordered to test various safety systems to clear the plant's jam-packed operating schedule. This button, that button, pressure up, pressure down, uranium rods in, uranium rods out. The test was ill-conceived and the reactor ill-designed – indeed, the entire technology was risky and dangerous.

A few days later, engineers in Sweden recorded a massive wave of radiation sweeping over their nation. Something at Chernobyl had gone seriously awry, sending out massive clouds of deadly radioactive fallout: 400 times the amount produced by the Hiroshima atomic bomb. The winds then brought the radiation across Europe, all the way to the mountains of Snowdonia, where the rain washed radioactive dust onto the slatey stones and peaty soils. The grass then soaked up the fallout and was eaten by sheep.

British officials rushed to ban the movement of Welsh sheep, including from field to market. As news and notices percolated across north Wales, some farmers – already right there in the stocks selling their sheep – were suddenly turned away and sent back home. Government inspectors then began testing Welsh sheep for contamination. Those animals causing the Geiger counters to click too rapidly would be banned from sale. Within weeks, more than 200,000 Welsh sheep – spread over thousands of farms – were consigned to isolation.

This situation was beyond the experience of Welsh sheep-farmers, and they could not argue with the inspectors about the weird new invisible pollution threatening the health of their sheep and of the people that might consume them. However, many farmers also said that if the inspectors had passed Geiger counters over their sheep before Chernobyl, they would have clicked anyhow due to the radioactive exposure from nuclear plants operating in Wales and England.

To be sure, no sheep died as a direct result of the explosion at Chernobyl. However, the high levels of radioactive caesium in some Welsh grass presented the spectre of future cancers and abnormal births. In the Ukrainian countryside around Chernobyl, human casualties from radiation exposure were still rising higher year by year throughout the final decade of the twentieth century. In north Wales, thousands of Welsh sheep were still failing the Geiger test more than twenty years after the disaster.

Just as the radiation tests in Wales were starting to show farms were growing slowly to be radiation-free, another disaster wreaked havoc on Welsh sheep-farming. In February 2001, foot-and-mouth disease reared its head in one single sheep at an abattoir at Gaerwen, Anglesey. Several farms that had sent sheep to slaughter that day were tested. Unfortunately, the results came back positive. Livestock scientists and veterinarians from various government departments then started communicating with each other, seeking advice, counselling opinions and assessing risks. All this took a few days whilst no action was taken. This meant sheep could move across the nation from farms to markets to abattoirs. Three days were lost before a ban on movement was declared. By then, thousands of sheep, cattle and pigs had been exposed to the virus. As testing proceeded, the outbreak was teetering towards epidemic status.

As the full scale of the problem reached the higher echelons of government, the agricultural ministry suddenly adopted a 'contiguous cull' policy. All animals that had been within three kilometres of known cases would be slaughtered. In this way, any confirmed case brought death and despair to surrounding farms even though they were probably disease-free. About one-quarter of the land area of Wales was designated as infected, locking out a vast area from agricultural production and sales. In the end, nearly a million sheep were slaughtered in Wales and the army had to be drafted in to bury the piled-up carcasses. These terrible scenes were relayed by mass media around the world.

The UK government banned the sale of sheep and cattle and pigs – alive or dead – within the country and for export. However, because horrific images of funeral pyres crossed their TV screens, many nations went further, banning the importation of a huge range of British foodstuffs.

The livestock farming sector was not the only industry to suffer. To contain the disease, many tourist activities were also curtailed. Any tourist not frightened away from Wales by burning carcasses found their entry to rural hiking trails and road routes either restricted or completely prohibited. Various events – big and small – ranging from countryside raves to the famed Royal Welsh Agricultural Show and the National Eisteddfod – were all cancelled. The mountains of Snowdonia and Bannau Brycheiniog, plus the Pembrokeshire Coast National Parks were closed to the public, thus wrecking the regular tourist trade. During the foot-and-mouth epidemic, Wales was a quiet, empty place.

The 1986 Chernobyl disaster and the 2001 foot-and-mouth outbreak still cast a long shadow over the Welsh farming sector. There is a lingering fear in rural Wales that another big disaster will eventually come along in the future. Such fears were heightened when heatwaves and droughts affected Wales in 2018 and 2019, followed by the coronavirus pandemic of 2020 and 2021. Although sheep were not susceptible to Covid-19, restrictions on human travel interrupted the easy transport of sheep and sheep products.

As though epidemics and nuclear pollution and heatwaves are not bad enough, more severe disruption to Welsh sheep-farming came in the form of Brexit. When Britain joined the European Union in 1973, the EU's Common Agricultural Policy heavily subsidised Welsh sheep-farmers to produce food sold around the EU. These payments stimulated the Welsh sheep industry and sheep numbers in Wales grew by millions of heads. By the early twenty-first century, the nation was awash with 10,000 sheep-farms and ten million living sheep. That was more than triple the human population of the country. As well as providing income for the farmers, this large sheep population supported ancillary jobs in shepherding and shearing, as well as propping up farmware suppliers and the road transport sector.

Brexit, though, has descended upon Welsh farmers like a ton of bricks. Firstly, the subsidies for food production have disappeared overnight. The Welsh Government promised to uphold EU-equivalent subsidies for a few years to cushion the blow but these are to be phased out within a decade. Secondly, Brexit set up a lot of new barriers between Wales and the EU, including new customs checks and taxes, new health and disease checks, and new transport regulations. It is as though some network of obstacles akin to the nineteenth-century tollgates has been resurrected, making it nigh on impossible for Welsh sheep-farmers to make money from sheep-farming.

Added to this, the British government is seeking free-trade agreements with its former colonies. This includes Australia and New Zealand, whose sheep-farmers are being set up to compete on free and equal terms against Welsh farmers to sell their sheep products into Britain. Because of these economic pressures, the number of Welsh sheep may drastically decline in the near future.

Although the food production subsidies are disappearing, all is not lost for Welsh farms. The Welsh Government is busily setting up new environmental support schemes whereby payments will be sent to farms for providing 'ecosystem services'. Farmers will thus be paid to support wildlife, thwart climate change, mitigate drought and help provide clean energy and water. As flocks disappear from the hilly Welsh landscape, they are likely to be replaced by wild woodlands, wetlands and wind farms. Many farmers in Wales these days believe the key to running a successful farm in coming decades will be diversification. Ecotourism is one potential money-earner and is becoming ever more popular. As I say this, I recall a 'sheep-walking farm' where Shelley and I forked out twenty pounds to take rare Welsh sheep for a walk over partially rewilded landscapes. Actually, it was a great experience. Somehow the sheep knew how to lead Shelley across wild meadows and through a regrowing forest whilst making him feel like he was the boss.

Despite the trend toward rewilding the Welsh landscape, many scientists and eco-responsible farmers believe that some form of sheep-farming can coexist with eco-friendly land management. For instance, if groups of farmers in highland Wales can work together to reduce and then rotate their flocks over much wider areas, they can free up other areas for the natural regeneration of wild meadows and peatbogs. If farmland meadows become highly diverse, or if they support rare species, the farmers will not only receive a state payment but they will also likely increase the recreational value of their land, attracting more ecotourists.

Also, to allow natural meadows and heathlands to regenerate, it is helpful to have sheep graze upon fast-growing grasses so that more varieties of slower-growing herbs and shrubs have a chance to emerge. Welsh ecologists have tried this trick in the field and it has shown great results. For example, rare species of wildflowers on the Llŷn Peninsula bloomed colourfully as sheep cleared away competing grasses.

Of course, realistically, this type of grazing conservation might only work in very particular sites. Yet there is work being done in Wales and around the world to transform sheep-farming into an eco-friendlier industry. For instance, veterinarians are working with farmers to concoct better recipes for wintertime feed that could minimise the greenhouse gases in sheep burps. Other teams of experts and shepherds are working to encourage sheep dairying in Wales since if sheep are milked, rather than just eaten, they could then be more efficient food producers. Added to this, the drive to insulate housing across Britain – in order to decrease fossil fuel use – could very well come to rely upon wool-based materials in order to get the job done quickly and easily. The Welsh wool trade, then, might yet experience something of a renaissance in the future. However, despite these projects, it is hardly likely that a large national flock of ten million Welsh sheep could altogether be transformed to be entirely eco-friendly.

These days, if you travel around the Welsh countryside, sheep still seem very abundant. Visit the castles of Pembrokeshire and Carmarthenshire: they will be framed by fluffy white sheep. If you jaunt up the hill to the National Library of Wales in Ceredigion, its slope is dotted with grey woolly sheep. If you ascend Bannau Brycheiniog or the peaks of Snowdonia, you'll look back over valleys bespeckled with sheep of many colours. As you know by now, I enjoy the sight of these fluffy beasts and wallow in the romantic idyll of their presence in the Welsh landscape. Yet, for a long time, I've also wondered if the country needs so many sheep.

The mountains of Wales have a strange beauty all their own. Visitors from foreign lands toss around adjectives like 'unearthly', 'otherworldly' and 'fantastical' to describe places like Bannau Brycheiniog, Snowdonia and the Preseli Hills. The alienness of the mountains also attracts various science fiction and fantasy filmmakers to use them as a backdrop, from *Willow* and the *Harry Potter* film series to the *Doctor Who* TV show. Yet as Shelley and I wandered over the crests and valleys of Bannau Brycheiniog, a nagging visual oddity worked its way into our heads. Where were the trees?

Shelley and I have walked alpine pathways across a number of countries as they wound through highland ranges. The slopes of these highlands, though, are usually covered in a myriad of beautiful trees: pines and spruces, ashes and oaks, hornbeams and beeches. Most of the mountains of Wales, in contrast, are devoid of trees despite their peaks being largely below the typical tree-line. Though most visitors to Bannau Brycheiniog are there to witness the grandeur of nature, the tree-less character of the range is not natural but artificial, maintained as such mostly to ensure pasture for sheep.

As much as I like sheep, woodlands and forests are beautiful and lovely to look at and to saunter through as well. The trees are probably a whole lot more useful, though, as they respond to twenty-first-century challenges like climate change and ecosystem breakdown. It seems that most Welsh people – Parliament included – are coming round to this viewpoint as well. Perhaps, when Shelley reaches my age, he will return to this amazing landscape and find great woods framing the odd sheep rather than the other way round. Such a composition would present a hopeful future whilst appreciating the past.

While the re-emergence of wooded landscapes across Wales should be welcomed, along with the reinvigoration of moorlands and wetlands, it would surely be wise to preserve traditional sheep-farming in some form as well. Apart from anything else, history has shown us that sheep-farming has enabled a number of cultures and civilisations to remain resilient in the face of catastrophic events, such as the Bronze Age Collapse and the Black Death, for instance. If, God forbid, the climate emergency becomes a global catastrophe or nuclear apocalypse is unleashed upon Europe, our woolly friends might well provide a pathway toward survival and recovery.

EPILOGUE

Through many short chapters, we've taken a long journey. Starting around 6,000 years ago, prehistoric peoples in Wales came face to face with their first sheep. We can only guess at their reaction to these strange new animals. The first people in Wales were Stone Age hunter-gatherers and they would have been accustomed to animals running away and hiding. However, these bewildering new sheep creatures just called out in a friendly way whilst standing stationary with curious looks on their faces. Perhaps the Welsh hunter-gatherers reacted like the Navajo Indians of sixteenth-century America, thinking the beasts to be gifts from the heavens.

Unlike the feral sheep that the Navajo discovered wandering past their camps, though, these first sheep in Wales were attended to by farmers – who had only recently arrived from mainland Europe. These farmers would have spoken in unknown tongues whilst adorned in strange attire and working with strange tools. Still, their care for the sheep would have left a profound impression on Welsh hunter-gatherers. Sheep were not to be hunted but nurtured and cared for.

By the time they arrived in Wales, sheep had already worked with humans to achieve great things. Sheep had helped set up trading routes across mountains and seas, they had co-created the world's first towns and cities, and they'd inspired the first forms of human writing. Evidently, caring for and nurturing these friendly soft-coated creatures could transform the world.

Eventually, the farming lifestyle became dominant in Wales. This might be because the farmers outcompeted the hunter-gatherers or because the farmers showed the hunter-gatherers how to farm. In any case, the primaeval woodlands of the Welsh lowlands and valleys started coming down, first from the stone axes of Stone Age farmers and then via the bronze axes of the Beaker folk.

As well as transforming the ecology of Britain, by 500 BC woolly sheep also served as a core commodity for the prehistoric Celts of Wales. Celtic tribes such as the Silures and Ordovices depended upon and robustly defended their flocks of sheep, often building great hillforts in a manner explicitly enabling them to do so. If travelling with a six-year-old around Welsh hillforts taught me anything, it is that they can realistically be conjured as 'sheepscapes', not warzones.

Meanwhile, sheep were empowering not only tribes but entire empires. The Babylonians, Greeks and Romans all had vast sheep-farms with gigantic numbers of sheep. In the first century AD, the Romans started extending their sheep-farms and wool workshops right into the lowlands of Wales both to support their soldiers and to extract wealth from the new province of Britannia. Little did they know that other sheep empires would follow in their ilk: the Mongolians in medieval times, the Spanish after Columbus, and then the British Empire in the eighteenth and nineteenth centuries. They all spread sheep as part of their efforts of conquest and control.

Of course, though tribes, kingdoms and empires have used sheep as agents of conquest or have fought wars over their pasturelands, most farmers were engaged in shepherding as a peaceful way to sustain their families – without harming anyone. Let's hear it for the sheep as well. Though they are probably unconscious of their amazing service to humanity and ignorant of their role in imperial conquest, they possess a specific creaturely agency that they act out in their local landscape. Sheep are industrious; sheep are clever; sheep are resilient. Although they are supremely social animals – like humans – each has its own personality. Many of them are playful, curious and determined. Sometimes this causes trouble, but the trouble they cause is at the scale of the farm and landscape. Sheep aren't imperious. Sheep do not pursue war. In fact, as we have seen in more than one chapter, they may be its innocent victims.

Though they've played their part in building empires, small-time subsistence sheep-farming is still a significant global lifestyle, especially in Asia and Africa. In Wales, though, since the coming of the Industrial Revolution, running sheep has been more of a capitalist venture than a traditional lifestyle. As such, it received a boost in support at the end of the twentieth century when Britain tied itself to the European Union. With Brexit, though, significant changes are afoot. Sheep-farming seems destined to give way to 'wilderness farming'.

Still, despite this transition, the Welsh nation and Welsh culture have just about assumed parity with the rest of Britain. Full independence also beckons, if the Welsh so wish to move that way. This journey to fairness and freedom has taken the best part of a thousand years. Whatever the exact political nature of Wales's future, Welsh sheep should be thanked for keeping Welsh people strong enough – for so long – that Wales has survived to reach these brighter times.

IMAGE CREDITS

The Standard of Ur: © The History Collection / Alamy Stock Photo.

The Little Shepherd Boy: Carlo Dalgas (1821/1851), Public domain, via Wikimedia Commons.

Ram-headed Khnum: Walters Art Museum, Public domain, via Wikimedia Commons.

Welsh Landscape with Two Women Knitting: William Dyce, Public domain, via Wikimedia Commons.

Highland Wanderers: William Watson (1840–1921), Public domain, via Wikimedia Commons.

The Sheep Drive: John Linnell, Public domain, via Wikimedia Commons.

Cader Idris from Kymmer Abbey: David Cox, Welsh Landscape Collection, © National Library of Wales.

The Emigrants: William Allsworth, Museum of New Zealand, © Album / Alamy Stock Photo.

Sheep gate in dry stone wall: © Realimage / Alamy Stock Photo.

Badger-faced mountain sheep: © Rebecca Cole / Alamy Stock Photo.

Near Llanbedr, Barmouth: © Penta Springs Limited / Alamy Stock Photo.

Tending Sheep, Betws-y-Coed: © Heritage Image Partnership Ltd / Alamy Stock Photo.

A flock near Tintern Abbey: © FLPA / Alamy Stock Photo.

A Welsh mountain sheep on Llangynidr moors: © Gordon

Scammell / Alamy Stock Photo.

A flock in front of a Cotswold 'wool church': © David Knibbs / Alamy Stock Photo.

Mountain sheep in a woodland: © John Dietz / Alamy Stock Photo.

FURTHER READING

The following publications are a short list of those that I have consulted over the years regarding the global history of agriculture and also Welsh history. I put them here to point toward further reading for those who wish to delve deeper into the topics or events outlined in the various chapters of this book.

Chapters 1 to 5 (the Stone Age)

Armstrong, P., *Sheep* (London: Reaktion Books, 2016).

Barker, G. and Goucher, C. (eds), *The Cambridge World History: A World With Agriculture* (Cambridge: Cambridge University Press, 2015).

Butler, A., *Sheep* (Oxford: O-Books, 2010).

Darvill, T., *Prehistoric Britain* (London: Routledge, 2010).

Hollander, D. and Rowe, T., *A Companion to Ancient Agriculture* (London: Wiley Blackwell, 2020).

Lynch, F. et al., *Prehistoric Wales* (Stroud: Sutton Publishing, 2000).

Pryor, F., *The Making of the British Landscape: How We Have Transformed the Land from Prehistory to Today* (London: Penguin, 2010).

Chapters 4 to 9 (the Bronze Age)

Barber, E. W., *Women's Work: The First 20,000 Years: Women, Cloth and Society in Early Times* (New York: W. W. Norton & Company, 1994).

Harding, A. and Fokkens, H., *The Oxford Handbook of the European Bronze*

Age (Oxford: Oxford University Press, 2013).

Manning, J. G., *The Open Sea: The Economic Life of the Ancient Mediterranean World* (Princeton: Princeton University Press, 2018).

Mazoyer, M. and Roudart, L., *A History of World Agriculture* (New York: New Monthly Review Press, 2006).

Redford, D. (ed.), *The Oxford Encyclopedia of Ancient Egypt* (Oxford: Oxford University Press, 2002).

Chapters 9 to 10 (the Iron Age)

Albarella, U. and Trentacoste, A. (eds), *Ethnozooarchaeology: The Present and Past of Human-Animal Relationships* (Oxford: Oxbow Books, 2011).

Cunliffe, B. W., *The Ancient Celts* (Oxford: Oxford University Press, 2012).

Davies, J., *A History of Wales* (London: Penguin Books, 1994).

Green, M., *Animals in Celtic Life and Myth* (London: Routledge, 1992).

Chapter 11 (the Roman Empire)

Bird, D., *Agriculture and Industry in South-Eastern Roman Britain* (Oxford: Oxbow Books, 2016).

Hollander, D. B., *Farmers and Agriculture in the Ancient Roman Economy* (London: Routledge, 2020).

Symons, S., *Roman Wales* (Stroud: Amberley Publishing, 2015).

Chapters 12 to 14 (the Dark Ages)

Flechner, R., *Saint Patrick Retold* (Princeton: Princeton University Press, 2019).

Holman, K., *The Northern Conquests: The Vikings in Britain and Ireland* (Oxford: Signal Books, 2017).

Jones, D. et al., *A History of Christianity in Wales* (Cardiff: University of Wales Press, 2022).

Kirkwood, A. C., 'History, biology and control of sheep scab', *Parasitology Today*, 2 (1986), 302–7.

Williams, A. et al., *A Biographical Dictionary of Dark Age Britain: England, Scotland, Wales, c.500 to c.1050* (London: Routledge, 1997).

Wood, M., *In Search of the Dark Ages* (London: BBC Books, 2022).

Chapters 15 to 24 (the High/Late Middle Ages)

Anderson, E. N., *Food and Environment of Early and Medieval China* (Philadelphia: University of Pennsylvania Press, 2004).

Burton, J. and Stober, K., *Abbeys and Priories of Medieval Wales* (Cardiff: University of Wales Press, 2015).

Fulton, H. (ed.), *Urban Culture in Medieval Wales* (Cardiff: University of Wales, 2012).

Griffiths, R. A. and Schofield, P. R., *Wales and the Welsh in the Middle Ages* (Cardiff: University of Wales Press, 2011).

John, M., 'Where are the Flemings?', *Journal of the Pembrokeshire Historical Society*, 23 (2014), *www.pembrokeshirehistoricalsociety.co.uk/category/2014-journal/*.

Johnson, C., 'The importance of sheep and their wool to the economy of Wales from 1100 to 1603' (unpublished doctoral thesis, University of Lampeter Trinity Saint David, Lampeter, 2006).

Lieberman, M., *The March of Wales, 1066–1300: A Borderland of Medieval Britain* (Cardiff: University of Wales Press, 2008).

Platt, C., *King Death: The Black Death and its Aftermath in Late-Medieval England* (London: Routledge, 1997).

Smith, Jr., J. M., 'Dietary decadence and dynastic decline in the Mongol Empire', *Journal of Asian History*, 34/1 (2000), 1–12.

Stephenson, D., *Medieval Wales, c. 1050–1332* (Cardiff: University of Wales Press, 2019).

Stevens, M., *The Economy of Medieval Wales, 1067–1536* (Cardiff: University of Wales Press, 2019).

Toorians, L., 'Wizo Flandrensis and the Flemish settlement in Pembrokeshire', *Cambridge Medieval Celtic Studies*, 20 (1990), 99–118.

Turvey, R., *Pembrokeshire: The Concise History* (Cardiff: University of Wales Press, 2006).

Chapters 23 to 28 (the Early Modern Period)

Bowen, L., *Early Modern Wales* (Cardiff: University of Wales Press, 2023).

Evans, C., *Slave Wales* (Cardiff: University of Wales Press, 2010).

Overton, M., *The Agricultural Revolution in England* (Cambridge: Cambridge University Press, 1996).

Thomas, H., *A History of Wales, 1485–1660* (Cardiff: University of Wales Press, 2011).

Chapters 28 to 35 (the Late Modern Period)

Anderson, V., *Creatures of Empire: How Domestic Animals Transformed Early America* (Oxford: Oxford University Press, 2004).

Brooking, T. and Pawson, E. (eds), *Seeds of Empire: The Environmental Transformation of New Zealand* (London: I. B. Tauris, 2011).

Chapman, J., *A Guide to Parliamentary Enclosures in Wales* (Cardiff: University of Wales Press, 1992).

Charlesworth, A., *An Atlas of Rural Protest in Britain, 1548–1900* (London: Routledge, 2017).

Christmas, S., 'An imperial sheep chase', China Dialogue, 25 April (2017), *https://chinadialogue.net/en/nature/9743-an-imperial-sheep-chase/*.

Collins, E. J. T. (ed.), *The Agrarian History of England and Wales: Part Two* (Cambridge: Cambridge University Press, 2000).

Conniff, R., 'What the Luddites really fought against', *Smithsonian Magazine*, March (2011).

Elias, T., *Trails of the Welsh Drovers* (Llanrwst: Gwasg Carreg Gwalch, 2019).

Godwin, F. and Toulson, S., *The Drovers Roads of Wales* (Stansted: Whittet Books, 1977).

Graham Jones, J. *The History of Wales* (Cardiff: University of Wales, 2017).

Hughes, P. G., *Wales and the Drovers* (Denbigh: Foyles Welsh, 1944).

Jones, R. E., *Petticoat Heroes: Gender, Culture and Popular Protest in the Rebecca Riots* (Cardiff: University of Wales Press, 2015).

Peden, R., *Making Sheep Country* (Auckland: University of Auckland Press, 2011).

Sanders, V., *Wales, the Welsh, and the Making of America* (Cardiff: University of Wales Press, 2021).

Williams, G., *The Desert and the Dream: A Study of Welsh Colonization in Chubut, 1865–1915* (Cardiff: University of Wales Press, 1975).